Law in Everyday Japan

Law in Everyday Japan

Sex, Sumo, Suicide, and Statutes

MARK D. WEST

The University of Chicago Press

CHICAGO AND LONDON

The University of Chicago Press, Chicago 60637
The University of Chicago Press, Ltd., London
© 2005 by The University of Chicago
All rights reserved. Published 2005
Printed in the United States of America

14 13 12 11 10 09 08 07   2 3 4 5

ISBN: 0-226-89402-9 (cloth)
ISBN: 0-226-89403-7 (paper)

Library of Congress Cataloging-in-Publication Data

West, Mark D.
    Law in everyday Japan : sex, sumo, suicide, and statutes / Mark D. West.
        p.   cm.
    Includes bibliographical references and index.
    ISBN 0-226-89402-9 (cloth : alk paper)—ISBN 0-226-89403-7 (pbk. : alk. paper)
    1. Law—Japan. 2. Law and economics. 3. Sociological jurisprudence. I. Title.
KNX442.W47 2005
349.52—dc22   2004024386

⊚ The paper used in this publication meets the minimum requirements of
the American National Standard for Information Sciences—Permanence
of Paper for Printed Library Materials, ANSI Z39.48-1992.

福田東子様へ

CONTENTS

FIGURES AND TABLES

FIGURES

TABLES

ACKNOWLEDGMENTS

Lots of people helped me with this book. Foremost is my family, which supported me throughout.

I am indebted to Don Herzog, Rick Lempert, Ronald Mann, Curtis Milhaupt, Mark Ramseyer, and Frank Upham, each of whom at one time or another read the whole manuscript, or at least most of it, and gave me invaluable comments. I also received particularly insightful comments on various chapters from Kent Anderson, Frank Bennett, Omri Ben-Shahar, Chris Boehning, Bob Ellickson, Hanoch Dagan, Eric Feldman, Sam Gross, John Haley, Hideki Kanda, Ellen Katz, Atsushi Kinami, Jim Krier, Deborah Malamud, Bill Miller, Bob Rasmussen, Jennifer Robertson, Carl Schneider, David Skeel, Lynn Stout, and Yoshiko Terao. I received helpful comments at presentations at Michigan, Georgetown, Harvard, Northwestern, Toronto, and Yale Universities and the Nichibei Hō Gakkai.

Of this group, a few deserve special re-mention. Atsushi Kinami was my official host and unofficial friend at the Kyoto University Faculty of Law, which was my second academic home for much of the project. Kinami helped in more ways than I can list, and I have yet to find anything that he can't do (or can't find someone who can). Herzog, Miller, and Schneider helped out in ways that are so difficult to pinpoint that I might be imagining them. They have my gratitude nonetheless. The idea for chapter 2 came from conversations with Lempert, the idea for chapter 5 came from conversations with Kinami, and Ramseyer raised the idea for chapter 7. I thank Emily Morris, who co-authored the article on which chapter 5 is based, for her gracious permission to publish a reworked version here.

My deans during the project, Jeff Lehman and Evan Caminker, and my secretary for most of the project, Cathy Brooks, together with other Michigan faculty, library and other staff, students, and alumni help make Ann Arbor the best place in the world outside of Japan to research Japanese law.

This book is dedicated to Fukuda Haruko, to whom I owe far more than a mere book dedication. You started this.

* * *

Chapters 2, 3, 4, and 5 are significantly reworked and updated versions of the following articles: Losers: Recovering Lost Property in Japan and the United States, 37:2 Law & Society Review 369 (2003); Legal Rules and Social Norms in Japan's Secret World of Sumo, 26 Journal of Legal Studies 165 (1997); The Resolution of Karaoke Disputes: The Calculus of Institutions and Social Capital, 28 Journal of Japanese Studies 301 (Summer 2002); and The Tragedy of the Condominiums: Legal Responses to Collective Action Problems after the Kobe Earthquake, 51 American Journal of Comparative Law 903 (2003, with Emily M. Morris).

I received funding from the Japan Society for the Promotion of Science (2001), the Japan–United States Educational Commission (Fulbright) (2002), and the University of Michigan Center for Japanese Studies (2003). I also benefited from the endowments of the Nippon Life Insurance Company and the Sumitomo Bank, Ltd. at the University of Michigan Law School.

AUTHOR'S NOTE

Names are given in American order: Yoko Ono and Ichiro Suzuki. Some names have been changed to preserve anonymity.

Unless stated otherwise, all yen amounts are converted to dollars at the rate of $1 = 100 yen. The actual rates published by the U.S. Treasury Department were 144.79 in 1990, 94.06 in 1995, 107.77 in 2000, and 108.82 in late 2004.

CHAPTER ONE

INTRODUCTION

The literature about law in Japan is dominated by studies of broad-based, high-stakes phenomena. At the center of this fetish with the big in Japanese law is a longstanding preoccupation with Japanese litigation rates. Some scholars argue that Japanese culture is responsible for low litigation rates; others argue that institutions and the economic disincentives to sue that they create are the causes.[1] Apart from that debate, much of the remainder of work on Japanese law, both in and outside Japan, is about similarly "big" topics such as corporate law and large-scale social issues.

It is time to move on. Although looking at lawsuits and large-stakes phenomena has enriched our knowledge, it has also created a potentially misleading and irrelevant model of Japanese law. Lawsuits are rare events in most people's lives in Japan as elsewhere, and high-stakes phenomena are by definition not commonplace. Basing our study of law in Japan, and especially of the role of law in Japanese society, on these sorts of events is a bit like assuming that the Super Bowl is played every day.

This book is about the role of law in *everyday* Japan. It examines the incentives created by law and legal institutions in everyday lives, the ways in which law intermingles with social norms, historically engrained ideas, cultural mores, and phenomena that cannot easily be explained. By ex-

---

1. See Takeyoshi Kawashima, Nihonjin no Hō Ishiki [Japanese Legal Consciousness] (1967); John Owen Haley, The Myth of the Reluctant Litigant, 4 J. Japan. Stud. 359 (1978); J. Mark Ramseyer and Minoru Nakazato, The Rational Litigation: Settlement Amounts and Verdict Rates in Japan, 18 J. Legal Stud. 263, 268 (1989).

amining how these concepts play out in everyday contexts, this book attempts to gain insight into Japanese law as it functions in society, and into Japanese society through a study of its laws.

WHY EVERYDAY JAPAN?

This book is a search for a richer, more resonant account of law through a study of its role in such everyday situations as sex, sumo, and suicide. The study of law in everyday life is not new. True, most legal scholars "generally prefer to pitch their tents in the shadow of the Supreme Court rather than on Main Street,"[2] but a fair amount of literature recently has appeared.[3] And at the same time, the study of everyday *life* in Japan is becoming more prevalent.[4]

What has not yet taken place is an in-depth study of law in everyday Japan. Anecdotal accounts have always been available. In one of my personal favorites, Melvin Belli, in a 1960 book with a foreword by Errol Flynn and Belli's name in the title ("Belli Looks at Life and Law in Japan"), attempted to describe law's role in Japanese everyday life in tales of chivalrous outlaws, illegal lottery tickets, and "mama-san, papa-san, and the geisha girl."[5] That's not quite what I have in mind.

The paucity of analysis is something of a surprise. When I teach Japanese law in the classroom, part of the struggle is to keep the conversation relevant, encouraging students, American and Japanese, to discuss their experiences in Japan without turning the class into one on "the role of law in my homestay experience." Students know, and are eager to talk about, the frustration of dealing with Japanese law on a daily basis. While discussions in my other classes often turn to examples from television movies-of-the-week (criminal law) or the business pages (corporate law), my students of Japanese consistently turn the comparative lens on the everyday.

2. David M. Engel, Law in the Domains of Everyday Life: The Construction of Community and Difference, in Law and Everyday Life, 123, 124, ed. Austin Sarat and Thomas R. Kearns (1995).

3. See, e.g., Patrick Ewick and Susan S. Silbey, The Common Place of Law: Stories from Everyday Life (1998); Sarat and Kearns, Law and Everyday Life, *supra* note 2.

4. See, e.g., Sheldon Garon, Molding Japanese Minds: The State in Everyday Life (1997); V. Lee Hamilton, Everyday Justice: Responsibility and the Individual in Japan and the United States (1992); Susan B. Hanley, Everyday Things in Premodern Japan (1997); James Mak, ed., Why It Works, Why It Doesn't: Economics in Everyday Life (1999).

5. Melvin M. Belli and Danny R. Jones, Belli Looks at Life and Law in Japan (1960).

In this book, I follow my students' lead to examine the role of law in everyday Japan in seven intriguing but ordinary settings: daily occurrences, sports, leisure, housing, sex, work, and the troubling nexus of personal finance and suicide.

I begin in chapter 2 with an analysis of lost-and-found practices. Japan is famous for the willingness of its citizens to return lost items to their rightful owners. What most observers do not realize is that these transactions are governed by recognized, centuries-old legal rules that mesh with norms, institutional structures, and economic incentives. Chapter 3 addresses sports through an analysis of sumo wrestling and the relation between law and norms in this culturally "Japanese" institution. Chapter 4 examines leisure though the lens of karaoke-based noise complaints, focusing on the social and legal reasons why people *don't* sue. In chapter 5, I look at the role of law in solving disputes about condominium reconstruction before and after the Kobe earthquake of 1995. In chapter 6, I turn to sex and love hotels, exploring the extent to which law and social change account for the popularity and usage patterns of these establishments. Chapter 7 examines the role of law in shaping long working hours in Japan, focusing on the role of working-hour statutes and judicially created rules regarding employee dismissal. Chapter 8 navigates the phenomenon of debt-caused suicide, where the evidence suggests that law is an important part of the mix of factors that lead to certain kinds of suicide.

Two elements unify these topics. First, each is commonplace for many people in Japan. Second, each is seen by many both in and outside Japan to be "Japanese." I regard the latter factor as important not only to hold your interest but also to deflect charges that I have skewed the inquiry toward a U.S. or Western legal tradition by choosing topics that are culturally "non-Japanese" and thus exceptions to our knowledge, or at least to our preconceptions, of Japanese culture.

Still, my topic selection might be criticized in at least two ways. First, a critic might argue that choosing "Japanese" topics marginalizes the inquiry or perhaps even stereotypes Japan. But as more than one scholar has pointed out, study of "the everyday" does the opposite; because the everyday exists everywhere, focusing on it is one way to broaden an otherwise limited analysis of that nation.[6] I have no desire to further the cute, misleading, and sometimes contemptuous coverage of Japan that has

6. See Harry Harootunian, History's Disquiet: Modernity, Cultural Practice, and the Question of Everyday Life (2000).

plagued accounts by the popular press. My goal is a rigorous analysis of several interesting Japanese phenomena, with the aim of showing the role of law in some ordinary, but perhaps quirky, places. The evidence presented in this book suggests that even the quirkiest of phenomena, and those subject to the usual claims of Japanese exoticism, are not beyond analysis.

Second, a critic might suggest that I focus more on "law" than on "everyday," choosing topics that enable a more rigorous comparative study of legal provisions. Although my first response to such a claim is to note the boredom entailed in such an inquiry, there is more at stake than intellectual hedonism. Especially given the dearth of research on the issue in the Japanese context, I share the view that "scholarship on law in everyday life should abandon the law-first perspective and should proceed, paradoxically, with its eye not on law, but on events or practices that seem, on the face of things, removed from law, or at least not dominated by law at the outset."[7]

For this book, then, I avoid subjects that simply are known spheres of legal regulation, even if those topics are "everyday," so as to avoid painting an unfairly legalistic picture of Japan. I chose topics that sounded interesting and Japanese. I tried to find areas that, at least on the surface, seemed unconnected to the law.[8] In many cases, the evidence that I uncovered for this book—both of law's importance and of its triviality—surprised me, and perhaps it will surprise you as well.

METHODOLOGY AND ARGUMENT

I rely primarily on three sets of analytical tools. First, I assume that institutions, the "rules of the game," matter. I focus not only on law but also on less formal humanly devised behavioral constructs such as social norms.

Second, in each case, my analysis is informed by the basic assumptions of rational choice theory: maximizing behavior, stable preferences, and market equilibria. Although rational choice theory has been extraordi-

7. Austin Sarat and Thomas R. Kearns, Beyond the Great Divide: Forms of Legal Scholarship and Everyday Life, in Sarat and Kearns, *supra* note 2.

8. Even gifts, often the subject of comparative U.S.-Japan social norms analysis (see James G. Carrier, Gifts and Commodities: Exchange and Western Capitalism Since 1700, 179–80 [1995]), have both contractual and tax consequences in Japan. See J. Mark Ramseyer and Minoru Nakazato, Japanese Law: An Economic Approach, 44–47, 227–28, 236–37 (1999).

narily useful and robust in the social sciences, these are merely assumptions, and often these assumptions are broken down by something as ordinary as anxiety, fear, joy, or a mistake. I try not to shy away from the areas in which individual behavior may not always comport with the assumptions. In other words, the cases are "problem-driven," not "theory-driven";[9] they are motivated by my own sheer curiosity, not grand theory. Still, without some model with which to begin, it would be hard to get much of anywhere at all.

Third and finally, I assume that in an exploration of how the world works such as this, empirical analysis, with all its requisite caveats, is more useful than other methods. In a couple of cases, I collected the kind of data that is amenable to statistical analysis, and I use regression and other techniques to develop or test hypotheses. But quantitative analysis alone produces results that are sometimes weak and almost always dry and yeastless. To inform this study, I also rely on evidence gathered from fieldwork. I visited sumo stables to learn about sumo rules, lost objects to learn about the lost-and-found system, visited debt counselors to learn about debt-suicide, toured Kobe condominium rubble to learn about reconstruction, and helped love hotel cleaning staff hunt for semen stains with black lights to learn about the love hotel trade. I did these things not so much to advance some kind of gonzo anthropology as to create opportunities to formulate and ask questions in context. Sometimes I asked questions in formal interview settings, but as these examples suggest, I gathered a lot of information from casual conversations as well.

Interviewing, or for that matter, conversing, is rare in studies of the law, and it was virtually unheard of in studies of Japanese law until very recently. Although I cannot be sure, I believe (and my Japanese colleagues agree) that many respondents were more open to me than they normally would be to fellow Japanese. This book attempts to utilize their candor to present a Japan rarely seen in print.

This combination of techniques is not easy to characterize succinctly. Consider two of the more dominant schools of legal scholarship, "law and economics" and "law and society." Law and economics "tends to focus on market processes, to emphasize efficiency, to assume rational behavior by individuals, and to use formal mathematical models." Law and society "tends to focus more on nonmarket processes, to emphasize norms, to

---

9. See Donald P. Green and Ian Shapiro, Pathologies of Rational Choice Theory, 6 (1994).

make few simplifying assumptions, and to adopt an empirical approach to understanding social behavior."[10] In this book, I do all of those things: in some cases, I treat individuals as the basic social unit, as does the law-and-economics view, but in others, I look more carefully at how social interaction affects behavior, as in the law-and-society view. I borrow tools from and blur the lines of both schools to create a richer and more accurate portrayal of the available evidence. If that approach does not satisfy purists, so be it.

Harrumph. As much as I'd like to leave it at that, having so boldly thumbed my nose at the purists, the difference is not merely methodological. If one were to read only the culture-and-society literature regarding Japanese law, one would assume that Japanese don't sue because harmony (*wa*) matters, respect duties but not rights (it's a samurai thing; you wouldn't understand), leave money on the table to keep the peace, and suppress the self for the sake of groups, shame, face, and appearance (*tatemae*) instead of reality (*honne*). Japan, like Cleveland, is certainly different, and sometimes these concepts help explain how. But Japan can't be boiled down to a few exotic Japanese keywords that explain everyone's behavior, and attempts to do so often result in beautiful models of circular reasoning.

The picture would be different, but not necessarily better, if one were to read only the economics literature about Japanese law. Were that your library, you would assume that Japanese people make decisions about suing based solely on court costs, expected damages, and attorney fees, they exercise rights with abandon, they bargain ruthlessly, and they always bow to the gods of efficiency, self-interest, cost-benefit, and rationality. As a starting point for analysis, sometimes this approach works well, and in many contexts, the framework produces interesting, often fascinating, results. But this just can't be the whole picture.

I am caricaturing the literature a bit. There are contexts in which one explanation works better than another, and for analytical purposes, it's often better to separate the parts. But when the economics-versus-society exercise is repeated again and again by Japanese and non-Japanese scholars alike, it creates the false impression that Japan is a monocausal, homogeneous exception to the rule that the world is a complicated place.

---

10. Lauren B. Edelman, Rivers of Law and Contested Terrain: A Law and Society Approach to Economic Rationality (Presidential Address), 38(2) Law & Society 181, 182 (2004).

To be sure, simplicity is often a virtue. I wish that I could distill the entirety of law in everyday Japan to the back of a business card that you could carry in your pocket, ready to impress at your next cocktail party with the announcement that Japan is 67.2 percent economics and 32.7 percent culture, with a 0.1 percent residual. (You'd be the life of the party!) I'm not so virtuous.

At the other extreme, we can't allow ourselves to become mired in the nihilistic carnival of throw-up-your-hands-in-desperation complexity that often threatens to envelop inscrutable Japan. By starting with an assumption of rationality and then exploring critically a few different contexts of everyday Japan, we can derive a few principles, or at least some hints as to how the world works. This approach allows us to examine the really interesting part of the story that has been lost in the dichotomy: the ways in which multiple causes intertwine in tangled, multifaceted ways to produce intriguing and colorful outcomes.

Law, as we shall see, matters in everyday Japan. But *how* law matters also matters. Beginning with chapter 2, we'll see that law matters in concert with social and other factors, it matters in unexpected ways, and it matters in different ways to different people—even in Japan.

CHAPTER TWO

LOST AND FOUND

We begin with an everyday occurrence: losing things. The Japanese system for reuniting owners with their lost possessions is said to be especially efficient. A recent survey of five hundred Tokyo and Osaka "businessmen" found that 41.4 percent had lost something in the past year and on average lost 2.7 items per year. Of the persons surveyed who recovered their lost items, only 22.5 percent found the item on their own; the remaining four-fifths received calls from strangers or found the items at lost-and-found stations.[1] All in all, in 2002, Japanese police received more than ten million items and cash totaling $129 million in voluntary finds from ordinary citizens. Find rates are highly correlated to loss rates, and more than 70 percent of the yen and 30 percent of noncash items are recovered by the original owner.[2]

For readers familiar with Japan, these figures may not be all that surprising. I have heard many a tale of cash, CDs, keys, cameras, briefcases, confidential legal memoranda, and books that reappeared after having been presumed lost forever, as well has a few stories of items that stayed lost (mentioning "lost property," I have learned, is an invitation for anecdotes). "Just think," a well-traveled Japanese friend said to me after re-

1. Shohisha Ishiki Chōsa, Bijinesuman no Otoshimono Hakusho [White Paper on Businessmen's Lost Property] (2000), available at http://www.cic.co.jp/introduce/20000411_1.html.

2. Keisatsuchō [National Police Agency], Keisatsu Hakusho [White Paper on Police] (2003).

covering his computer in Tokyo, "what would have happened if I had left my laptop on the subway in New York."

Among other tasks, this chapter presents the results of experiments conducted to determine whether my friend actually had a better chance of recovery in Tokyo or New York (the relatively unsurprising answer: Tokyo) and to uncover the reasons why. As for the latter, the focus of this chapter, most accounts attribute Japan's apparent success at lost-and-found to social factors or Japanese ethics. As the *Los Angeles Times* put it, "Drop something in a public restroom or in a subway corridor in Tokyo and there's a good chance you'll get it back, here in one of the most honest nations on Earth."[3]

Maybe people in Japan *are* honest and altruistic. I do not argue that they are not, and I happily acknowledge that some of the factors that support honesty appear to be in abundance in Japan. In this chapter, though, my central claim is that the Japanese lost property system works well in large part because of well-designed formal institutions that efficiently allocate and enforce possessory rights. Those formal institutions at least coincide with, perhaps are caused by, and may in addition foster informal institutions, the informal enforcement of which coerces outliers who might not otherwise do the right thing.

The Japanese approach to found property is not unique; as this chapter shows, similar regimes appear in the United States. But at least four important potential differences emerge from the details of Japanese property rights allocation and enforcement:[4]

First, compared to the legal regime of the United States (and most other systems in the world), Japanese finders' law is simple and uniform.

Second, the system has a long and relatively unwavering history and appears to be well known.

---

3. Mark Magnier, Many Happy Returns for Lost and Found, L.A. Times, Nov. 29, 1999, at A1.

4. This chapter is the first discussion of Japanese finders' law in English and the first historical discussion of the scheme in any language. Even in Japan, there is little about the subject other than a handful of case commentaries and practical guides for police who administer the scheme; the only article remotely on point that I was able to uncover is a three-page essay comparing Japanese and U.S. newspaper clippings and court cases concerning lost property. Masami Otsuka, Hanrei ni Miru Nichibei Bunka Hikaku No. 7: Otoshimono wo Hirotta Hito no Kenri no Nichibei Hikaku [A Comparison of Japanese and U.S. Culture through Court Decisions No. 7: Legal Rights of Lost Property Finders], 2–4 Kokusai Hōmu Senryaku 82–85 (1993).

Third, the reporting of lost objects is made more efficient by the *kōban* (police box) institution and the establishment of a legal duty of police to search for owners. The ubiquity of the kōban helps ingrain law-supporting norms in everyday Japan from childhood.

Finally, Japanese finders' law creates well-defined incentives to encourage finders to report their finds and disincentives to misappropriation. The law provides a simple system of carrots and sticks.[5] Japanese civil law provides that a person who finds a lost article shall deposit it with the police or with the security office of the building in which it is found, if such an office exists. The law then provides two carrots. First, if the owner claims the object, he or she is required to pay the finder a fee of 5 to 20 percent of the object's value. Second, if no one claims the object in six months and two weeks, the object is returned to the finder.

Now the stick, from Japanese criminal law. Although Japanese law contains no penalties for nonrescue (a finder is free to ignore lost property), a finder who misappropriates the property for his or her own has committed embezzlement and is subject to fine of up to $1,000 and imprisonment of up to one year. I find that although prosecution of adult offenders for the ordinary appropriation of lost property is rare, embezzlement of lost property is second only to larceny in the number of juvenile cases brought by police to prosecutors, and adults are often prosecuted in particular situations, such as when the acquisition is connected with a more serious crime or when intent is particularly obvious. Even when prosecution is not initiated, the time-consuming and degrading process of investigation in Japan, as we shall see, often is a punishment in itself.

Because the above four factors are interrelated, it's hard to formulate a precise order of importance in explaining Japanese success at recovering lost property. The kōban system and carrot-and-stick incentives might be the most important in influencing individual behavior, and in the absence of either the system would likely be much less effective. But both may be reinforced by simple rules and an educated citizenry, and social norms, in turn, may be both cause and effect for each factor.

The chapter proceeds as follows. First, I present quantitative evidence about Japanese item recovery that suggest a relatively efficient regime. Still, the data are equivocal. To better understand comparative lost-and-

---

5. On carrots and sticks in finders' law, see Saul Levmore, Waiting for Rescue: An Essay on the Evolution and Incentive Structure of the Law of Affirmative Obligations, 72 Va. L. Rev. 879 (1986).

found systems, following Milgram's famous lost-letter technique and subsequent "lost dollar" studies,[6] I conducted an experiment involving the intentional loss of property. In short, I dropped wallets and cell phones in Tokyo and New York and waited to see how much I recovered.

I then attempt to explain these findings through an investigation of lost-and-found institutions. I discuss the Japanese finders' law, outline its historical origins, and compare it with that of other legal systems, particularly those of the United States. Next I analyze how those legal rules are applied in practice.

Finally, I attempt to unpack the knotty relation among social norms, honesty, altruism, and the formal institutions discussed in the chapter. I examine the sparse social scientific evidence about honesty and altruism in Japan in general and about the return of lost property in particular. In part because of the dearth of such studies, I then attempt to build on that database with two empirical studies of my own. First, I conduct a survey of issues relating to finders in Japan and compare it with existing U.S. survey data. Second, I follow up on the lost-wallet experiments presented in the beginning of the chapter by talking with those who returned the property and police officers who handled the returns.

HOW MUCH IS LOST AND FOUND?

Japan maintains some of the most extensive and detailed data about lost and found property in the world. I examine those data to attempt to determine how much property is lost and found in Japan. I look at national statistics and then compare those data with the available data from the United States. Finally, I present the results of a unique experiment designed to compare lost-and-found rates in Japan and the United States.

Official Japanese Data

Compare Tokyo, obviously an urban area, with Aomori, a rural area. Table 2.1 presents data about items lost and recovery rates for the two ar-

---

6. Stanley Milgram et al., The Lost-Letter Technique: A Tool of Social Research, 29 Public Opinion Q. 437 (1965); Louis A. Penner et al., Lost Dollar: Situational and Personality Determinants of a Pro- and Antisocial Behavior, 44 J. Personality 274–93 (1976).

Table 2.1 Lost Property in Tokyo and Aomori, 2003

	Tokyo	*Aomori*
Population	11,830,000	1,478,000
Kōban per 100 km²	96.5	7.9
Found objects		
Most popular	1. Umbrellas (396,696)	1. Umbrellas (7,947)
	2. Clothes (238,151)	2. Wallets (6,229)
	3. Wallets (175,579)	3. Bags (1,298)
Total number	1,867,397	19,725
	(1 per 6.3 residents)	(1 per 74.3 residents)
Percent returned to owner	21.7	40.76
Percent awarded to finder	59.3	22.38
Found Cash		
Total value of found cash	¥2,492,024,204	¥239,804,427
	($25 m)	($2.39 m)
Percent returned to owner	71.9%	70.56%
Percent awarded to finder	18.4%	21.40%

Sources: Kōban data are from Sōmucho Tōkeikyoku, Shakai Seikatsu Tōkei Shihyō [Social Indicators by Prefecture of Japan], 188 (2000); Tokyo data from Tokyo Metropolitan Police, http://www.keishico.metro.tokyo.jp/toukei/kaikei/kaikei.htm. Aomori data are from Amori Prefectural Police, available at http://www.police.pref.aomori.jp/keimubu/otoshimono.htm. Objects not returned or awarded are sold or thrown away.

eas in 2003. The urban-rural comparison reveals both interesting similarities and interesting differences. The percentages of objects and cash that were returned to owners are quite high, roughly the same, and near the national average. In both cases, more than 60 percent of objects and more than 90 percent of cash was recovered by either the finder or the original owner.

But the distribution of found objects between finders and losers differs. Tokyo awarded a much higher percentage to finders than Aomori, and Aomori returned a much higher percentage to original owners. Perhaps Tokyo finders are more aggressive in pursuing their claims. Perhaps Tokyo losers give up more easily. Or perhaps Tokyo losers lose different items that have different recovery rates. The data for Aomori were not broken down by object, but in Tokyo, the objects most likely to be recovered by owners were cell phones (76.1 percent), identification cards (67.8 percent), and wallets (62.4 percent); no other item had more than a 50

Figure 2.1. Lost-and-Found Reports, 1973–2002

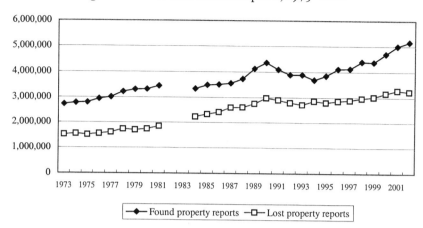

percent recovery rate. The objects most likely to be awarded to the finder were umbrellas (93.3 percent), clothing (80.9 percent), stock certificates (70.9 percent), and cameras (66.2 percent).

This difference aside, the rest of the data line up about as one might expect. The most frequently found objects in both areas were umbrellas, with wallets coming in second in Aomori and third in Tokyo. Most interestingly, the disposition of cash is nearly identical. In roughly three-quarters of the cases of found cash, the owner turned up—and only a very small portion of the cash went to neither the finder nor the owner.[7]

To get a sense of whether Tokyo and Aomori data accurately represent national lost-and-found patterns over time, I examined national lost-and-found data for the period 1973–2002. Figure 2.1 details the number of loss reports and finder's reports for the period. Finders' reports are filed much more frequently loss reports, resulting in data that appear to show more finds than losses. Most basically, as the figure shows, loss rates and find

7. The Tokyo Metropolitan Police also keep data for twelve categories of found objects for the period 1989–2003. The top three finds are included in table 2.1, but the time-series data show some interesting trends. First, electronics finds have grown astronomically in the past few years, largely because of the increase in portable communications. Although electronics accounted for only about 10,000 finds annually before 1995, in 1995 the number was 22,000, and by 1998, 77,248 finds were reported annually. Second, losses of big-finders'-fee items such as stock certificates are not rare, averaging about 10,000 finds per year. See Tokyo Metropolitan Police, http://www.keishicko.metro.tokyo.jp/toukei/kaikei/kaikei/htm.

Figure 2.2. Lost and Found Cash, 1973–2002

Figure 2.3. Lost and Found Items, 1973–2002

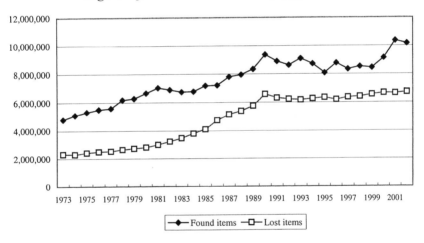

rates have generally increased over the period (data are unavailable 1982–1983), with a "bubble" coinciding with Japan's economic bubble in the late 1980s and early 1990s.

To get a more complete picture, it is useful to divide the data into objects and cash. Figures 2.2 and 2.3 show the amount of cash and the numbers of items that are listed in the loss reports and finder's reports.

These two figures suggest some interesting trends. First, note that reported cash finds as a percentage of reported cash losses decreased significantly over the thirty-year period (from nearly half in the mid-1970s to less than one-third in 2002). Again, multiple phenomena may account for the change; among other things, finders might be less honest than they were in the past, or losers might be reporting more cash losses.

Second, note that the opposite phenomenon occurred for object finds. Reported object losses as a percentage of reported object finds increased significantly (from less than half in the 1970s to more than two-thirds in 2002. Perhaps fewer object losses are being reported (perhaps items may be more replaceable), or more object finds are being reported.

Third, note that the loss rate for cash exceeds the find rate, while the find rate for items exceeds the loss rate. In this connection, note also that the find rate and loss rate exhibit roughly the same trends in both figures. Although the report rates have changed over time, the same basic ups and downs appear. To check the relations more precisely, I compared the correlation of the first differences—the annual rates of change—between (1) cash lost reports and cash found reports and (2) object lost reports and object found reports. The correlation for cash was a highly significant 0.853 ($p = 0.000$). The correlation for objects was only 0.176 ($p = 0.360$), not even marginally significant. Although the data may be imperfect, these results may indicate that the system is more effective in reuniting losers with cash than with noncash items because find report rates more closely track loss rates.

To further explore incentives, I examined the data for the disposition of found property, as detailed in figure 2.4. As the figure indicates, owners have become more aggressive in retrieving both property *and* cash in the past thirty years, but cash has a higher return rate. Again, multiple explanations may be possible, including the easier identification of cash owners (cash is often lost in wallets that contain identification). In any event, the data suggest that although cash finds exceed reported cash losses, cash losses that are reported are more likely to be returned to the owner than object losses. The increase in the percentage of returned items over time may be indicative of an increase in the value of portable objects such as electronics in the past two decades.

Comparison to the United States

Unlike Japan, the United States keeps no national statistics on lost-and-found property, and I was unable even to locate any state that maintained such data. Accordingly, I turn to city-specific data for insights, but note that any unit of comparison is imperfect. In any two systems, and cer-

Figure 2.4. Found Cash and Items Returned to Owner, 1973–2002

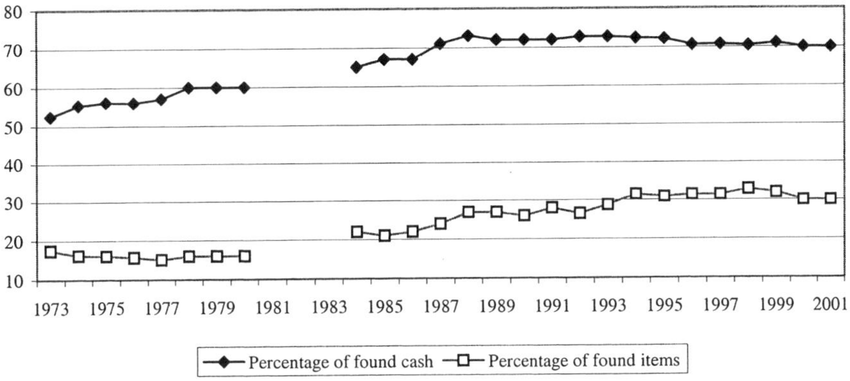

tainly in comparisons between Japan and the United States, there are likely to be differences in objects lost, objects carried, the nature of places frequented, and conceptions of what objects should be turned in to authorities. The data do not compensate for such factors.

That stated, the best comparison in the United States with Tokyo, at least, is probably New York. New York's lost-property statute requires police to accept property, give receipts, and give notice of the finding if they "have reason to believe that a person has an interest in found property" (New York Personal Property Law §253). As I show below, the New York statute is also somewhat similar to the Japanese statute in awarding the property to the finder after a specified period of time. But when I called the precincts specifically designated by the New York City Taxi and Limousine Commission to receive lost property, I was informed that those precincts only keep logs, not statistics. I filed a Freedom of Information Act request with the New York Police Department. After several rounds of phone calls, I received my answer nearly two years later: my request was denied because (unlike Japan) the data do not exist.

I also tried Los Angeles. With its low reliance on public transportation, Los Angeles is a difficult comparison to Japan, but the police function could conceivably be the same for lost items found on public property. The Los Angeles Police Department Property Division informed me that it logs all lost property. But it does not keep related statistics and in fact does not distinguish between property found by citizens and property retrieved by officers in the course of a crime investigation.

I then turned to an alternative: Grand Central Terminal in New York City. According to a spokesperson for the regional commuter rail system

Metro-North, the lost-and-found at Grand Central Terminal, which averages about 140,000 passengers per day, receives about one thousand found items per month. In 1995, the return rate was said to be 20 percent or less "at best." Since that time, thanks at least in part to an enterprising former police officer who attempted to make the office more efficient through better labeling, the return rate for found items in 2000 is said to be "sixty percent or higher."[8]

The Grand Central figures are not scientific, and the fact that they were formulated by a Metro-North spokesperson might make them suspect. If they are accurate, they are high, approximately equal to the Japanese national rates. But Grand Central is a relatively closed environment, and as such may not be compared easily with the national Japanese figures.

For a better comparison, I attempted to obtain figures from Japanese train stations. Although I was unable to obtain official figures from major Japanese railways, I was told unofficially that at Shinjuku Station in Tokyo, which averages three million passengers per day according to East Japan Railway (and unlike Grand Central is a station on many lines and not simply a terminal), the owner recovers about 80 percent of lost items. If that figure is accurate, it is significantly higher than that for Grand Central[9]—even though greater passenger volume at Shinjuku might make it

8. Kate Stone Lombardi, Electronics Store? No, Lost and Found in Grand Central Terminal, N.Y. Times, July 28, 1996, at 13WC1.

9. The Shinjuku data, like those for Grand Central, may be suspect. Shinjuku Station sits on the very busy twenty-nine-station Yamanote line, which encircles central Tokyo in an infinite loop and on which four hundred thousand objects are lost annually; see Eki Shanai no Wasuremono Soku Kensaku [Unified Search for Objects Lost in Stations and on Trains], Nihon Keizai Shinbun, July 10, 2002 (evening edition), at 18. A unified computer system for locating objects on that line did not enter a testing phase until May 2002 (before then, workers phoned and faxed from station to station to find objects), shortly after Shinjuku personnel reported the 80 percent figure to me. There are no data available for the Yamanote line, but for rough comparison, I obtained data for the thirty-eight stations of Japan Railways' Hokkaido Railway Company on the Hakodate Line and in the Sapporo suburbs. In those stations, the lost item return rate rose from 26 percent to 32 percent in the week that a computer system was introduced (ibid.), a figure much lower than that reported in Shinjuku. Although the Hokkaido figure may be lower than Shinjuku's simply because recovery at thirty-eight stations is more difficult to manage than at one, there is little reason why the computerless Yamanote line should significantly outperform the computer-aided Hokkaido lines and little reason why Shinjuku should significantly outperform the rest of the Yamanote line. Accordingly, I suspect that the Shinjuku figure is an anomaly, is exaggerated, or employs a denominator that somehow limits the field to Shinjuku losses, but I was unable to obtain further details.

more difficult for officials to administer lost-and-found procedures and for losers to locate their objects.

In short, Japan generally appears to do a much better job of gathering data relevant to lost-and-found property than does the United States. The evidence regarding the efficacy of the system is equivocal, but the available data, combined with the lack of organized U.S. data and anecdotal evidence, suggest that the Japanese lost-property system functions well in comparison with the U.S. system.

An Experiment

But yes, the evidence regarding efficacy is equivocal. To investigate further, I conducted an experiment based largely on various "lost" techniques of psychologists to study helping behavior, honesty, cooperation, and a variety of other social and political phenomena. Perhaps the most famous such procedure is the "lost-letter technique" described and developed by Stanley Milgram. To avoid the pitfalls inherent in the survey process, Milgram devised a method of direct experimental observation: "At the root, the technique is a simple one. An investigator distributes—drops—throughout a city a large number of letters, addressed and stamped but unposted. A person who comes across one of these 'lost' letters on the street must decide what to do: mail it? disregard it? destroy it?"[10]

In Milgram's first study, conducted in 1963, he found that while more than 70 percent of finders returned by mail letters addressed to "Medical Research Associates" or to an individual, only 25 percent returned letters addressed to "Friends of the Communist Party" or "Friends of the Nazi Party." Subsequent studies, as well as modifications such as the "lost e-mail method," found similar results.[11]

Expanding on Milgram's technique, other researchers studied human behavior using lost dollar and lost wallet experiments. In lost dollar experiments, psychologists examined reactions to a lost dollar in a wallet, in an envelope belonging to an institution, and without an identifiable owner. Collapsing various situations and owner characteristics, they found that

10. Stanley Milgram, The Individual in a Social World: Essays and Experiments, Reading 296 (1977).

11. Steven E. Stern and Jon E. Farber, The Lost E-Mail Method: Milgram's Lost-Letter Technique in the Age of the Internet, 29 Behav. Res. Methods, Instruments, & Computers 260 (1997).

31.2 percent returned the dollar, 39.6 percent ignored it, and 29.2 percent took it.[12] Similar popular studies replicated these sorts of tests, finding, for instance, that 70 percent of wallets left on the street were taken, despite the fact that the wallets contained the owner's address.[13] These results surely are discouraging to losers. Even when surveyed, a situation in which respondents can easily lie, 21 percent of eighteen-to-thirty-four-year-olds told *Money* magazine pollsters that they would keep a wallet with complete identification that contained $1,000.[14]

Finally, in the most recent manifestation of the genre, economists Martin Dufwenberg and Uri Gneezy conducted an "experimental lost wallet game" in which they attempted use a bargaining game to determine the factors that might lead a finder to return a lost wallet. Not surprisingly, they found that the higher the stakes, the more likely the participants in the experiment were to keep the wallet. They also found some interesting altruistic effects, consistent with the Dictator game, in which one player decides how to divide a pot of money. But this experiment—and the discussion—rest on the assumption that players in the game, as well as wallet-finders in real life, have no economic reasons to report the find. The finder "simply keeps the wallet," they note, when he or she realizes that "the owner *does not reimburse* the finder if she picks her wallet up at the police station."[15]

In Japan, as this chapter has shown, the dynamics are different. Although the owner does not fully reimburse the finder, leaving some moral hazard, the finders' fee and the possibility of full reimbursement after six months and two weeks encourage many people to turn in wallets.

To find out more about how these incentives operate in the real world and in cross-cultural settings, I conducted a similar test. In two locations in New York and one in Tokyo, I dropped objects and cash. New York's lost property statute is relatively simple; objects with a value of more than $20 are required to be turned in to police (New York Personal Property Law §252). The statutory waiting period in New York for a find of less than $100 is three months, and the finder has a right to the property for ten days after the expiration of that period (New York Personal Property

---

12. Penner et al., *supra* note 6.

13. Ibid. at 294.

14. Denise M. Topolnicki, You'd Be Surprised What Folks Will Do for Money Today, Money, Aug. 1994, at 12.

15. Martin Dufwenberg and Uri Gneezy, Measuring Beliefs in an Experimental Lost Wallet Game, 30 Games & Econ. Behav. 64 (2000), emphasis added.

Law §253). Before the end of the period, the property goes to the loser if claimed.

Here's what I did.[16] To test the return of objects, I dropped one hundred mobile phones in each location. To test the return of cash, I dropped twenty wallets in each location. (I had obtained sixty wallets from a lost-and-found auction and inserted in each a small amount of cash and an identification card.) In Japan, each wallet contained two 1,000-yen bills. In the United States, each wallet contained two $10 bills to reach the New York $20 statutory minimum (not that a New Yorker would have any clue about the statutory minimum, but to create the legal obligation). This methodology may tell us little about how people react to valuable finds, such as a briefcase stuffed with cash, but it should help us understand more about returns of more everyday finds.

I expected to find higher return rates for property than for cash. Property is relatively illiquid; an unknown person's mobile phone not connected to a service is not all that useful or valuable. Return of mobile phones may give a good indication of altruism, while return of cash may add an additional element of honesty. Of course, the actual calculation may differ by individual.

The first two locations I used were mixed business-and-shopping districts of Tokyo (Shinjuku) and New York (midtown Manhattan). I designed the third location to test possible cross-cultural differences: I dropped objects in front of a New York grocery store (with the owner's permission) that caters almost exclusively to a Japanese expatriate clientele. I expected relatively good return rates from this location because of the clear identity of the person to whom the find should be reported. Still, if differences in lost property recovery rates are based primarily on cultural traits, we might expect to see similar return rates among Japanese finders in Tokyo and New York. But if institutions are a large part of the difference, we might expect return rates to differ by country, not ethnicity.

The results of the drops are as reported in table 2.2. As the table shows, for both phones and cash, the highest return rates came from Tokyo (ninety-five phones, seventeen wallets), and the lowest from New York (seventy-seven phones, eight wallets, including two *empty* wallets).[17] The

16. For details of the project, see the appendix to Mark D. West, Losers: Recovering Lost Property in Japan and the United States, 37:2 Law & Society Rev. 369 (2003).

17. Although details are not available, these results are comparable to those of a previous popular survey that found a 70 percent take rate. See Penner et al., *supra* note 6, at 294.

Table 2.2. Results of Property Drops

	Tokyo		New York		New York Japanese	
	Phones	*Cash*	*Phones*	*Cash*	*Phones*	*Cash*
(a) "Lost"	100	20	100	20	100	20
		(¥40,000 total)		($400 total)		($400 total)
(b) Returned by finder	95	17	77	6 intact, 2 empty	84	12
(c) Of (b), # returned to police by finder	88	16	6	2	8	2
(d) Of (c), # in which rights not waived by finder	5	15	N/A	N/A	N/A	N/A
(e) Of (d), # recovered by finder after waiting period	2	6	0	1	0	1

differences are statistically significant (phones, $\chi^2(2) = 13.1569, p < 0.01$; wallets, $\chi^2(2) = 12.48, p < 0.01$). The same distribution was true for the ratio of objects returned via the police; eighty-eight phones and sixteen wallets were given to the police in Tokyo even though the objects contained identifying information that would have allowed that finder to contact me directly. In New York, almost all returns were made by phone calls to the phone mailbox listed on the object even though a police station was located nearby.

Finders' recovery rates tell a similar story. New York has no procedure by which a finder waives rights to claim unclaimed property, but in Tokyo, the finders of eighty-three of eighty-eight phones waived such rights (wisely, because they had little value), and the finders of only one of sixteen wallets waived (wisely, because the contents were worth two thousand yen). Of the five phones to which rights were not waived, two were recovered by finders after the waiting period, and of the fifteen returned wallets to which rights were not waived, six were recovered by finders.[18] In New York, only one of the wallets delivered to police was recovered by the finder after the statutory period.

18. Presumably the other nine nonwaived wallets were not recovered because the finders forgot about them or decided that the trip to pick them up wasn't worth the two thousand yen, because the trip cost a lot, because the action seemed petty, or because they simply didn't care.

The results of the New York Japanese drop were interesting; return rates were higher than those for New York but lower than those for Tokyo. Several explanations seem plausible. First, perhaps the drop location made returns easier than in the general New York case, because the most logical return location was the store clerk. But note that a few finders returned items to the police nonetheless, a response that does not comply with the law even in the Japanese system (which mandates return to the store) but may be an understandable product of a socially ingrained legal system, discussed below, that encourages returns to police. Second, perhaps all Japanese finders are simply more honest or altruistic than non-Japanese counterparts. Although this explanation is certainly possible, note that the New York Japanese return rates were higher than the New York rates but lower than the Tokyo rates, suggesting that Japanese altruism is not monolithic. It may be that Japanese who come to New York are somehow "contaminated" by New York, a finding that could be explained by many different factors, including both formal and informal institutions. I return to these causal questions in the final part of the chapter.

Although no location had return rates as high as Tokyo's, no location had abysmal return rates. Given that New York devotes virtually no public resources to the recovery of lost property, the return rates there may not be all that bad, suggesting, perhaps, that Japan is spending considerable resources for what may be a relatively small direct payoff. Although Japan may be in fact gaining indirect payoffs in the form of greater societal comfort (which might result in greater economic activity), it might have the luxury of devoting its resources to what seems like a relatively insignificant endeavor because of its low violent crime rates. However, if police attention in Tokyo to such minutiae as lost bicycles is *driving* low rates of violent crime there, policymakers in New York and elsewhere would do well to take note. The available data do not unequivocally support either causal story, and some combination of both may be at work.[19]

---

19. Although New York and Tokyo are similar, the national data might be more significantly affected by geography. Japan is a relatively small, densely populated country with a more or less centrally administered law enforcement agency and with resources devoted to kōban for many purposes, among which is lost property management. As such, the system would appear to be able to operate at lower cost than a similar system might in the United States, with its automobile culture, wide-open spaces, and patchwork law enforcement system.

LEGAL CONTOURS

The success of the Japanese system is attributable at least in part to the incentives created by legal institutions. I now examine the modern system, discuss its historical origins, and compare it with that of the United States.

The Modern Japanese System

Japan's modern legal system has its origins in the late nineteenth-century Meiji Era (1868–1912). The Meiji legal reforms, based largely on French and German models, included the introduction of formal legal education organs and higher courts and the establishment of the first Constitution, Criminal Code, Code of Criminal Procedure, and Civil Code. Article 240 of the Civil Code, adopted in 1896 and still in force, provides that lost articles are the property of the finder if the actual owner does not appear within six months of the date of public notice of the loss, computed as two weeks after the recovery. The Civil Code then provides that the provision is to be administered "in accordance with other special laws."

The relevant "special law," the Law Concerning Lost Articles (*Ishitsu-butsuhō*, Law no. 40 of 1899), was adopted in 1899 and remains in force. The Law Concerning Lost Articles provides a concrete set of rules on the basis of which to administer lost property. A person who finds lost property must to return it to its owner or submit it to the chief of police within seven days of the find (articles 1, 9). Lost property includes articles left behind by other people and domestic animals that have run away (article 12). If a person finds lost property inside a private establishment (such as a department store, a ship, or inside the turnstiles of a railway), he or she must submit it to the management of the establishment within twenty-four hours (article 10).

Note that the system applies to all property, with no minimum value threshold. According to the law, a penny found on the ground cannot be pocketed but must be taken to the police.

The law establishes a reward system. On recovery, an owner "shall pay" the finder a sum of between 5 and 20 percent of the value of the lost property (article 4). A finder has a civil right to the reward (assuming the find was reported within the seven-day period), but nonpayment is not a criminal infraction. If the property is found in a private establishment, one-half of the reward goes to the establishment's owner, giving the owner incentive to secure lost property (and less incentive for the individual finder in such establishments). If no one claims the property, and the finder waives or forfeits his or her rights to it, then it becomes government property (articles 9, 15). The finder forfeits rights by not turning in within seven days.

The carrots here, possession after six months and the finders' fee, can be significant. Japanese courts, normally not known for judicial activism, have attached some guidelines to aid in its administration. The value of the property is to be determined at the time of its return to the owner.[20] The exact fee within the 5–20 percent range depends on the type of property and the surrounding facts, but if the parties cannot agree, the court may determine the appropriate fee. The court generally compromises at 10 percent of the value.[21] Some special property deserves special treatment; negotiable notes are valued at one-third to one-half of face value, but nonnegotiable notes are valued at only 2 percent of face value.[22]

The flip side is article 254 of the modern Japanese Criminal Code, adopted in 1907 and still in force today, which creates the crime of embezzlement of a lost article: a person may not wrongfully appropriate a lost article. In perhaps the best-known case in Japan, a group of fisherman in northern Akita prefecture, with the governor's permission, stocked a pond with carp. These were not just ordinary carp, but *nishikigoi*, big, colorful carp that sell for $1,000 or so and eat out of your hand at Japanese gardens. The fishermen stocked their pond with about a thousand of them. About sixty of them escaped their net and were subsequently "found" by Ono. Ono knew what he'd gotten, and he knew their source, but he nevertheless sold them for 380 yen per pound, for a total of 20,520 yen (they were supposedly worth 54,000 yen at the time). The court had little problem finding embezzlement and imposed on Ono a suspended sentence of six months' imprisonment.[23]

20. *Sugisaki v. Hayakawa Building Brokers Bank*, Tokyo District Court, 2386 Hōritsu Shinbun 14 (Feb. 2, 1928).

21. *Nagaoka v. Okuyama*, Great Court of Cassation, 27 Minroku 2199 (Dec. 26, 1922); *Satō v. Shimizu K.K.*, Nagoya District Court, 404 Hanrei Jihō 47 (Mar. 4, 1965).

22. *Kōno v. Tokyo Renga*, Tokyo District Court, 1420 Hanrei Jihō 103 (Mar. 5, 1991); *Yoneda v. Tōkai Bank*, Tokyo District Court, 1043 Hanrei Jihō 140 (Mar. 15, 1982).

23. *State v. Ono*, Supreme Court, 999 Hanrei Jihō 127 (Feb. 20, 1981). Many cases are not so clear-cut. A recent Japanese law–related variety television program asked its panel of four attorney experts whether a crime was committed when a hypothetical suspect found a

Drafters of the Criminal Code apparently imported the criminal law category of "embezzlement of lost articles" from the German system, which made a distinction, subsequently adopted in Japan, between two types of embezzlement: lost-property embezzlement and entrusted-property embezzlement.[24] The latter, as in the United States, is the misappropriation of property in custody. In contrast to the case of lost-property embezzlement, the property is entrusted to the "finder." In lost-property embezzlement, there is no such entrustment. More than 98 percent of all embezzlement arrests are for lost-property embezzlement.

A third category of property theft, larceny, is more difficult to distinguish from lost-property embezzlement. Larceny occurs when one deprives another of possession of an object; embezzlement occurs when one wrongfully appropriates an object that belongs to another. The key in distinguishing the two is possession.[25] Japanese courts have held that a camera left on a tour bus for five minutes within twenty meters of the owner remains in the owner's possession, so taking it would be larceny, not embezzlement.[26] Bicycles are especially problematic and do not automatically invoke a theft charge. A bicycle left out at night less than two meters from one's home is still the owner's possession and thus the charge is theft,[27] but if a drunken owner misplaces his bicycle, it is merely lost, so a subsequent taker is guilty only of embezzlement.[28] Objects found without an owner in sight, mail mistakenly delivered, and personal effects left on

---

large quantity of cash, attempted to report it but changed his mind at the last minute in front of the police station, took it home, and eventually returned it ten days after the find. The panel split 2–2; the suspect's two supporters argued that he lacked mens rea to keep the find and should be rewarded for doing the right thing, while the other two argued that his change of heart at the police station evidenced mens rea.

24. Hiroshi Satakura Sen'yū Ridatsubutsu Ōryōzai [Embezzlement of Uncontrolled Objects], in Chūshaku Keihō [Annotated Penal Code], ed. Shigemitsu Dandō (1964).

25. Sadahiko Takahashi, Settō to Ishitsubutsu (Sen'yū Ridatsubutsu) Ōryō to no Genkai [The Line between Theft and Lost-Property Embezzlement], Keihō no Sōten [Points at Issue in Criminal Law], Jurisuto Zōkan 25 (1987).

26. State v. Hosoda, Supreme Court, 147 Jurisuto 86 (Nov. 8, 1957).

27. State v. Yamamoto, Fukuoka District Court, 8 Kokei 418 (April 25, 1955).

28. State v. Masuda, Tokyo High Court, 281 Hanji 31 (Aug. 8, 1961). In practice, a "found" bicycle is tagged by police with a notice that if the bicycle is not moved by a certain date, it will be removed. If the owner does not move it, police remove it and hold it for the six-month period. If not claimed, it goes to the initial finder who first reported it to police, or, if there is no such person, to auction. Without such a practice and an occasional campaign, many train stations would be deluged with abandoned bicycles.

a train have all been held to constitute lost objects for purposes of distinguishing the charges.[29]

If a person has been "punished" (*shobatsu*) in the past for embezzlement of lost property, the Law Concerning Lost Articles (article 9) states that he is not entitled to finders' rights. It seems unlikely that the provision is applied very often, but note its severity and the incentives it creates. If you embezzle lost property once, you're not entitled to claim it again, or receive the finder's fee for that matter, even if you follow the legal procedures to a T. Just leave the thing there, you with the dirty hands. Although the provision might mitigate serial fraud, it does so by making an outcast of even the most reformed embezzler.

In short, finders of lost property in Japan have three options. First, they may ignore it with no consequence. Second, they can turn in the property to the police or to a private substitute. If they do so within seven days, they normally are entitled either to (1) the property, after six months and fourteen days, or (2) if recovered, a finder's fee of 5 to 20 percent. Third, finders may keep the property, but if they do so, they may be punished by fine or imprisonment.

History

The orderly scheme outlined above was adopted as part of the late Meiji reforms, in which German influence was strong. Some facial similarity to the German scheme exists. But closer analysis reveals a different, earlier origin, for as it turns out, these Meiji schemes were not novel, either. A nearly identical regime functioned in the Edo Period, Japan's feudal era (1603–1868). In 1742 the shogunate promulgated the *Kujikata Osadamegaki* (roughly, Official Collection of Legal Rules), Japan's first attempt at a national compilation of preexisting local laws for shogunate-controlled territories.

Article 60 of the *Osadamegaki* contains three provisions pertaining to lost property. First, it incorporates a 1721 edict requiring that a finder submit lost property to authorities within three days. If the owner appears

---

29. *State v. Sekiguchi*, Supreme Court, 2 Keishū 1877 (Dec. 24, 1948); *State v. Boku*, Supreme Court, 4 Keishū 190 (June 27, 1950); *State v. Gochi*, Great Court of Cassation, 23 Keiroku 1113 (Aug. 15, 1917). The greater discretion said to be given to common-law judges (to expand the scope of larceny) may explain why lost-property embezzlement is a highlight of civil systems and not common-law systems: it fills in a gap in theft law.

and the property is cash, he or she must halve it with the finder. If other than cash, the owner must pay the finder an unspecified reward. Second, incorporating a 1738 edict, the *Osadamegaki* states that if the owner does not claim the property within six months, possession is awarded to the finder. Finally, incorporating a customary rule of law with no fixed date, the *Osadamegaki* provides that a finder who appropriates the property will be fined.[30] Although it is difficult to find the exact origin of this customary rule, prosecutions, some of which resulted in the "fine" of a death sentence, from the late seventeenth and early eighteenth centuries reflect its existence.[31] Thus, depending on how one counts, the system has been in existence nationally for at least 125 years and perhaps in excess of 300. If lost property practices are socially ingrained, this length of time seems sufficient for the process.

Prosecution and Enforcement

Of course, few modern cases of embezzlement of lost property are punished by death. But cases are indeed reported, and some are indeed prosecuted.

Trivial cases. The Code of Criminal Procedure permits police to dispose of criminal cases when prosecutors authorize them to do so (article 246). Prosecutors do so by sending guidelines to police. Although there are no national guidelines, the standards and operations reported by Johnson in his in-depth study of Japanese prosecutors are typical:

---

30. A 1784 official handbill reprinted in the *Koji Ruien*, or Encyclopedia of Ancient Matters, seemingly modifies the law (though perhaps for a limited time; the evidence is unclear) by specifying that ships and bamboo lumber that float into harbors are property of the state to be sold at public auction, no matter who finds them. Harigamirui, reprinted in 2 Koji Ruien [Encyclopedia of Ancient Matters], Hōritsu vol. 44, Ran'ibutsu, p. 799, 1896–1914, ed. Jingōshichō (rev. ed. 1928).

31. An example is Rizaemon's case of November 22, 1683. Although the details are unclear, Rizaemon apparently appropriated and hid 50 *ryō* (very roughly $50,000 today) that his employer had lost. Unfortunately for Rizaemon, his sister found it and reported the find to the authorities. It is unclear how the employer initially lost possession of the money, but it had occurred in such a way that the prosecuted crime was not one of larceny but one of embezzlement of lost property. The shogunate, perhaps noting the close relation to larceny (which was heavily punished) and the large amount of the loss, sentenced Rizaemon to death. Harigamirui, *supra* note 30.

In the early 1990s deputy chief prosecutors instructed police to drop theft cases on three conditions: if the value of the stolen goods was less than 10,000 yen (about $85); if the offender had a fixed residence (this standard disqualifies transients, many of whom are foreigners); and if the offender repented. . . . [P]rosecutors know that police stretch the standards (often by relaxing the 10,000 yen cap in order to fit stolen bicycles and mopeds under the ceiling), though they insist worrisome abuses are rare and deviations from the guidelines seldom depart from their own definition of a "minor" case.[32]

Still, these "trivial" cases can be time-consuming and distressful for those accused of the crime. I spoke with a total of fifteen persons accused of lost-property embezzlement but whose cases were disposed of by the police because of low stakes. All fifteen, who were accused of appropriating a range of objects from wallets to electronics to small appliances, told stories of long questioning by police and short notice for appointments; the shortest time for questioning was six hours. In one case, the accused was asked to bring in his wife, who took time off from work to hear her husband's apology to the police. In three others, the suspects were asked to sign confessions that painted their actions in what they felt to be a much more sinister light than the circumstances warranted.

Arrests. For nontrivial cases, the pipeline begins with arrests. Consider first the annual numbers of arrests and cases sent by police to prosecutors, as shown in figure 2.5.[33] With the exception of a slight dip in 2000, the figure indicates a rising and not insubstantial number of arrests each year. The number of cases sent to prosecutors post-arrest is approximately equal to the larceny rate and more than twenty times the murder rate.[34]

Prosecution: juvenile. Figure 2.5 reveals only the number of persons who meet thresholds for arrest and forwarding to prosecutors—prosecution

32. David T. Johnson, The Japanese Way of Justice: Prosecuting Crime in Japan, 55 (2002).

33. Arrests and prosecutions are taken from Hōmushō, Kensatsu Tōkei Nenpo [Annual Report of Prosecutorial Statistics], various years.

34. Virtually every measure of crime has increased over the last decade in Japan; the crime rate rose from 1,324 criminal offenses per 100,000 people in 1990 to 1,926 per 100,000 in 2000 and increased every year but one in the period. National Police Agency officials inform me that the number of lost-property embezzlement incidents may be much higher in recent years than arrest figures indicate, because police have focused much of their attention on crimes that they believe to be more serious.

Figure 2.5. Incidents of Embezzlement of Lost Property, 1989–2001

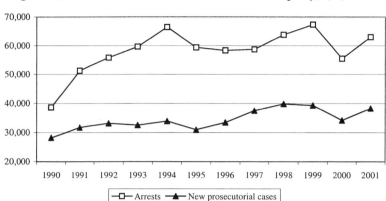

itself is another matter. Consider next the prosecution figures. Figure 2.6 details the total number of cases and the two major categories of disposition for lost-property cases during the thirty-year period ending in 2002.

The figure shows that more than three-quarters of all cases are sent by prosecutors to family court; in other words, more than three-fourths of the offenders in lost-property embezzlement crimes disposed of by prosecutors are minors under the age of twenty. Teenagers are most likely to commit the crime; the distribution of juveniles disposed of by family courts in lost-property embezzlement cases between 1990 and 1999 is roughly 28 percent for juveniles under sixteen, 41 percent for juveniles between sixteen and seventeen, and 29 percent for juveniles aged eighteen to nineteen.[35]

The distribution of crime among adults and minors is significant and implies several possibilities. Perhaps minors are treated more leniently than adults: adults might be charged with larceny (with penalties of up to ten years' imprisonment), while juveniles are merely charged with lost-property embezzlement (with penalties of up to one year's imprisonment), which would distort the statistics. This explanation is certainly plausible, but arrest rates tentatively suggest that it may be incomplete. Although adults do indeed comprise less than 25 percent of the lost-property embezzlement pool, they only account for 43 percent of the lar-

---

35. Saikō Saibansho Jimusōkyoku, Shihō Tōkei Nenpo [Annual Report of Judicial Statistics], various years.

Figure 2.6. Prosecutorial Disposition of Lost-Property Cases, 1973–2002

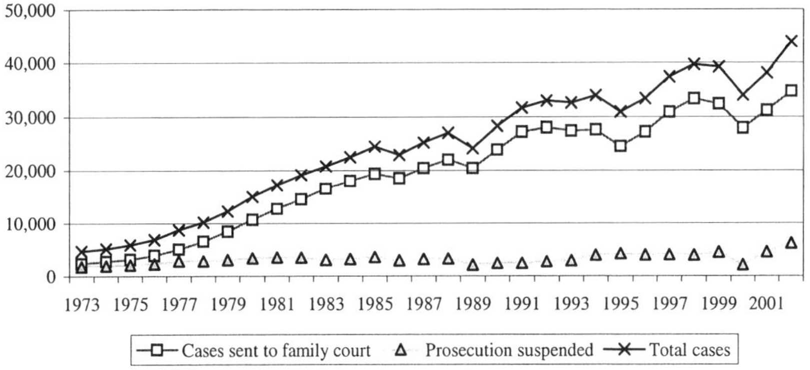

| | Cases sent to family court   △ Prosecution suspended   Total cases |

ceny pool.[36] Moreover, larceny is the only crime for which juveniles are arrested more than they are for lost-property embezzlement. Larceny accounted for 65.8 percent of all juvenile arrests in 1998, suggesting that larceny remains an option for juveniles as well.

My discussions with police and offenders suggest a different explanation: juveniles actually do commit more lost-property embezzlement than adults. More than half of arrests of juveniles for this offense are due to misappropriated bicycles. The most common scenario is the taking of bicycles from train stations, where bicycles are in abundance, some are not locked, and those that are locked are usually locked only with a small spoke-stopper that prevents the rear wheel from turning.

When the ownership of the bicycle is clear, larceny is generally charged; if not, lost-property embezzlement is charged, suggesting that these arrests are for misdeeds more akin to theft than to the everyday lost-property situation. But bicycle cases are not the object of misappropriation. Police, prosecutors, and juveniles to whom I spoke detailed a long list of embezzlement scenarios not listed in any statistical survey: a cornucopia of failures to return or report cash, wallets, shopping bags full of purchases, mobile phones, purses, electronic games, jewelry, skis and other sporting equipment, and so on. Although I have no systematic method of matching loss reports with state enforcement, police officers whom I in-

36. Of 152,379 cases, 85,473 were sent by prosecutors to family court. See Hōmushō, *supra* note 33, at 78–79.

terviewed estimated roughly that about one-half to three-fourths of lost-property embezzlements could be so linked.

Prosecution: adults. If arrest figures accurately reflect frequency, about 25 percent of lost-property embezzlement is committed by adults, and 18 percent of cases are settled by suspension of prosecution, a disposition by which prosecutors release suspects without declaring a lack of guilt or insufficiency of evidence. During the period 1973–2002, prosecutors nationally filed charges against an average of 251 adults each year, including a high of 558 in 2002 and a low of 129 in 1993. About 10 cases of adult lost-property embezzlement cases are decided each year in district court and about 35 in summary court. Cases never end in not-guilty verdicts. More than 90 percent of cases result in jail sentences, and about half of those sentences are suspended. Fines are imposed about twice a year.

Prosecutors whom I interviewed suggested that many of the cases in which adult defendants are criminally punished involved cases in which the lost-property embezzlement was not the only crime committed. To check, I turned to the *Hanrei Taikei* CD-ROM database, which contains 40,754 criminal cases. A search found seventy-four unique cases of potential lost-property embezzlement. Of these seventy-four cases, eighteen involved additional serious crimes. Murder is common; the relevant issue in that situation is whether the murder victim retains "possession" of the property after his or her death for purposes of distinguishing between larceny and embezzlement.[37] Courts have found, for instance, that when a defendant immediately takes a victim's watch after killing her, the crime is larceny,[38] but when a defendant kills his lover and takes her cash and bankbook five to ten days after her death, the crime is lost-property embezzlement.[39]

In the remaining fifty-six cases, serious crimes were not involved. The court had to decide between larceny and embezzlement in thirty-six of the cases; for instance, when a defendant watched a victim "lose" his wallet for less than two minutes at a space of fifteen meters at Tokyo Station while purchasing a bullet train ticket, the court found larceny, not embezzlement. About half of this group of potential lost-property embezzle-

---

37. Manzaburō Shōda, Shisha no Sen'yū ni Tsuite [Regarding Control by Deceased Persons], 320 Jurisuto 69 (1959).

38. *State v. Kawaguchi*, Supreme Court, 447 Hanrei Jihō 97 (April 8, 1956).

39. *State v. [unidentified]*, Niigata District Court, 560 Hanrei Times 199 (Jul. 2, 1985).

ment cases thus were simply larceny cases. The remaining twenty were "pure" lost-property embezzlement cases; that is, they neither featured another serious crime nor required the court to distinguish larceny. Most of these twenty cases did not involve property that was "lost" in the traditional sense, such as the removing of money from an automobile accident victim in one's care four to eight hours after the accident.[40] Only a few cases involved simple lost-property facts, such as the finding of criminal liability for persons who take lost objects from trains, including rolls of cloth, blankets, and raincoats.[41]

Comparison to the United States

Compared to the Japanese system, the U.S. lost-property legal regime is complex and unpredictable.

Law. Finders' law doctrine in the United States is conceptually difficult, making contradictory statements and arbitrary distinctions that are difficult for courts, not to mention laypersons, to follow and apply. When the facts are simple, there is little problem. In the paradigmatic case of *Armory v. Delamirie*, for instance, a chimney-sweep's boy found a jewel while cleaning a chimney.[42] The court simply found that he was entitled "to keep it against all but the rightful owner." But even this distilled holding is not entirely accurate,[43] and as Helmholz has noted, "When the facts become more tangled . . . , the limitations of the hornbook rule appear."[44]

Part of the doctrinal complexity lies in the distinction made in the common law between lost property and property that is merely mislaid. Subject to claims of the true owner, lost property goes to the finder, and

40. *State v. Matsuo,* Morioka District Court, 582 Hanrei Jihō 110 (April 16, 1979).

41. *State v. Katō,* Great Court of Cassation, 27 Keiroku 545 (June 18, 1921); *State v. [unidentified],* Great Court of Cassation, 2630 Hōritsu Shinbun 6 (Nov. 2, 1927); *State v. [unidentified],* Tokyo High Court, 761 Kōken Sokuhō (Nov. 5, 1958).

42. *Armory v. Delamirie,* 1 Str. 505, 92 Eng. Rep. 664 (K.B. 1722).

43. The chimney-sweep boy's claim would be subject to claims of a prior possessor.

44. R. H. Helmholz, Wrongful Possession of Chattels: Hornbook Law and Case Law, 80 Nw. Univ. L. Rev. 1221, 1231 (1987). Helmholz finds that courts disallow possession in cases of wrongdoing on the part of the finder; a hint of dishonesty may cause the property right to transfer to a more honest finder. See *Niederlehner v. Weatherly,* 73 Ohio App. 33, *aff'd,* 142 Ohio St. 366 (1943); *Willsmore v. Township of Osceola,* 106 Mich. App. 671, 308 N.W.2d 796 (1981).

mislaid property goes to the owner of the locus. Many commentators have found the lost-mislaid distinction artificial.[45] Again Helmholz is instructive: "Commentators have pointed out that normally the only objective evidence of the owner's state of mind is the place where the object was found, and it has repeatedly been shown that this is an uncertain guide. One can as easily lose an item on a bench as he can mislay it there. The distinction invites arbitrary decision. Even if it could be consistently applied, the distinction depends upon a largely fictional difference in mental attitude on the part of the true owner. . . . The distinction is built on sand."[46] In the United States, unpredictability and inconsistency plague finders' law from the moment an object is found—the exact moment at which we should be most eager to influence behavior and control moral hazard problems. Virtually all that is certain at that moment is that the true owner has a legitimate claim; the validity of claims made by others is much less clear.

Moreover, finders' law in the United States, unlike the unified Japanese system, is a state-by-state hodgepodge of common law, modern statutes, and haphazard local regulations.[47] In a reaction to the difficulties of the common-law doctrine, more than one-third of the states have adopted lost property statutes,[48] but these statutes differ widely in scope, operation, and remedy.[49]

---

45. Comment, Lost, Mislaid, and Abandoned Property, 8 Fordham L. Rev. 222, 235 (1939).

46. R. H. Helmholz, Equitable Division and the Law of Finders, 52 Fordham L. Rev. 313, 316–17 (1983).

47. A marginally more organized system exists for abandonded property, a category that usually is defined as dormant accounts at financial institutions and unclaimed items from safe deposit boxes. Although laws differ by state, banks and similar institutions are usually required to deliver these funds and items to state treasurers' offices (in California, for instance, funds held by business associations escheat to the state after three years of account inactivity, see Cal. Code tit. 10, ch. 7 [Unclaimed Property Law], §1513).

48. Jennifer S. Moorman, Finders Weepers, Losers Weepers? *Benjamin v. Lindner Aviation, Inc.,* 82 Iowa L. Rev. 717, 717 and note 8 (1997).

49. Oregon (Or. Rev. Stat. §98.025 [2003]), for instance, compensates finders for costs incurred in finding, giving of notice, and care and custody of the lost object. Wisconsin (Wis. Stat. Ann. §170.09) awards the same plus "a reasonable compensation to the finder for his trouble." Montana (Mont. Code Ann. §§70-5-103 to 70-5-105, 70-5-201 [2004]) requires a finder to return a find with a value of more than $10 (including a starving animal) to the owner if the owner is known or suspected. The finder receives compensaton for expenses and a "reasonable award," and may sell the object if it is perishable, if it is in danger of losing half its value, or if the cost of keeping it exceeds two-thirds of its value. New York (Personal Property Law §§252–254) requires a finder to deliver any item with a value

Courts apply state law in ways that make the underlying statute confusing. The Iowa court (ruling 4–3) in *Benjamin v. Lindner Aviation, Inc.*,[50] following the common-law distinction between lost and mislaid property, held that the Iowa lost-property statute did not apply to mislaid property, despite the fact that the Iowa statute apparently was enacted "almost a full year before any United States court even recognized the common-law classifications of found property."[51] The Second Circuit Court of Appeals, interpreting the New York lost-property statute, similarly held that the law did not apply to common-law "mislaid" property, a finding that "baffled" the dissent in part because of "the fact that the distinction has been statutorily abolished in New York."[52]

The point is not that U.S. law is an unworkable mishmash. Diversity is an integral part of the U.S. federal system, and each individual system might work well on its own. I also have little doubt that if Montanans do not know their state's finders' law, their ignorance is not primarily because New York's law differs. The point is merely that in Japan, there in fact is only one law and one system. Uniformity may lead to lower general levels of statutory ignorance.

Enforcement. It is difficult to determine the enforcement and prosecution patterns of lost-property cases in the United States. Misappropriation of lost property is a widely recognized criminal offense. But because it is considered a form of larceny and not a separate form of embezzlement, statistics are unavailable. A leading criminal law treatise suggests that under most schemes, prosecution is difficult because at the time of the finding, a finder must (1) intend to steal the property and (2) either know the identity of the owner or have reason to believe that he or she can learn the identity.[53] Modern statutory schemes such as that of the Model Penal Code that

of more than $20 to the police within ten days and awards the property to the finder after a period of three months to three years, depending on value. Iowa (Iowa Code Ann. §644.7), which has had a lost-property statute since 1839, requires a finder to report the find to the county auditor within five days. It also awards a 10 percent finders' fee for "the taking up of boats and other vessels, and for finding lost goods, money, bank notes, and other things," but provides that vessels, rafts, logs, and lumber become the property of the county (Iowa Code Ann. §§644.1, 644.4, 644.13).

50. *Benjamin v. Lindner Aviation, Inc.*, 534 N.W.2d 400 (Iowa 1995).
51. Moorman, *supra* note 48, at 730.
52. *Saritejdiam, Inc. v. Excess Ins. Co.*, 971 F.2d 910 (2d Cir. 1992).
53. Wayne R. LaFave and Austin W. Scott, Criminal Law, 712 (2d ed. 1986).

are adopted in most states release from liability finders who initially steal but later change their minds and attempt to locate owners.[54]

In a Lexis database search of legal cases, I uncovered about sixty cases of larceny of lost property, about half of which were more than fifty years old. None of them concerned minor incidents such as theft of bicycles or cameras; most had much larger stakes. Nor did I find any cases in which the appropriation accompanied a violent crime, as is the Japanese pattern. Perhaps these cases are plea-bargained, or perhaps the decisions simply are not reported; I harbor no illusions that Lexis is a representative set of all disputes. My conversations with defense lawyers, police, and prosecutors suggest that arrests, not to mention prosecutions, for misappropriation of lost property are extremely rare. As a New York City assistant district attorney to whom I spoke explained succinctly, "The Japanese are fucking insane. I've never heard of that sort of thing. We don't have the resources to go after people who find lost shit."

RECOVERY IN PRACTICE

The legal regime that governs lost property is an integral part of the Japanese lost-and-found system. Equally important is the everyday process by which police and other officials administer the legal rules.

When one finds lost property in Japan, the first place to visit is often the local police box, or kōban. Much heralded as an integral part of community policing, kōban, and their rural equivalent, *chuzaisho*, are small police posts manned by as few as one or two officers. In 1999 there were 6,600 kōban and 8,100 chuzaisho, which I will discuss collectively as kōban.[55] In Tokyo, they are widespread; there are more than ninety-six police stations and kōban for every one hundred square kilometers of space. In outlying areas, the distance between kōban is greater, but the average in Japan is still about eighteen for every one hundred square kilometers, meaning that on average, one is never more than three or four miles away from a kōban. Because many kōban are located near areas that attract crowds (train stations, department stores, parks, and so on), a kōban is likely to be within walking distance from one's find.

Kōban perform a wide variety of tasks, most of which are not directly

---

54. Ibid. at 712 and note 45.

55. Keisatsuchō, *supra* note 2; see also Walter L. Ames, Police and Community in Japan, 17–55 (1981).

related to crime control, such as giving directions and counseling local residents.[56] Accordingly, most residents are familiar with their local system; a recent survey found that 94.6 percent knew where their kōban is, and 13.8 percent knew the name of someone there.[57]

Managing lost-and-found is an integral function of the kōban.[58] A survey conducted in the late 1980s found that 35 percent of all people who visit a kōban do so in connection with lost property.[59] When 3,000 people (2,200 responding) were asked in a 1997 survey what tasks they thought were most important for the kōban, 71.8 percent chose the disposition of lost property, second only to neighborhood "patrol" at 82.6 percent. Of the 636 polled persons who had visited a kōban in the previous two to three years, 40.7 percent stated that they did so in relation to lost property (in second place, with 18.6 percent, were visits to ask directions).[60] In a more recent survey of 2,211 voters conducted in 1998, when asked what they would do if they misplaced ten thousand yen (about $100) on the street, 38 percent responded that they would report it to the police, while 60 percent said that they would give up. Although quitters outnumber reporters by a wide margin, it is significant that nearly four of ten persons say that they would report lost cash *even with no identifiable or traceable marks*.[61]

The details of lost-and-found practice—down to the sizes of the

56. Shingo Suzuki and Jūichi Kobayashi, Keisatsu no "Komarigoto Sōdan" ni Kansuru Bunseki [Analysis of Police Consultations], 39 Kagaku Keisastu Kenkyūjo Hōkoku 66–81 (1998).

57. Shingo Suzuki et al., Jūmin no Chiiki Mitchakudo to Kōban ni Tsuite no Ninchi/Hyōka to no Kanren [Relation of Kōban Knowledge and Appraisal to Citizens' Regionalism], 33 Kagaku Keisatsu Kenkyūjo Hōkoku 85–94 (1992).

58. A recent news report suggests that many Japanese have begun to use 110, the Japanese equivalent of the emergency phone number 911, for nonemergency inquiries such as lost property; in Tokyo, nonemergency calls outnumber emergency calls. In addition to lost property inquiries, citizens are said to use 110 to ask such decidedly nonemergency questions as the location of a twenty-four-hour animal hospital and the procedure for driver's license renewal. Okigaru ni 110ban Kyūzō [Drastic Increase in Nonemergency Calls to 911], Nihon Keizai Shinbun, Nov. 2, 2001, at 19 (evening edition).

59. David H. Bayley, Forces of Order: Policing Modern Japan, 95 (1991).

60. Sōrifu [Prime Minister's Office] Kōban/Chuzaisho ni Kansuru Seron Chōsa [Survey Regarding Kōban], available at http://www.sorifu.go.jp/survey/koban.html.

61. Asahi Shinbun Survey, April 1, 1998, available at Roper Center for Public Opinion Research, University of Connecticut, at http://www.ropercenter.uconn.edu/jpoll/home.html.

forms—are meticulously laid out in the law and in various companion ordinances and cabinet orders.[62] The orders provide, first, that on delivering the object to the police, the finder complete a finder's report (*shutokutodoke*). The finder's report details the nature of the lost object, the amount of any cash found, the place of the find, and contact information about the finder. The finder then receives a finder's receipt (*shutoku-mono azukarisho*) that instructs the finder of his or her rights as a finder and where to claim the property. Kōban police treat finder's reports for even trivial items seriously, which may result in a psychological benefit for the finder that he or she might not receive in another lost-property system.

In the process of filing a finder's report, finders also have the option of waiving their rights to the property and to the finder's fee. Determining exactly how often this waiver occurs is extraordinarily difficult, and no formal record of waivers is kept. At one kōban, police permitted me to examine all 542 finder's reports on file. Ninety-five percent of reports of cash finds did not waive rights; only in small-change cases were rights waived. In 60 percent of the reports of noncash lost objects, the finder waived rights. My interviews with police stationed at kōban further suggest that finders only waive rights for the trivial (small change, umbrellas), the old, the embarrassing (I was often told tales of found items with various sexual connotations), and items that they may already own (mobile phones). Police suggestion may also affect waiver rates. Some officers encourage waiver for trivial objects ("Sign here, you don't need such a thing, right?"), while others discourage waiver by requesting that finders complete the bare minimum of information ("Name, address, description, sign here, sign here, we'll do the rest").[63]

---

62. Ishitsubutsu Toriatsukai Kisoku [Lost-and-Found Rules], Kokka Kōan Iinkai Kisoku 4, Mar. 2, 1989; Ishitsubutsuhō Shikō Kisoku [Lost-and-Found Enforcement Rules], Sōrijurei 52, June 10, 1958; Ishitsubutsuhō Shikōrei [Lost-and-Found Enforcement Order], Seirei 172, June 10, 1958.

63. Police in the Tokyo kōban in the experiment described above tended to fall into the former category, which may have resulted in a high number of waivers. They may have been especially encouraging (subconsciously or otherwise) if they suspected that the objects were part of my experiment, in which case the experiment may not accurately reflect everyday practice.

Kōban police also informed me of several lost-property ventures and scams that take advantage of the institutional structure. Some entrepreneurs scout for abandoned bicycles, report them to police or turn them in themselves, fill out the forms, collect them after the waiting period, and resell them in used-bicycle shops that they own. Others attempt to file

For the next fourteen days, the police must attempt to locate the owner and post a brief notice of the find. The language matters —the police *must* attempt to locate the owner. Article 1 of the Law Concerning Lost Property imposes a duty on police to attempt to look for the owner. If reasonable measures are not taken, the owner has a claim against the prefecture.[64] Notices must be posted at police stations and kōban either in brief bulletin board notices or in a log of lost items, the form of which is dictated by ordinance and lists only the item and the time and place of the find. Particularly valuable items are also listed in newspapers. If police are not successful in locating the owner in two weeks, the property is usually transferred to a central location such as the Tokyo Metropolitan Lost and Found Center. The property is held at the central location for the shorter of six months or the locating of the owner.

If the owner of the lost property is located and wants the property, he or she may retrieve it at the kōban soon or at the central holding facility later. If police have incurred any costs in storage, the police submit to the owner a request for reimbursement. When the owner retrieves his or her property, the police call the finder. Within one month, the finder may request the 5–20 percent finders' fee from the owner. My interviews suggest that parties almost always settle at 10 percent of the object's value, the percentage often mandated by Japanese courts when disputes arise. I was unable to locate any case in which an owner refused to pay, perhaps because the legal provisions are spelled out clearly both on the finder's receipt and the receipt received by the owner at the time that the property is returned, perhaps because the police encourage payment or perhaps because of underlying norms. If the parties disagree as to the value or the percentage of the fee, their only remedy is to resort to the courts.

If the owner of the property is not located within six months and four-

---

false loss reports to attempt to recover others' lost property. Although police in charge of returns claim to be rigorous in requiring accurate descriptions and to have stopped several fraud scams, it would nevertheless seem easy to claim the loss of a black umbrella on a rainy day if possession of the same were one's goal. Still others attempt to manipulate the system using more elaborate insurance scams.

64. Kokka Baishōhō [State Redress Law], Law No. 125 of 1947; Jitsumu Ishitsubutsu [Lost Property Law Practice], 208–9, ed. Ishitsubutsuhō Kenkyūkai (1998). I know of no such cases, but Japanese police tell me that they are aware of the potential threat. On the increase in lost property returned on the basis of information access, see Richard S. Goldstein, Finders, Keepers? An Analysis and Validation of a Free-Found-Ad Policy, 11 J. Applied Behav. Analysis 465 (1978).

teen days, the finder may retrieve the object for a period of two months from the central holding facility. Although most high-value items are retrieved, many items of lesser value are not, despite the nonwaiver of rights by the finder. Many factors could account for the nonretrieval: finders may simply forget their find, misplace the finder's receipt, or simply be unable or unwilling to retrieve the object during the specified time. Items not retrieved are sold at public auction or thrown away.

The procedure that an owner follows if she loses an object is in some ways the mirror image of the finder's process. The owner visits the kōban and files a loss report (*ishitsubutsutodoke*) detailing the loss.[65] If the item is found, the owner is contacted and pays the finder's fee; if not, she is usually out of luck. If an item is found and the owner contacted before the owner can file a loss report, the owner simply visits the kōban after the contact and files a loss report on that occasion. Police have various procedures (from notebook registries to computer databases) in place to match owners with property, the details of which are too varied to warrant detailed discussion other than to note that computerization is increasing.

Interestingly, in no official literature have I seen any appeal to altruistic or norm-based considerations in the return of lost property. Many reasons might explain why this might be so; perhaps it is superfluous, perhaps it is ineffective, perhaps is seems excessively paternal, or perhaps officials predict more compliance with appeal to legal rules rather than moral ones. Whatever the case, kōban police and related officials take extra care to advertise the potential economic rewards of submitting lost property. The annual *White Paper on Police* often lists the year's biggest winners in the lost-and-found lottery, and the popular press follows up on the stories.[66] The Tokyo police issue a brochure that details the lost-and-found

---

65. Credit-card companies and insurers often require the filing of a loss report. Although such factors may affect the statistics discussed above, they would not affect my experiments in any material way. In 2004, Sanwa Supply started a lost-and-found service by which members affix a tracking sticker to their valuables. If lost and found, the service, for a fee, will fill out the forms, pick up the item, pay the finder's fee, and courier the find to the owner. See http://www.landf.jp.

66. In 2004, a Chiba waste disposal company employee found ¥28 million ($28,000) in the trash in Soka City and turned it in to the Soka municipal government. The original owner never materialized. The Soka government denied the claim of the finder on the ground that he was never authorized to work for Soka, filed a criminal complaint against the man, and kept the money for itself. See Saitama: Sōka no Genkin Shutoku [In Saitama, Soka Keeps Cash], Mainichi Shinbun, Sept. 8, 2004, at 1.

process. The cartoonlike story begins with a boy who finds a lost bag in the street and ends with his reward—the bag itself. One implication is that in this case, at least, virtue need not be its own reward.

In his extensive study of Japanese police, Bayley observed a similar but perhaps more ambiguous phenomenon:

Around parks [children] often find coins that have dropped out of pockets of people who have sat on the benches. If the children turn them in, as well as other lost items, many kōban reward them with a small printed card filled in with the child's name, the date, and the particular deed performed. Officers often make a show of receiving lost coins and putting them in a lost-and-found box. Then they give the child a reward of equal amount, which in fact comes from their own pockets. The lesson is that lost money belongs to the loser but virtue has a tangible reward.[67]

The printed "reward cards" discussed by Bayley may indicate a sort of moral approval, but the cash, as Bayley notes, may carry a different message. In any event, the ubiquity of kōban and the lack of a statutory minimum value for lost property allow the inculcation of the norms codified in the statute at an early age (and, as we have seen, if they're not inculcated, and you are caught keeping the find, you're out of the system altogether the next time). In turn, the law is reinforced by the underlying inculcated norms.

The use of kōban is thus closely tied to social norms, and the success of kōban might be dependent on such norms. But the kōban are fundamentally a legal institution, a formally devised unit of the state. Accordingly, in the remainder of this chapter, I primarily treat kōban as a formal institutional variable in the same class as legal rules.

TOWARD A CAUSAL STORY

Above I outlined the law and showed how it works in practice. In this section I analyze experimental evidence to attempt to unravel the relation of legal and social influences on lost-and-found practice. The question might be phrased as follows: "Even in the absence of a law that efficiently allocates (through clear rules) and enforces (using the kōban system and crackdowns on crime) possessory rights to lost property, might Japan

---

67. Bayley, *supra* note 59, at 26.

nevertheless have a successful lost-and-found practice because of internalized social norms or high levels of altruism?" This what-if sort of question is essentially unanswerable, but various techniques can point toward one set of factors as more likely causes than others. First, I briefly examine the available general literature from a variety of disciplines on altruism and honesty. Next, I report the results of a survey of found property in Japan and compare it with a similar test conducted in the United States. Finally, I report the results of the follow-up to the lost-property experiment discussed at the beginning of this chapter. The evidence, taken in total, suggests that institutional incentives play a large role in explaining the efficacy of Japan's lost-and-found system but are not a complete explanation.

Evidence of Honesty and Altruism

All other things being equal, we might expect honest, fair, and altruistic people to report lost property more often than their opposites. If Japanese people are more honest or altruistic (two separate concepts that I discuss together here), we would expect more recovery of lost property in Japan. But the available evidence—and it is sparse—from sociology, psychology, economics, and anthropology is ambiguous at best. Consider the following four studies, the first three of which are comparative:

· In his comparative study of trust, sociologist Toshio Yamagishi surveyed 928 university students and nearly 500 randomly sampled persons in Japan and the United States. Yamagishi asked several questions directly related to honesty. In response to the statement "I keep in mind the spirit of fair play in every situation," Yamagishi found statistically significant higher levels of honesty in American men in both the university and random samples and no statistically significant differences among American and Japanese women. In response to the more direct statement "I do not want to be dishonest in any situation," Americans rated significantly higher in virtually every subsample. From these questions and others, Yamagishi constructed an index of honesty and fairness in which Americans rated significantly higher than Japanese in every category.[68]
· Psychological studies examine honesty and helping behavior in chil-

68. Toshio Yamagishi, Shinrai no Kōzō [The Anatomy of Trust] (1998).

dren. Two Japanese researchers attempted to measure deception in Japanese and American three-to-six-year olds by hiding a toy and telling a child not to peek. Most children peek, and most children lie about peeking. But the experiments revealed no significant differences among U.S. and Japanese children in regard to deception.[69]

- In an economic study of altruism, Charles Yuji Horioka and three co-authors analyzed the Comparative Survey of Savings in Japan and the United States, a survey conducted in 1996 by the Japanese government. Using a variety of data on saving and bequest motives in the two countries, they found the evidence to be "remarkably consistent" with the theory that "the selfish life cycle model," in which "individuals are selfish and do not care about their children or about anyone else," is "the dominant model of household behavior in both countries but that it is far more applicable in Japan than it is in the U.S."[70]

- From the field of anthropology, in another study of helping behavior in adults and children, Takei Sugiyama Lebra administered a thematic apperception test in which she asked approximately two hundred Japanese adults and high school seniors to finish the phrase "if you are kind to others . . . ." The two most popular categories of responses were "autistic satisfaction" such as "you will feel better" or "your feelings will be enriched" (34.3 percent for adults, 34.1 percent for high schoolers) and "reciprocal return in other forms" such as "you will be rewarded" (30.3 percent for adults, 31.9 percent for high schoolers). But among male high school students, the reward was the most popular answer (35.6 percent).[71]

I don't mean to suggest that Japan somehow revels in dishonesty or that altruistic behavior is any less prevalent in Japan than elsewhere. Nor do I claim that the evidence concerning honesty, altruism, and social norms comprises the entire spectrum of Japanese society. Cultural differences may lie elsewhere, such as in concepts of luck and desert, underlying class structure and resource distribution, or views regarding

69. Kiyobumi Kawakami and Kiyoka Takai-Kawakami, Kodomo no Kyogi Kyōdō [Deception in Children], 36 Jidō Aonen Seishin Igaku to Sono Kinsetsu Ryōiki [J. Child and Adolescent Psychiatry] 223 (1995).

70. Charles Yuji Horioka et al., Are Americans More Altruistic Than the Japanese? A U.S.-Japan Comparison of Saving and Bequest Motives, NBER Working Paper 7463. http://econpapers.hhs.se/paper/fthosakae/487.htm (2002).

71. Takei Sugiyama Lebra, Japanese Patterns of Behavior (1976).

the value or nature of ownership,[72] and this chapter does not attempt to investigate the entirety of culture.[73] I merely note that after searching the literature for data that might shed light on the ethical model that may be most relevant to lost property in Japan, the above studies seem to constitute some of the best available formal empirical evidence about the topic, and their results are far from certain. At best, some of them only predict questionnaire responses and not necessarily real-world actions.

The studies suggest a conclusion and a conjecture. As for the former, at least in comparison to the United States, the Japanese propensity for returning lost property does not appear to be due largely to more widespread or deeply rooted Japanese norms of honest behavior. Some other factor or set of factors is likely at work.

As for the latter, this chapter has shown a striking correlation between lost-property practice and lost-property institutions in Japan. The correlation can lend itself to two opposing interpretations of historical causality: either lost-property practice spawned institutions, or lost-property institutions encouraged the development of lost-property practice. Although the historical record can support either interpretation, there is an analytical way to gain a better—though, I recognize, very tentative—understanding of the causal relation. Assume that honesty can be divided into two types, "general" and "specific." Specific honesty is the practice of honest reporting of lost property; general honesty is the broader phenomenon examined in the studies above. General honesty, as some of

72. My interviews of kōban police and others suggest that many people distinguish umbrellas (and sometimes bicycles) from other objects. Umbrellas are often seen as a sort of fungible communal property, especially during downpours in Japan's spring rainy season. A clear vinyl umbrella, available just about anywhere, usually costs five hundred yen (about $5). Alternatively, at thirty (of a total of ninety-nine) Osaka subway stations, one can borrow an umbrella from a group that charges advertisers for logo placement. Regarding return rates, the group's chairman states that "if it suddenly starts to rain at 9 A.M., all our umbrellas will be gone. But fewer than 10 out of 100 people will return them." See Muryō Kashikasa [Free Umbrellas for Borrowing], asahi.com MYTOWN, available at http://mytown.asahi.com/osaka/news01.asp?kiji=293 (2002).

73. Even the name of the property-holding facility may have some cultural connotation. One Japanese commentator, writing in Japanese, describes the connotation of the English phrase "lost & found" as "We might find your lost property!" and the connotation of the equivalent Japanese phrase "*ishitsubutsu hokan*" as the less hopeful "We'll hold on to your lost property for you." Makia Matsumura, Lost & Found, asahi.com MYTOWN, available at http://mytown.asahi.com/usa/news02.asp?c=22&kiji=2 (2002).

those studies suggest, is arguably similar in Japan and the United States, but lost-property institutions in those two countries differ. Assuming that specific honesty and general honesty are correlated, it seems relatively unlikely that differences in the practice of specific honesty led to institutional differences (in the form of codification of practice), because similar general honesty structures should have led to similar institutional structures in both countries. The fact that institutional differences have arisen despite similar honesty structures leads to the conjecture that Japanese institutions may have "carved out" specific honesty as separate from general honesty.

Still, general honesty may not necessarily correlate with lost-property specific honesty, and applying these studies directly to the lost-property context may be problematic. Although honesty and fairness may play a role in some decisions of whether to report lost property, other concerns (including not only the potential cultural factors listed above but also the business of one's schedule, for instance) may be important as well. It is also unclear whether these studies of largely interpersonal honesty measure the same sort of factors that comprise the sort of societal helping behavior that characterizes property return. Accordingly, I conducted two new studies to more directly examine the lost-and-found context.

Survey

In 1939, Arvin Donner surveyed 2,188 elementary and secondary school students in Iowa and Texas regarding their knowledge and opinions regarding finders' law and their reactions to various lost-property hypotheticals. She found, first, that 86 percent of the students' judgments on the hypotheticals were roughly in line with existing case law. But she also found that "students do not possess the statute information regarding what to do in cases of lost and found property. None of the 2188 students tested could give the state statute regarding lost and found property, and seventy-eight percent of their responses to questions dealing with the state statute concerning lost and found property were answered, 'Don't Know,' or their responses were gross inaccuracies."[74]

Donner's study raises many questions. What does "give the state statute," for instance, mean? Despite the survey's eccentricities, it is in-

---

74. Arvin N. Donner, A Survey of Students' Concepts Concerning Lost and Found Property, 34 J. Educ. Res. 288, 294 (1940).

teresting as a serious effort to examine the phenomenon, and Donner's sample choice, at least, is intriguing. Note that one of the jurisdictions tested, and in fact the source of two-thirds of the students in the sample, was Iowa. As discussed above, Iowa has since 1839 had a statutory scheme that entitles a finder to 10 percent of the value of her find. The timing is also interesting; just five years before Donner's survey, in a case that accounts for eleven of the thirteen references in the Iowa Code Annotated, the Iowa Supreme Court decided the constitutionality of the provision and declared that it served laudable public policy goals.[75] If there has been any U.S. jurisdiction at any point in time in when knowing the law could be particularly advantageous, or perhaps when we might expect people to know the law, it might be Iowa in 1939. Yet none of the students in Donner's survey knew the law. I would not expect the results of a more recent survey to differ considerably.

For comparison, with the help of assistants (and as part of regular courses of instruction), I conducted a simple survey regarding lost property of 615 ninth-graders in Japan. The written survey contained four open-ended scenario-type questions. The instructions stated that the test was one of legal knowledge. The primary questions and summarized responses were as follows:

1. *A finds a wallet on the sidewalk with thirty thousand yen inside and takes it to the police.* B, *who lost the wallet the previous day, goes to the police and claims the wallet. The police give* B *the wallet. Does* A *have a legal right to collect a reward from* B? *If so, how much?* Eighty percent of students (497) correctly responded that *A* has a legal right to a reward (a figure similar to that found in Donner's Iowa study). An additional 30 students incorrectly answered that *A* has no legal right to the reward but still should receive one. Of the 497 who answered correctly, 410 responded with award amounts that fell in the correct range of 5 to 20 percent of thirty thousand yen. Most (339) stated that the reward would be 10 percent, or three thousand yen.

2. *A takes the wallet in Question 1 to the police.* The person who lost the wallet never recovers it. What happens to the wallet and the money inside? In one formulation or another, 510 students (83 percent) correctly stated that the finder has a right to the property. The most common other answer was that the police take the property.

---

75. *Flood v. City National Bank of Clinton*, 20 Iowa 935, *cert. denied*, 56 S. Ct. 749 (1935).

3. *After finding the wallet in Question 1, A keeps it. Is this a crime?* Five hundred and fifty-two students, or about 90 percent, correctly stated that keeping the wallet is a crime.

4. *A sees the wallet in Question 1 and in fact sees money sticking out of the top, but he ignores it and keeps walking. Is this a crime?* Three hundred and thirty-two students, or 54 percent, correctly stated that ignoring the wallet is not a crime.

The survey data suggest two primary points. First, Japanese students seem to have a high degree of knowledge of lost-property law; or, alternatively, lost-property law might coincide with norms, and students have knowledge of those norms. The origins of this knowledge appear to be dual; home, as discussed above in relation to kōban visits, and school. As for school, lost-property law per se is not part of the Japanese classroom curriculum; teachers clearly are not reading the statute in class. But methods of instruction are important; the Japanese elementary education system's holistic focus on "children's long-term internalization of values"[76] might lead to tacit knowledge of the rules or perhaps to an inculcation of the norms that underlie lost-property institutions, regardless of whether students can "give the statute."

A second point worth noting from the survey data is that when students erred, they generally erred on the side that would facilitate return of lost items. In response to question 4, nearly half of the students answered incorrectly that ignoring the wallet is a crime. Although the response is incorrect, if such opinions are widespread in the population, they might lead to a high level of recovered lost property.

Interviews

The data presented above suggest that (1) Japanese people know finders' law and (2) measurable differences in lost-property recovery can be seen among New Yorkers, Tokyoites, and Japanese expatriates in New York. But the data do not necessarily show a linkage between (1) and (2), that is, that law accounts for the differences. Japanese lost-property recovery rates might be higher not because of the law, legal institutions, or enforcement but because of social norms or altruism. The conjecture raised

76. Catherine C. Lewis, Educating Hearts and Minds: Reflections on Japanese Preschool and Elementary Education, 212 (1995).

earlier in this section—that institutions may have spawned practice—refers only to the origin and direction of *historical* causality (which came first, institutions or practice?), and not necessarily to the daily thought process that characterizes *motivational* causality (which plays a larger role in explaining actions, institutions or practice?). To explore these causal factors, I turned to interviews.

I was able to speak with thirty-eight persons from the Tokyo experiment, twenty-two persons from the New York experiment, and ten persons from the New York Japanese experiment. Even without additional analysis, these numbers say something about the lost-and-found process. The number was relatively high for Tokyo because finders are requested to fill out a found property report by the police that lists contact information. The number was perhaps higher than one might expect in New York, because most persons who returned the property contacted me by phone instead of using the police or a merchant as an intermediary. The number was relatively low for New York Japanese because most finders simply returned property to the store clerk and left no additional information. Of course, in all cases, more interviews are better, but I simply was unable to interview any additional persons in the data set.

In these interviews, I attempted to ascertain why persons returned lost property. Three primary groups of answers were given in all three locations. The categories have some overlap, but some basic distinctions can nevertheless be made. First, some explanations focused explicitly on formal institution-based rewards. I recorded these answers, such as "If the owner doesn't claim it, I have a right to it" or "I want the reward money," as institutional explanations. Note that for an answer to be coded as "institutional," a returnee did not have to be able to recite the statute or know where to find it. A finder did not even need to be aware that the rule was a creature of the state, though I attempted to determine more precisely finders' knowledge about this point.

These institutional explanations are relatively easy to distinguish from the second and third categories of answers, which were more difficult to separate. The second category includes explanations that centered on social norms and civic duties that may be informally enforced but are unregulated by formal institutions. I recorded these answers, such as "It's what you're supposed to do" or "Everybody does that," as social norms explanations.

Finally, some explanations were based in notions of altruism and similar internal other-regarding preferences that had no obvious link to either formally enforced institutions or informally enforced social norms. Although some of these internal factors might in fact be internalized social norms,[77] I simplified the inquiry by categorizing answers like "Honesty is the best policy" as other-regarding.

Cross-cultural surveys are, of course, imperfect; it is possible that observed differences in result are based on differences in the way that a question is understood or in interviewees' response styles. As for perception of the question, although I attempted to mitigate the problem by vetting the survey with experts and amateurs in both countries, differences may arise nonetheless.

As for response styles, in this particular case, social psychology literature suggests that Japanese people have low self-esteem and are self-critical (for instance, they are reluctant to conclude that they perform better than average classmates), while North Americans have high self-esteem and are self-enhancing (and are reluctant to conclude that they perform worse).[78] Given these studies, one might argue that Japanese interviewees would be less likely than New Yorkers to give self-enhancing explanations that boast of their honesty,[79] which could result in fewer "other-regarding" responses. Although no study can completely avoid such difficulties, in this case, the inclusion of relatively self-neutral responses in the other-regarding category may mitigate the concern. For instance, "I felt sorry for you" or "So sad!" (*"Kawaiiso"*) was a common response of Japanese interviewees and is an often-used Japanese phrase. Some scholars formally distinguish sympathy from "pure" altruism,[80]

77. Richard H. McAdams, The Origin, Development, and Regulation of Norms, 96 Mich. L. Rev. 338 (1997); Lynn A. Stout, Other-Regarding Preferences and Social Norms, Social Science Research Network, Georgetown Law and Economics Research Paper No. 265902, available at http://papers.ssrn.com/sol3/papers.cfm?abstract_id=265902 (2001).

78. Steven J. Heine and Kristen Renshaw, Interjudge Agreement, Self-Enhancement, and Liking: Cross-Cultural Divergences, 28 Personality & Soc. Psych. Bull. 442 (2002); Shinobu Kitayama et al., Individual and Collective Processes in the Construction of the Self: Self-Enhancement in the United States and Self-Criticism in Japan, 72 J. Personality & Soc. Psych. 1245 (1997).

79. Steven J. Heine, Toshitake Takata, and Darrin R. Lehman present evidence suggesting that lower self-esteem in Japan is internal and not simply a matter of self-presentation. Steven J. Heine et al., Beyond Self-Presentation: Evidence for Self-Criticism among Japanese, 26 Personality & Soc. Psych. Bull. 71 (2000). If so, the modesty in such responses might not be false.

80. David Sally, Two Economic Applications of Sympathy, 18 J. L. Econ. & Org. 455, 456–57 (2002).

following other empirical studies of altruism in Japan and the United States,[81] but I include them together in the third category of other-regarding responses. If, as David Sally discusses,[82] sympathy is based in social interaction, physical distance, and psychological affinity, it would not be unreasonable to expect a large percentage of Tokyo responses relative to New York responses to fall in the "other-regarding" category, but other interpretations of distance are of course possible.

Crucially, very few interviewees gave only one type of explanation. I found that if I listened carefully and persistently, interviewees tended to offer two, and sometimes all three, explanations. I recorded all explanations. Two primary factors motivated this strategy. First, by not forcing interviewees into a single explanation or a binary choice, I hoped to mitigate further some of the cross-cultural concerns mentioned in the previous paragraph, because multiple responses may allow for more self-praise or self-criticism and because there is no a priori reason for a self-critical person to choose one self-neutral option rather than another. Second and more basically, human motivation is complex, and although multiple responses may be somewhat imprecise, they may be better able than binary choices, Likert scales, or short-answer surveys to capture some of this complexity. As table 2.3 shows, the mix of responses differed enough to suggest real differences among the locations.

When asked why they returned the property, Tokyo finders typically offered one of two explanations. First, many saw returning lost property as a civic duty and explained that such values had been inculcated in them since childhood. About half of these social norms explanations also included mentions of kōban. Although these explanations touch on institutions, and I regard kōban themselves as an institutional variable, because of the focus on civic duty and values, I recorded such responses as social norms explanations in the absence of more explicit mentions of formal institutions. Had I included these explanations in the institutional category, that response would have accounted for more than 90 percent of the responses. In any event, explanations involving kōban were not honesty-based and arguably were not altruistic or otherwise other-regarding.

Second, many Tokyo interviewees, often in addition to the social

81. See Hiroshi Matsui et al., Aitasei no Kōzō ni Kansuru Kokusai Hikaku Kenkyū [Comparative Analysis of the Structure of Altruistic Behavior], 13 Shakai Shinrigaku Kenkyū [Studies in Social Psychology] 133 (1998).

82. Sally, *supra* note 80.

Table 2.3. Explanations for Returns of Lost Property

	Tokyo	New York	New York Japanese
Institutions	32 (84%)	1 (.5%)	8 (80%)
Social norms	20 (53%)	7 (32%)	4 (40%)
Regard for others	7 (18%)	20 (91%)	4 (40%)
Total number of interviews*	38	22	10

*Interviewees gave multiple explanations.

norms explanations, volunteered more explicit institutional carrot-and-stick explanations. Seven interviewees cited the stick, noting that not turning in the property was a punishable form of theft. All thirty-eight Tokyo finders knew of the reward system, and ten referred explicitly to the reward as "one-tenth" (*ichiwari*). To be sure, most finders did not know the exact fee mandated or other statutory details. But all knew of the system's existence, and only two finders seemed unsure as to whether the reward system was created by formal institutions (one thought it was a local police custom, another thought it to be merely urban legend).

At least in the case of the phones, the carrots and sticks may not be explicit. A finder is always free to ignore the phone, eliminating the stick. Neither does the carrot seem large or even certain; 10 percent of the value of a phone often is a pittance, finders seldom need another's phone after six months, and a finder's only remedy against an owner who refuses to pay a reward is a civil suit—all plausible reasons why the waiver rate for phones in Tokyo was relatively high. Still, the Tokyo interview responses suggest that people act as if the carrots and sticks matter, whether because of incomplete familiarity with the law, because of the ingrained nature of the system, because the thought process does not begin until the object is already in one's possession, or for some other reason or combination of reasons.

Sympathy-based predictions notwithstanding, it was in New York, not Tokyo, that the reasons for returning lost property were more likely to be stated in other-regarding terms. New York interviewees stressed that "I'm an honest person," that "I couldn't live with myself if I kept your money," and that "I just thought about how [inconvenienced] I'd be if I lost my phone." I classified these explanations as other-regarding, and though I recognize that they might also be social norms, they certainly are not institutional. One vocal male interviewee put it more succinctly.

After he gave me several individual-honesty explanations, I tried leading him by saying, "Oh, come on. I'm sure a lot of people return stuff just because they want a reward, right?" He responded, "You brainiacs might think so, but you don't know human nature. Not everybody does everything for money. I called you because it's the right thing to do." Only a handful of New York interviewees focused on social norms, and only one mentioned the possibility of reward—and he knew of no legal basis for it (none exists).

The results of the interviews with the New York Japanese, like those of the experiment itself, fell somewhere in between those of Tokyo and New York, though the small sample size yielded less-than-conclusive results. Interviewees focused largely on institutions but seemed to give greater weight to altruistic factors than the Tokyo interviewees. Few spoke of social norms, perhaps because they did not feel familiar with New York norms. Interestingly, however, while these interviewees seemed confident in their institutional assessments, their knowledge of New York institutions often was simply incorrect. Many New York Japanese interviewees incorrectly assumed an institutional reward structure similar to that of Japan. Some were surprised to hear that New York has no kōban system (most made returns to the store clerk). In other words, New York Japanese relied heavily (80 percent) on institutions but got the institutions wrong.

From the evidence from finder interviews, I conclude that formal institutions are a central factor but certainly not the only factor in the recovery of lost property. In Tokyo, where finders' law and related institutions are good and recovery rates are high, interviewees focused on institutions. Among New York Japanese, where recovery rates were good but not as good as in Tokyo, interviewees continued to focus on institutions despite the fact that they got the institutions wrong. And in the general New York setting, in which finders' law institutions are poor and recovery rates are relatively low, the few New Yorkers who returned the property did so for reasons independent of institutions.

The New York setting in the comparative context further suggests that although altruism gets results, altruism alone may not provide the same benefits as altruism plus institutions. It may be that finders are in a moral double-bind; they are guilty if they keep the property and suckers if they turn it in. The existence of institutions like those in Tokyo may be one factor that encourages people at the margin to solve the double-bind by reducing their "sucker" feelings with rewards. Of course, these marginal calculations are imprecise and muddled. Institutions may result in a net increase in returns, but they may in fact do so via a reduction of underlying altruism as the reward incentives crowd out internal ones.[83]

To obtain an additional reference point, I supplemented these post-experiment interviews with police interviews in Japan. In the course of researching this chapter, I spoke to forty police officers at thirty kōban. Each of these officers is engaged in lost-property "practice" of some sort on a daily basis. The officers also gave multiple explanations. Most (thirty-seven), like the post-experiment interviewees, suggested that people return lost property because of institutional concerns. Thirty-two suggested social norms, and twenty suggested altruistic explanations.

The data given in this section warrant a final caution. Although I have categorized explanations for analytical clarity, I make no claim that law can be separated from underlying societal and other informal institutions. The relation between law and society is undeniably complex, and the lost-property context is no exception. On one hand, a major reason for the Japanese lost-property regime's consistency over time may be that it reflects established informal practices that might function effectively today even in the absence of formal institutions.[84] On the other, the general-honesty evidence on historical causality tentatively suggests that as the law has become more embedded in society it has standardized nascent norms, or perhaps even created them from scratch, suggesting greater institutional importance. Then again, perhaps the relation is better described as one of mutual reinforcement, as suggested in the discussion of kōban above.

The issue is complex, and I see little analytical value in imposing a total dichotomy here. But the data presented above may at least offer insights into individuals' *perceptions* and conceptualizations of their behavior regarding this issue at a static point in time. The individuals in my interviews appear to have had little problem categorizing "law" sepa-

83. Bruno S. Frey and Reto Jegen, Motivation Crowding Theory: A Survey of Empirical Evidence, University of Zurich Working Paper No. 26, available at http://papers.ssrn.com/sol3/papers.cfm?abstract_id=203330 (2000); see also Richard Titmuss, The Gift Relationship: From Human Blood to Social Policy (1997); Margaret M. Blair and Lynn A. Stout, Trust, Trustworthiness, and the Behavioral Foundations of Corporate Law, 149 U. Penn. L. Rev. 1735, 1764–175 (2001).

84. I suspect that dismantling one particular institution, the kōban, would lead to substantially less compliance, but note that Tokyoites in the Edo and Meiji Periods returned objects to the police long before kōban were established as institutions for that purpose.

rately from other explanations. In Tokyo, everyone knew the rules, almost everyone knew that those rules were formal, and most said that they
relied on them. In New York, virtually no one knew the rules, and almost
no one said that they relied on them.

With these cautions in mind, the evidence presented above thus suggests that finders are motivated by a complex interaction of altruistic and
legal factors. The available evidence also suggests that conceptions of
correct behavior are strongly intertwined with the legal environment into
which one is socialized. Whether the specific lost-property institutions
that comprise the Japanese legal environment are a product of such conceptions, a cause, or both, they play a major role in explaining the efficiency of the Japanese system.

CONCLUSION

Japan is in many ways a loser's paradise. I have attempted to show that
much of the strength of the Japanese lost-and-found system lies in the
civil and criminal legal system that creates clear and longstanding carrots
and sticks for the return and nonreturn of lost property, as well as in the
corresponding legal institutions that dictate police duties and create the
kōban enforcement system. The enforcement of nascent juvenile crime
may also be an important variable. Although it is difficult precisely to
place the importance of these variables in a hierarchy, each appears to play
an important role, and together they appear to have synergistic effects.
Other factors, including altruism and social norms, are both important
and interrelated with these institutions, but by various methods—statutory exposition, data analysis, surveys, experiments, and interviews—I
have suggested that legal institutions, and socialization of those institutions over time, may play a bigger role in explaining the system's success
as well as differences between Japan and the United States.

Still, the Japanese system has drawbacks. First and perhaps foremost,
it seems expensive. If Japan is able to justify such administrative expense
because it has very low violent crime rates, it is unlikely that many other
countries can copy the Japanese model. But Japan may have very low
crime rates in part precisely because it devotes administrative resources
to such factors as the kōban system and zero-tolerance enforcement of
low-level crime. As Wilson and Kelling put it in "Broken Windows,"
their famous essay on community enforcement, "[u]ntended property becomes fair game for people out for fun or plunder who ordinarily would

not dream of doing such things and who probably consider themselves law-abiding."[85] If Japan's low crime rates are a result of broken-windows-based community enforcement that creates incentives for property not to become "untended," further investigation may be in order.

Second, even if one wanted to mimic the Japanese system, it might not be exported easily. The Japanese experience suggests that for the system to work, it must rely not only on the correct tweaking of civil and criminal incentives but also on well-oiled administration systems and an educated populace. Modification of institutions in a different historical and social context may not engender as efficient a lost-property market as that which has apparently functioned efficiently for many generations.

Although we cannot sort out with absolute precision the relative causal impact of various factors or even be certain that some variables are causes, it is reasonable to postulate that the behavior of finders in Japan provides in microcosm a good and clear example of the many factors that working together make for social control in society and illustrate how law, norms, institutional structures, and economic incentives can mutually reinforce the message that each sends. In Japan, the law commands the return of lost property, it punishes those who fail to return it, and it guarantees rewards to those who do. Police are close by to accept lost objects. Recognized, centuries-old routines exist for turning in lost property and protecting finders' interests, children are taught in visits to kōban the norm of returning lost objects, and they are socialized by praise and rewards when, as youngsters, they turn in small sums. Adults are rewarded twice: once for turning in lost property and once when their lost property is found, perhaps thereby creating greater allegiance to formal and informal lost-property institutions. The result is that many people return valuable property, even in situations in which the chance that they would be found out if they kept it is relatively low. If only the mix of law and social control norms meshed as well when more significant matters were at stake.

85. James Q. Wilson and George L. Kelling, Broken Windows, Atlantic Monthly, Mar. 1982, at 29, 38.

CHAPTER THREE

SUMO

Step into a Tokyo noodle restaurant or hop into an Osaka cab at 5 in the afternoon, and you will hear it on the radio. Walk into an electronics store on a Sunday afternoon, and you are likely to find groups of men staring at it on television the way that people in college towns stare at the screen to watch football. Some matches are better than others, sometimes the sport is more popular than at other times, but sumo's place as a pervasive element of Japanese everyday life is constant.

Still, most people, even in Japan, do not know what makes sumo tick—how wrestlers organize, how they make their money, and how that money is distributed. In the Japan Sumo Association, relations primarily are shaped by rules and norms relating to the ownership and transfer of 105 shares of "elder stock" that are held by the association's senior members. The elder share regime determines how and by whom the association is governed, the time at which a wrestler retires, and the nature of a wrestler's life following retirement from the ring at around thirty years of age. The outcomes of matches determine the shape of the sumo governance regime, and at times, the reverse may also be true.

These elder share rules and norms are part of the association's idiosyncratic institutional environment. As a legal matter, the association is technically a foundation, but it has borrowed qualities from the corporation and the partnership to create a unique institution that serves its interests. As a business enterprise, the association promotes and sells a sport, competes with other sports such as baseball and soccer, receives revenues, and distributes profits to investors. Yet at its heart it is a cultural entity, with historical ties to Shinto religion and the imperial family, and as such is charged with such lofty responsibilities as the "education of young persons and students."[1]

Historically, the association has been notoriously insular and tight-lipped about its organization and its affairs in general. The following reaction of the association to a simple inquiry, as described a former University of Tokyo law professor, is typical: "A writer friend of mine deliberately went to the Sumo Association and asked to see a copy of its internal rules. The Association asked him, 'What is your purpose?' In the end he was shown nothing."[2] Controlling the flow of information—both negative information such as scandals and the timing of positive information such as the announcement of a new champion—helps preserve the positive image and cultural mystique of sumo. A lack of disclosure from some business enterprises might cause consumers to assume the worst. But sumo's somewhat mystical pseudo-religious roots create in the public an expectation of secrecy. The association has kept the curtain closed because peeking behind it might spoil the fun, which might result in reduced public interest and ultimately in reduced income for the association. Much of the information on which this chapter is based is withheld from the public.[3]

The focus of this chapter is the myriad of formal legal rules and informal social norms that sumo has developed outside the usual confines of the law to structure and define its internal relationships. "Social norms" are informal societal constraints that generally are not enforceable under law. My definition of "legal rules" is broad. It refers to legislative and judicial provisions, of course, but such provisions generally play no particular role in sumo. More specifically, I use the term to refer to the organizational rules of the association. These rules are not simply norms that the association happens to writes down. They are approved by the Ministry of Education, Culture, Sports, Science, and Technology in its capacity as

1. Zaidan Hōjin Nihon Sumō Kyōkai Kifu Kōi [Act of Endowment of the Japan Sumo Association] ("Association Act"), art. 4.

2. Kōji Shindō, Hōritsu-teki na Mono no Kangaekata (2) [Thinking about Things Legally (Part 2)], 503 NBL 20, 25 n.5 (1996).

3. In 1998, partially in response to tax scandals and decreased revenues, the association released for the first time the names of all elder stockholders. But share information before that date, and the details of all share transactions, remain private.

sumo's supervising agency on behalf of the state,[4] and as such have the force of law within the association's organizational boundaries.

I use sumo's rules and norms to examine two relatively unexplored areas of the literature. First, most firms that have been the subject of academic discourse are constrained by Western cultural and historical baggage—but sumo is arguably the most Japanese of Japanese institutions. Second, studies of rules and norms of close-knit groups have largely focused on substantive and remedial rules and norms that govern transactions and punishment.[5] I use sumo to examine constitutive rules and norms—those that determine structure and interrelations of an enterprise. Doing so can help us better understand a central problem of the book: how people in Japan legally and socially define the contours of everyday interaction.

WHAT IS SUMO?

Before discussing what sumo is, it is useful to clarify what sumo is not. Sumo is not necessarily a sport for overweight slobs. The average wrestler in the top division, despite weighing in at 354 pounds (157 kilograms), reportedly has a fat-to-body-weight ratio of less than twenty percent.[6] Chiyonofuji, one of the most successful wrestlers of all time, had only eleven percent body fat in his prime.[7] Nonetheless, when the goal is to stay in the

4. The association operates under the loose supervision of the ministry (see Minpō [Civil Code], art. 34; Monbu Daijin [Minister of Education], No. 347, Zaidan Hōjin Dai-Nippon Sumō Kyōkai Setsuritsu Daihyōsha Jūhachimei [In re Eighteen Representatives' Establishment of the All-Japan Sumo Association], Dec. 28, 1925), which supervises all cultural activities; see generally Bunkazai Hogo Hō [Cultural Assets Protection Act], Law No. 214 of 1950. The ministry approves the association's charter documents and certain amendments thereto. See Association Act, *supra* note 1, arts. 43–45.

5. Ellickson categorizes each rule and norm as one of five types: *substantive* (rules or norms that "define what primary conduct . . . is to be punished, rewarded, or left alone"), *remedial* (provisions that dictate "the nature and magnitude of the sanction to be administered"), *procedural* (provisions that "govern how controllers are to obtain and weigh information"), *constitutive* (provisions that "govern the internal structures of controllers"), or *controller-selecting* (provisions that govern the "division of social-control labor among the various controllers"). See See Robert C. Ellickson, Order without Law: How Neighbors Settle Disputes, 132–36 (1991).

6. See Mark Schilling, Sumo: A Fan's Guide, 72 (1994).

7. See Tsutomu Kakuma, Sumo Watching, 70 (1993).

ring, weight is undeniably a weapon. Some wrestlers have placed a bit too much emphasis on the weight factor and have become terribly obese—the most obvious case being Hawaiian-born Konishiki, who approached 625 pounds (284 kilograms)—but generally a wrestler who is simply fat will not be successful.[8]

Sumo has simple rules. The first wrestler to step out of the ring or to touch the ring with any part of his body other than the soles of his feet loses. There are seventy officially sanctioned winning moves, each of which can be classified as a pushing, thrusting, throwing, or leverage technique. Lighter wrestlers, ecological research shows, use a wider range of moves.[9] Certain moves are prohibited—poking in the eye, twisting fingers, kicking in the abdomen, punching with a closed fist, pulling hair, and so on—and result in automatic disqualification. Most bouts take five or ten seconds; longer contests may run for a few minutes.

But sumo is much more than sport. Fights proceed in accordance with ancient ritual. Each bout begins with the ring announcer's calling the names of the two wrestlers. The wrestlers step into the ring, and the announcer again calls their names. The wrestlers then perform an elaborate series of rituals that includes foot-stomping (to drive out evil spirits), rinsing the mouth with "power water" (for strength), salt-throwing (for purification), and hand-clapping (to show lack of weaponry). When the allotted time has elapsed, the referee summons the two wrestlers to the middle of the ring to begin the bout. After the wrestlers fight, the referee points his paddle toward the winner's corner. The wrestlers bow to one another, and the loser leaves the ring first. The winner squats in front of the referee, makes a gesture of thanks to the three gods of creation, then receives an envelope containing money from the referee.

8. Before 2001, a new recruit was required to be 173 centimeters (5 feet, 8 inches) tall and 75 kilograms (165 pounds), with special exceptions for new recruits with outstanding backgrounds in college or amateur sumo. See Zaidan Hōjin Nihon Sumō Kyōkai Kifu Kōi Shikō Saisoku [Detailed Rules Regarding the Enforcement of the Act of Endowment of the Japan Sumo Association] ("Association Act Rules"), art. 54. Although the weight requirement can be overcome by eating and drinking, it was rather difficult for a short potential wrestler to increase his height. Some, however, succeeded; some by bumping their heads into a wall, others by adding silicon implants. In the most notorious case, a sixteen-year-old implanted 6 inches (15 centimeters) of silicone into the top of his head. In 1994 the association banned head implants. In 2001, the association dropped the requirement altogether, allowing wrestlers of all sizes who have "athletic ability."

9. See John Whitfield, Small Sumo Mix It Up, Nature, July 15, 2002, available at http://www.nature.com/nsu/020708/020708-21.html (discussing work of Perri Eason).

Approximately seven hundred to nine hundred full-time wrestlers compete in the association's six annual fifteen-day tournaments. A committee of the association decides pairings. Wrestlers in the top division compete once each day; lower-ranked wrestlers have only seven bouts during a tournament. The wrestler with the best record in each division wins the division. If two or more wrestlers are tied on the last day, a play-off is held to determine the winner. Seldom does a wrestler in the top division win a tournament with a record of fewer than twelve wins (and three corresponding losses), and victories with perfect (15–0) records are not uncommon.

The journey from entry into the sumo world to celebrity status is usually long and difficult. Typically, sumo stable scouts recruit boys who are in their mid-teens. Although a growing number of new recruits have finished high school (11 percent) or college (12 percent), most (77 percent) have only a basic compulsory junior high school education. Until a wrestler-recruit retires from the sumo world, his home is one of fifty training stables. Larger stables may have forty wrestlers; smaller stables, only three or four. Wrestlers sleep in a communal room, prepare and eat all meals together, and do little else besides sumo. Most of a wrestler's day is spent practicing sumo in one way or another: fighting, technical training, and, since the late 1990s, weight training. Each stable has a social structure that at once resembles a family home and a paramilitary organization. The elder in charge of the stable is always a former wrestler and takes on a paternal role.[10] He teaches and coaches the pupil and gives him his sumo name, which often contains characters used in the elder's own sumo name. Because wrestlers do not fight members of their own stable in tournaments, there exists in the stable a certain fraternal sense of unity and loyalty.

The stable is founded on a rigid hierarchy based on rank. On entry into the stable a recruit is assigned to a more experienced wrestler. In theory, the senior wrestler's job is to assist the recruit on his journey, but in reality the recruit becomes a sort of personal slave. The recruit waits on his senior wrestler, performing tasks as menial as scrubbing the wrestler's back and washing the wrestler's underwear.

10. The Japanese word for elder, *oyakata*, literally means "parent." The elder is assisted in his task by his wife, who counsels the recruits, helps out with cooking, and acts as a sort of second mother to the boys. See Seigoro Kitade, Sumōbeya no Okamisan [Wives of the Sumo Stables] (1993); Yoshihiro Oinuma, Sumō Shakai no Kenkyū [Research on Sumo Society], 84–86 (1992).

With the exception of outstanding college sumo stars, all wrestlers begin their sumo careers in the "pre-sumo" (*maezumō*) division, which is really not a formal division at all. Pre-sumo wrestlers compete in only three bouts in the fifteen-day tournament and are immediately promoted to the next level, *jonokuchi,* at the next tournament. From that point on, promotion and demotion are based solely on a wrestler's win-loss record and decided by the association's Committee on Rankings (Banzuke Henseikai).

In general, the Committee on Rankings promotes wrestlers with winning records and demotes wrestlers with losing records. Some weight is given to a wrestler's absolute win-loss record in a tournament (especially in higher divisions), but promotion and demotion are largely determined by whether a wrestler had a net balance of wins or losses; that is, whether the wrestler had more or fewer than eight wins in a fifteen-day tournament. Accordingly, a wrestler who achieves his eighth win or eighth loss in a tournament before the fifteenth day often has less incentive to continue with the same level of vigor during the remaining days of the tournament because his promotion or demotion for the next tournament is already decided. This system has led to rumors that the outcome of some sumo bouts is fixed. This would not be altogether unsurprising, because sumo's rituals and history, like those of kabuki and other traditional Japanese arts, tend to make it as theatrical as it is competitive. But the association vehemently denies such allegations and has taken the extraordinary steps of suing Diet members (for example, Shintaro Ishihara in 1963) for libel and lodging formal accusations of criminal libel with prosecutors against weekly magazines (for example, *Shūkan Post* in 1996) because of their statements that sumo is rigged.[11] In particularly fishy situations, the association has publicly reprimanded wrestlers whose performance was lackluster and has launched internal investigations.

The greatest temptation for fixing matches comes on the final day of the tournament as a wrestler with a seven-win, seven-loss record on the fifteenth and final day may receive a little extra help (to finish with a winning 8–7 record) from an opponent whose promotion or demotion is already sealed. Mark Duggan and Steven Levitt found that wrestlers "on the bubble" on the final day win about 25 percent more often than would be expected—but that match-rigging vanishes in times of media scrutiny.[12] The root of the phenomenon is the promotion rules. Taking a dive

---

11. See "Umi" Areba Dase [If There Is "Pus," Drain It!], Asahi Shinbun, May 23, 1996, at 16; Ōnaruto, Yaochō [Fixed Matches] (1996).

can be rational because a cooperative wrestler may have the favor returned when he finds himself in a similar situation. The system tends to benefit the association, which can more easily keep its popular and revenue-producing stars in the spotlight for longer periods of time (whether by deliberate choreography or mere willful blindness) than it could with an absolute win-loss promotion system. Most people who care about the rules of promotion are already such fans that a rule change is not needed to keep them supporting sumo financially.

Rumors or no rumors, wrestlers who win bouts are promoted through the *jonokuchi, jonidan, sandanme,* and *makushita* divisions. A particularly strong wrestler may make this series of jumps to makushita in less than a year. Most wrestlers never advance past that point. But for the lucky few who successfully persevere, the next step is the promised land of the *jūryō* division, the second-highest, which contains twenty-six wrestlers. A wrestler in this division may be allowed to have his own junior recruit to tend to his needs. He is allowed to have his own room, and if he is married, he can move out of the stable. He trades in his old "uniform" for a fancy new one, and he finally is given a modicum of respect. Most important, he begins to earn a salary and is no longer considered a mere apprentice.

The next leap, promotion from jūryō to the top division of *makuuchi* (alternatively, *makunouchi*), is something like a minor league baseball player's being called up to the major leagues. Makuuchi division wrestlers are on the covers of sumo magazines, are interviewed by the media, and can make a lot of money. Within the stable, they are treated like kings. But the journey is not yet over, because wrestlers fiercely compete for rank within the top division. The top ten wrestlers in the division are the cream of the crop, and they are ranked, in ascending order, as *komusubi, sekiwake,* and *ōzeki,* which collectively are known as the "three ranks" (*san'yaku*). All wrestlers strive to enter the three ranks, if only for one tournament. Elders who did not advance to the three ranks while they were active are doomed to be second-class champions for their entire post-ring careers.

At the top of the heap stands the *yokozuna,* usually translated as "grand champion." More than simply a rank, promotion to yokozuna is virtually an anointment of a wrestler as the embodiment of sumo. There have only been thirty yokozuna in the postwar era, and only sixty-eight since the

---

12. Mark Duggan and Steven D. Levitt, Winning Isn't Everything: Corruption in Sumo Wrestling, 92 Am. Econ. Rev. 1594 (2002).

title was created three centuries ago. Unlike members of all other ranks, a yokozuna can never be demoted; he is simply expected to retire when his performance begins to slip. Because the rank is permanent, the decision of whether to promote an ōzeki ("champion") to yokozuna is made very carefully and with great consideration of public expectations. The initial recommendation is made by the Yokozuna Deliberation Council, a committee established in 1951 composed of fifteen prominent outsiders, including university professors and industry leaders (and, as of 2001, one woman).[13] The council's recommendation is usually routinely accepted by the Committee on Rankings on behalf of the association.

Compensation in the sumo world is directly related to a wrestler's rank and success in the ring. The formulas for determining compensation are somewhat complex, but the basic rule is that wrestlers receive only a small stipend until they reach the second-highest division (jūryō) and become true professionals. In other words, of the eight hundred or so wrestlers currently competing, only the top sixty-six are professionals. But once a wrestler reaches the second-highest division, he begins to receive a salary, a daily travel allowance, prize money for certain victories, and other compensation that correlates to victories in individual bouts (to discourage sloth at any level). Monthly base salary levels in 2003 were as follows: yokozuna, ¥2.82 million ($28,200); ōzeki, ¥2.347 million ($23,470); komusubi and sekiwake, ¥1.693 million ($16,930); other top-division wrestlers, ¥1.309 million ($13,090); second-division wrestlers, ¥1.036 million ($10,360).[14] At the top of the sumo world, the sport can be quite lucrative; in 1993, yokozuna Akebono earned ¥79,199,250 (approximately $800,000), more than three times his base salary.

At the end of a wrestler's career in the ring when he is about thirty years of age, he must decide whether to stay in the firm as an elder or to abandon his firm-specific human capital and look for a job in the outside world. Wrestlers who do not remain in the association as elders usually

13. See Masaya Urado, Ōzumō Marugoto Zatsugaku Jiten [The Unabridged Encyclopedic Dictionary of Grand Sumo], 216 (1995) (list of members); see also Yokozuna Shingiiinkai Kisoku [Rules of the *Yokozuna* Deliberation Council], in Zaidan Hōjin Nihon Sumō Kyōkai Kifu Kōi Shikō Saisoku Fuzoku Kitei [Special Provisions Attached to Detailed Rules Regarding the Enforcement of the Act of Endowment of the Japan Sumo Association], 53 (rules for promotion); Lee A. Thompson, The Invention of the Yokozuna and the Championship System, Or, Futahaguro's Revenge, in Mirror of Modernity: Invented Traditions of Modern Japan, 174, ed. Stephen Vlastos (1998).

14. Association Act Rules, *supra* note 8, arts. 76, 77.

become amateur coaches, open specialty restaurants, or become professional (theatrical) wrestlers. A handful of popular wrestlers become entertainers and politicians.

The Sumo Association

Since its establishment in 1927, the association has governed every aspect of professional sumo. The association is composed of approximately twelve hundred people, including elders, wrestlers, hairdressers, announcers, referees, and clerical workers. Although select wrestlers and referees have nominal input in the decision-making process, for all practical purposes the association is the elders, and every major decision is either made or approved by some or all of the 105 holders of elder stock. Elders control every aspect of the association, including countryside exhibition tours, health insurance, examination of new applicants, operation of the sumo museum, security, and public relations.

Only the skimpiest of skeletal frameworks is dictated by the default rules of the Civil Code. Formally, the association is a nonprofit "public welfare juridical person" (*kōeiki hōjin*) as defined by the code.[15] Pursuant to the code, the association's Act of Endowment (*kifu kōi*, a legal document similar to a corporation's charter documents) provides for ten directors (*riji*), three supervisors (*kanji*), and various other officers (*yakuin taigu*) who supervise the workings of the association.[16]

This Act of Endowment, a document privately negotiated with and approved by the Ministry of Education, elaborates on this simple structure. The board of directors is led by its chairman (*rijichō*), who serves as the association's representative, both legally and in the media, and usually is a former yokozuna.[17] All executives are required to be elders.[18] The Act of Endowment further provides for a Deliberative Council (*hyōgiin-kai*), which is the decisive core of the association for all matters other than those that must be decided by the board of directors.[19] The Deliberative

---

15. Article 34 of the Civil Code provides that a public welfare juridical person is an association or foundation relating to worship, religion, charity, science, or art or otherwise relating to the public interest and not having a profit-making objective, subject to the permission of the relevant governmental authorities. Minpō [Civil Code], art. 34.

16. See Minpō [Civil Code], arts. 52, 58.

17. Association Act, *supra* note 1, art. 20.

18. Association Act Rules, *supra* note 8, art. 31.

19. Association Act, *supra* note 1, art. 25.

Council is composed of the 105 elders, four wrestlers, and two referees.[20] It serves as a pseudo-shareholder organ and elects all directors and supervisors every other year just after the January tournament.[21]

Association rules require that elections be conducted "with instruction from the heart of the sumo path, and in strict fairness, so as not to lose honor and dignity."[22] Reality is more complex. The outcome of elections—especially the election of those who will fill the powerful directors' positions—is usually decided in advance according to a "camp" system. Historically, stables have been grouped into five camps (*ichimon*), or groups of affiliate stables. Each stable is associated with a camp. Although no formal rules are established, it is generally understood that each of the five camps—Dewanoumi, Nishonoseki/Fuatagoyama, Takasago/Kokonoe, Tokitsukaze, and Tatsunami/Isegahama—is entitled to elect two directors.

This basic system of decision-making applies not only to elections but to almost all significant decisions of the association. In theory, the Deliberative Council has specific charge over matters pertaining to the association's budget and real estate, the economic welfare of elders, wrestlers, and referees, and such other matters as may be decided by the board of directors.[23] In practice, the Deliberative Council governs the association in conjunction with the board. Camps generally make decisions as blocs, and the ninety-five nondirector elders informally monitor the ten director elders.

The association currently is comprised of fifty-three stables. Only elders may open stables, and they may do so only with the permission of the association. The association provides stablemasters with at least ¥70,000 ($700) in "training payments" monthly for each wrestler in the stable not in the top two divisions, which, combined with various other payments, reach ¥1.8 million ($18,000) per unranked wrestler per year. Extra training payment is provided for higher-ranked wrestlers; stables receive ¥2.16 million ($21,600) for ōzeki and ¥2.76 million ($27,600) for yokozuna. Larger stables may receive total amounts that approach ¥100 million ($1 million) per year. This system provides incentives for elders

20. Association Act Rules, *supra* note 8, arts. 34–35. The referees and wrestlers are elected for two-year terms. Ibid. Representative wrestlers are usually the highest-ranked wrestlers, and representative referees are almost always the top two referees.

21. Association Act, *supra* note 1, art. 23.

22. Association Act Rules, *supra* note 8, art. 30.

23. Association Act, *supra* note 1, art. 26.

to recruit and train winning wrestlers by ensuring that more successful stables are more highly compensated.

But stable maintenance costs can be high; food bills alone can run thousands of dollars a month. Accordingly, in addition to funds received from the association, a stablemaster elder seeks and usually receives funds from stable support groups (*kōenkai* or *tanimachi*) and individual supporters. Each stable usually has at least one support group. Support groups are expensive fan clubs in which members pay dues in return for a relationship with the stable, drinks with their favorite wrestlers, and tickets for good seats (tournaments are often sold out). Dues are a substantial source of income for a stable. The Kyushu Sadogatake support group (an average group), for example, charges regular members annual dues of ¥20,000 ($200) and special members ¥30,000 ($300). The three thousand members of the group generate at least ¥60 million ($600,000) annually for the Sadogatake stable and its wrestlers in dues alone.[24]

Many stables and individual wrestlers also have wealthy individual supporters who make large contributions. Although most large transactions are secret, some relationships are well known. The newly expanded Futagoyama stable is said to have been created (by a 1994 merger with the Fujishima stable of the same camp) with the help of a ¥500 million ($5 million) contribution from the head of a Buddhist sect. Potentially more reliable data come from Japanese tax authorities, who report that in 1995 the Futagoyama stablemaster, his wife, and his two wrestling sons paid ¥190 million ($1.9 million) in income taxes on an estimated combined income of ¥430 million ($4.3 million).[25]

Smaller transactions with supporters are more visible; patrons often slip wrestlers ¥20,000 ($200) or so to have a formal picture taken together or to dine at a wrestler's table. A wrestler often shares these funds with his stablemaster. Financial rewards such as these ensure a steady stream of elders who are eager to take over the responsibilities of a stablemaster.

---

24. Seiji Nozaki, Tanimachi to iu Ikikata [The Life of the Sumo Supporter], in Sumo Dosukoi Tokuhon [Sumo Reader], 166, 177 (Bessatsu Takarashima no. 160, ed. Shinji Ishii, 1992).

25. Tōkyō Shōkō Risaachi, Zenkoku Kōgaku Nōzeisha Meibo [National List of High-Tax Payers] (1995); Futagoyama-beya Zeimushō Chōsa de "Kakukai no Kane" ni Mesu ga Hairu [Tax Investigation of Futagoyama Stable Drives a Stake into the Heart of "Sumo World Money"], Shūkan Post, June 28, 1996 at 242, 243. In 1995, tax authorities penalized an elder named Kokone for failing to report $600,000 received from supporters in 1992. See Ex-Chiyonofuji Slapped with Tax Penalties, Sumo World 8 (Sept. 1995).

THE ELDER SHARE REGIME

The Problem

All firms face the basic organizational problem of how to utilize personnel to maximize revenue. In the sumo firm, the specific problem is how to get the people who could best perform this task for the association to stay involved with the sport. For two reasons, one easily identifiable group of people who are able to maximize revenue (though not necessarily the best) is composed of retired wrestlers. First, elders know each other well and have a common culture. They also have developed unique firm-specific knowledge of the inner workings of the association.

Second, popular retired wrestlers are needed to continue in the sport to keep demand for the sport high among both fans and new recruits who want to train with the superstars. Elders are extremely visible. Although revenue-producing potential new recruits and longtime fans may not know an elder by his elder name, they will often know the elder's fighting name and face from his glory days in the ring. This visibility allows elders to serve as the association's economic ambassadors and to keep sumo competitive in the sports marketplace.

That ex-wrestlers are in the best position to maximize revenue is not obvious. Generally speaking, professional sports leagues are owned by outsiders, not ex-players. One reason that this is so is that entry costs in conventional professional sports leagues are often prohibitively high. A wealthy ex-player—a Michael Jordan—can purchase an interest, but very few others can. Conventional sports leagues generally are also managed not by ex-players but by outsiders. The heads of sports leagues usually are businesspeople or lawyers who are chosen by the owners.

In theory, the association's ex-player owners similarly could hire outsiders. But the former have built trust-based relationships over many years, beginning in adolescence. Given the importance of secrecy in the association, the cost of determining the validity of an outsiders' reputation and educating them in the ways of the organization are said to be simply too high when compared to self-management.

Finally, most professional sports leagues also do not rely on retired players to keep the popularity of the sport high, relying instead on the players themselves, who give interviews and appear in commercials. But the association strongly discourages active wrestlers from doing so because, they say, the public expects sumo to maintain a modicum of mystique.[26] These constraints have led the sumo firm to structure its management and ownership differently from conventional sports leagues.

The Solution: Elder Shares

Sumo has not always been Japan's semiofficial national sport. In the seventeenth century, sumo was a constant source of trouble to the Japanese shogunate government. At that time sumo was unorganized, and countryside tournaments often led to gambling and fights among spectators. Worried about this unsavory situation, the shogunate repeatedly issued bans against the sport.

Despite the bans, bored townsfolk wanted to see sumo as an alternative to theater. Beginning in 1684, the shogunate occasionally allowed sumo tournaments to be held as charity events, with profits going to the building of temples and shrines and other worthy causes. Such tournaments could only be held with the express permission of the shogunate. To obtain such permission, a responsible party would deliver a formal request to the shogunate. As sumo became more respectable in the eighteenth century, retired wrestlers began to deliver these requests to the shogunate under the stage names under which they had fought. These ex-wrestlers were the first elders.[27] By the late nineteenth century the elder share system had crystallized, and the Tokyo Sumo Association was composed of 88 elders. Each share now carried a specific name in honor of a previous owner, and an elder who acquired a share assumed the attached name.

When the Tokyo Sumo Association merged with the Osaka Association in 1927, Osaka's 17 elder shares were added to Tokyo's 88 to create the current system of 105 shares. The association maintains a list of these 105 names, and only eligible retired wrestlers are entitled to hold the shares (a physical piece of paper like a stock certificate) to which those names are attached. A few clerical and assistant coaching positions aside, a wrestler who wants to remain associated with professional sumo after

26. See Keiji Isaji, Ōzumō "Kindaika" to Hōritsu Mondaiten ni Tsuite [The "Modernization" of Sumo and Legal Problem Points], Jiyū to Seigi [Liberty and Justice], 67, 70 (Nov. 1994).

27. See Tarō Nase, Toshiyori Kabu Kara Miru Sumō no Hen na Keizaigaku [Sumo's Strange Economics as Seen in the Elder Share System] in Ishii, *supra* note 24, at 137, 142–44.

retirement must acquire one of the shares and become an elder (and as-sume the elder name) on his retirement.[28] An elder may hold more than one elder share during the course of his career. Elders may exchange shares, and they usually do so in order to affiliate with a specific stable or to become a stablemaster. Exit is permanent; a wrestler may not leave the association and then reenter (either as a wrestler or as an elder).[29]

The basic rules as to who may obtain a share and become an elder are fairly straightforward. To be eligible to purchase a share, a wrestler must have appeared in the top (makuuchi) division for one tournament or have appeared in the second (jūryō) division in twenty consecutive or twenty-five total tournaments.[30] At any given time, only about fifty wrestlers of about eight hundred meet this requirement. Keeping eligibility require-ments high helps ensure that only the most visible wrestlers have an op-portunity to become elders.

One exception to the general eligibility requirements pertains to so-called "master" elder shares: shares that belong to the fifty-three stable-masters and carry the same name as the stable (all other elders affiliate with stables as coaches). Many stables have long histories and utilize par-ticular training methods. It might well be inefficient for an outsider who has no knowledge of the inner workings of the stable to take over as sta-blemaster. To remedy this potential problem, the association provides that if the board of directors approves, a stablemaster elder may transfer his share to a wrestler (from his own stable) who has competed in only one tournament in the second division.[31]

Association rules and norms create several restrictions on share trans-fer. First, shares may not be transferred or even loaned to wrestlers or others who do not meet the above criteria, ensuring once again that only the fittest survive. Second, the share of a deceased elder reverts to the as-sociation if it is not transferred within five years of his death or retirement from the sumo world.[32] This provision prevents shares from lying on the shelf when they could be put to good use by a revenue-producing elder. Third, although the association does not formally have the power to approve or refuse transfers provided that they comply with the above

28. See Isaji, *supra* note 26, at 69 (discussing non-elder positions for wrestlers who wish to remain with the association).

29. Association Act Rules, *supra* note 8, art. 95.

30. Ibid., art. 48.

31. Ibid. See Oinuma, *supra* note 10, at 136–38.

32. Association Act Rules, *supra* note 8, art. 48.

requirements, a wrestler retiring from the ring to become an elder must submit to the association an "elder name succession/inheritance notice" (*toshiyori shōmei, keishō todoke*) advising of his plans to assume the elder name.[33] Although the inner workings of the association on this point are unclear, it appears that on at least one occasion its board of directors exerted significant pressure on receipt of this notice to prevent an elder from selling his share to a qualified buyer because of the buyer's suspected role as a broker in fixing matches.[34]

Some potential revenue-producers cannot become elders because shares are scarce or the price is too high. Accordingly, the association has adopted four rules to help certain wrestlers obtain shares. First, a wrestler who has become a yokozuna is allowed to remain in the association as an elder under his sumo fighting name for five years. Only if he is not able to acquire an elder share after the five-year period expires is he required to leave.[35]

Second, the association may award a truly great yokozuna a "single-generation" or "lifetime" share. The standard, if there is one, is unclear, but the achievement of twenty championships appears to be a prerequisite. These shares carry the wrestler's fighting name and are only valid for one generation; that is, the elder may not transfer the share on his retirement from the association, and it may not be inherited upon his death. Only three such shares have ever been awarded and registered. Adding these single-generation shares to the number of "regular" shares brings the total number of elder shares to 108.

Third, historically, a wrestler was allowed to rent a share from another elder. This rule was especially helpful in the case of an elder who died with no apparent eligible heir or of a competing wrestler who, though eligible to purchase an otherwise available share by virtue of success in the ring, was ineligible to participate in the association until his formal retirement from the ring. In 1998 this system collapsed, at least in part because of a 1996 tax scandal in which share rental income was not reported. To prevent further scandals, the association banned the renting of shares (grandfathering already rented shares through 2003) and the holding of multiple

33. Ibid.

34. Ōnaruto, *supra* note 11, at 53–55 (the former elder Ōnaruto's account of board chairman Futagoyama's success at preventing the wrestler Itai from borrowing an elder share, ostensibly on the ground that he had not significantly participated in the association's regional tours).

35. Association Act Rules, *supra* note 8, art. 48.

shares. In its place a fourth rule was instituted to ensure adequate personnel: associate elders (*jun-toshiyori*). The association created slots for a maximum of ten associate elders, who must have competed in one tournament in the top three ranks, twenty in the top division, or thirty in the top two divisions combined. Associate elders may stay in the association for two years (three for ōzeki, five for yokozuna), during which time they must acquire a permanent share or leave.

But portions of this regime soon backfired. By eliminating the rental market, elders had deprived themselves of a potential source of income. Moreover, the number of associate elder slots (ten) was fewer than the number of shares generally on loan (in 1998, the number was seventeen), resulting in personnel shortages and open shares (nine in 2002). Elders who held multiple shares had few options. In late 2002 the association lifted the ban on rentals and reduced the number of associate elders from ten to five (and the waiting period from two years to one for ordinary wrestlers). This attempt to balance supply and demand thus combines the rental and associate elder systems.

At some point, most elders lose their popularity, and with it their ability and desire to drum up demand for the sport. Like many law firms, the sumo firm does not allow its members to continue in the venture forever. To ensure that shares are put to their highest use, the association mandates that elders relinquish their shares at age sixty-five.[36]

But unlike a law firm, the association does not require an elder to relinquish his share to it on retirement; he merely has to find an eligible individual buyer. In fact, the entire transfer process is generally decentralized.[37] At least two reasons account for the difference. First, unlike rules at law firms, the rule-based qualifications for becoming a buyer in the association are so stringent that very few people other than popular wrestlers who could increase revenues have any chance to purchase shares. Because the requirements are so strict, the association need not suffer the collective decision-making costs it might incur in evaluating a potential elder's human capital. The occasional lemon can be kept out by pressure from the board.

36. Teinen Taishoku Kitei [Retirement Age Rules], art. 1, in Zaidan Hōjin Nihon Sumō Kyōkai Kifu Kōi Shikō Saisoku Fuzoku Kitei [Special Provisions Attached to Detailed Rules Regarding the Enforcement of the Act of Endowment of the Japan Sumo Association], 41.

37. When the association's chairman, Sakaigawa, proposed in 1996 that the buying and selling of shares be prohibited and that the association instead control exchanges, he was soundly defeated, forced to withdraw the proposal, and eventually run out of office.

Second, not all transactions are left to individual elders. Just as a law firm can elect a new partner, the association can elect a new elder by issuing a lifetime share if a spectacular candidate appears. It can thus ensure that a potential revenue producer does not fall through the cracks simply because he cannot afford a share or a share is not available at the time of his retirement.

The Incentives: Elder Share Benefits and Valuation

The association encourages share ownership by attaching economic benefits to elder shares. Because it is not a corporate entity and elder shares do not entail ownership in the corporate sense, profits are not distributed as dividends but as an annuity-like fixed monthly salary. As of 2003, all elders were entitled to receive a salary of at least ¥12.18 million ($122,000). Elders who have advanced in the association's hierarchy—largely a function of longevity, rank as a wrestler, and stable ownership—receive larger amounts; elders who are directors receive ¥18.45 million ($184,500), and the chairman receives ¥20.87 million ($208,700).[38]

Unlike a university or a law firm, becoming an elder in the association does not result in a quantum jump in earnings. In fact, a junior elder's salary is always less than his salary was as a wrestler. But unlike junior partners and tenured professors, a wrestler's ability to generate income for the association usually decreases as he leaves the ring to assume the administrative or coaching position of a junior elder. Just as star basketball players can earn more than their coaches, star wrestlers can earn more than their elders.

Elder salaries correlate roughly to the economic performance of the association. Consider one particularly interesting time in the association's history, and perhaps the zenith of its popularity, the mid-1990s. As seen in table 3.1, both gross revenues and elder salaries have increased every year in the period. From 1989 to 1991, the elders gave themselves six-percent salary increases each year. In 1991, both the popularity of sumo and ticket prices increased, resulting in a 33 percent increase in distributable income from ¥1.15 billion ($11.5 million) in 1990 to ¥1.54 billion ($15.4 million) in 1991. The mere 6 percent increase in elder salaries approved in late

---

38. Association Act Rules, *supra* note 8, arts. 73–74. Causal factors are from regressions in Takanobu Nakajima, Ōzumō no Keizaigaku [The Economics of Sumo], 46–47 (2003). Elders receive their salaries net of taxes. See Ōnaruto, *supra* note 11, at 45.

Table 3.1. Association Revenues and Elder Distributions, 1989–1995

Year	Gross income (millions)	Gross elder salaries[a] (millions)	Net residual earnings after expenses[b] (millions)	Elder take of net income (%)	Salary increase declared at year-end for subsequent year (%)
1989	$ 79.60	$4.5	$12.30	36.59	6
1990	$ 94.60	$4.8	$11.50	41.73	6
1991	$ 99.69	$5.1	$15.40	33.11	56
1992	$102.87	$8.0	$12.11	66.06	6
1993	$108.15	$8.5	$15.10	56.29	6
1994	$110.61	$9.0	$13.49	66.71	6
1995	$142.60	$9.5	$13.40	70.89	6

[a]Assuming equal salary distribution among ten directors, three supervisors, five officers, seven committee heads, and eighty-two regular elders.

[b]Because elder salaries are (appropriately) considered expenses, net income figures provided by the association exclude amounts distributed to elders. To determine the size of elders' take as a percentage of distributable funds, I have regarded elder salaries as shareholders' equity, and have added gross elder salary amounts back into the association's net income figures. The association reports net income as follows: 1989—¥780 million ($7.8 million); 1990— ¥670 million ($6.7 million); 1991—¥1.03 billion ($10.3 million); 1992—¥411 million ($4.11 million); 1993—¥660 million ($6.6 million); 1994—¥449 million ($4.49 million); 1995— ¥390 million ($3.9 million). These amounts are required to be deposited in a bank account or invested in securities. Zaidan Hōjin Nihon Sumō Kyōkai Kifu Kōi [Act of Endowment of the Japan Sumo Association], art. 7.

1990 for 1991 was not made with the thought of such economic success in mind, and accordingly profits distributed to elders as salary in 1991 dipped to only 33 percent of net income. To increase elders' take of the larger and seemingly growing pot, the association approved a whopping 56 percent elder salary increase for 1992. With the new salary structure in place, elder salaries accounted for a more comfortable share of distributable revenues, and the association returned to its standard six-percent salary increases.

By linking elder income to the association's financial performance, elder shares create incentives for elders to keep demand for the sport high. The more elders increase sumo's popularity, the higher the firm's revenues will be. The higher the firm's revenues, the greater the return on

an elder share both as salary and in deferred compensation that can be realized by selling the share.

   But there's a problem here. Why don't elders shirk? Surely some shirking occurs, but it is mitigated by the relatively small size of the association,
which increases monitoring. In addition to dirty looks and gossip, shirking elders may be monetarily sanctioned, because stables and camps can
refuse to nominate shirking elders for more lucrative positions in the association such as that of director.

   Elders as a group refrain from grabbing a larger share of the profits.
Elders could modify their pay structure to distribute all (or almost all)
distributable funds to themselves as bonuses at the end of the year. Two
factors suggest why they do not change the system. First, grabbing could
leave the association without sufficient funds to make the wealth-
maximizing investments that would be necessary for the firm. Keeping
sufficient funds in the association helps keep the price that an elder can demand for his share high. Second, the annual increases that the association
approves for elders usually apply to wrestlers; when elder shares are
increased by six percent, wrestler salaries (the salaries of the sixty-six
wrestlers in the top two divisions) are increased by the same margin. This
arrangement may serve as a precommitment device for elders against
grabbing a larger share of the pie, and in turn it creates incentives for
wrestlers, like elders, to keep revenues high.

   In pricing shares, elders and wrestlers calculate the present value of
the future income stream generated by share possession. Assuming a discount rate of five percent and a thirty-five-year annuity stream, the minimum market price for an elder share should be approximately ¥137 million ($1.37 million).[39] An elder who expects to be a director (and receive
the higher director's salary) for fifteen of his thirty-five years between retirement from the ring and retirement at age sixty-five will value the share
under otherwise identical constraints at ¥265 million ($2.65 million).
Lowering the discount rate to one percent changes these valuations to
¥246 million ($2.46 million) and ¥427 million ($4.27 million), respectively; raising it to ten percent changes the valuations to ¥80 million
($800,000) and ¥192 million ($1.92 million).

   In the only court case on point to date (perhaps the only one that the
association could not mediate internally—they don't want their dirty

---

39. The annuity was calculated using the formula $1 - (1 + r^{-n})/r$.

laundry shown), the Tokyo District Court in 2003 found appropriate a price of ¥175 million ($1.75 million) for the Tatsunami share. The facts are a bit messy, but they illuminate some otherwise vague practices. In 1995, the wrestler Asahiyutaka, then twenty-seven years old, married the daughter of the Tatsunami elder and was formally adopted, a not uncommon method for a wrestler to stay in the sumo family. In 1999, the elder passed the Tatsunami share to Asahiyutaka. Shortly thereafter, Asahiyutaka's wife filed for divorce. Tatsunami sued Asahiyutaka for payment on the share. Asahiyutaka claimed that no agreement existed and that share purchases were forbidden by the association. The court rejected each claim. Instead, the court found that "an oral agreement existed under which [Asahiyutaka] would pay an appropriate price for share transference, as is customary" and awarded the elder the ¥175 million that he demanded.[40]

Current salary is not the only factor considered in pricing shares. Elders and wrestlers include in their calculations the likelihood of salary increases and the possibility of additional income that can be earned as a stablemaster. Wrestlers also make purchase bids based on their own age. Although very young wrestlers cannot amass the funds necessary to purchase a share, in general younger purchasers receive the annuity over a longer period of time and accordingly should be willing to pay more for a share. Scarcity also plays a role. When there is a surplus of available shares, an elder approaching age sixty-five may be forced to take a lower price for his share than he otherwise would.[41] Finally, an elder may choose to sell his share at a substantial discount to a wrestler who marries that elder's daughter, as in the Tatsunami case.

The actual market prices at which shares are bought and sold are very close to the prices that the above calculations suggest. Although the terms of share transfers are generally kept secret, elders, wrestlers, and other insiders confirmed for me in the mid-1990s that the market price for a share was generally in the range of ¥100 to ¥400 million ($1 to $4 million).

40. See, e.g., Toshiyori Myōseki Soshō de Gen Tatsunami Oyakata ni 1 Oku 75000 Man'en Shiharai Meirei [Elder Tatsunami Ordered to Pay ¥175 Million in Elder Share Suit], Asahi Shinbun, Feb. 24, 2003, available at http://www.asahi.com/sports/etc/TKY200302240098.html.

41. The available elder share pool is shrinking owing to increased longevity of elders. Through the 1970s, only a few elders lived long enough to reach the mandatory retirement age of sixty-five, but an increasing number now reach that age. See Lora Sharnoff, Grand Sumo, 139 (rev. ed. 1993).

Prices are said to have been around ¥100 million ($1 million) in the 1980s[42] but increased in the mid-1990s as former elder ōnaruto claimed to have sold his share in 1995 for ¥300 million ($3 million), ¥30 million ($300,000) less than his original asking price.[43] Prices are said to have leveled off in the late 1990s. Elders tell me that the price in 2003 was between ¥150 million and ¥200 million ($1.5 to $2 million), as seen in the Tatsunami case. The decrease might reflect sumo's somewhat lower popularity in 2003 (the stadium is now only 90 percent full) or the lower discount rate.

This financial analysis is not meant to imply that sumo wrestlers sit down with calculators and annuity tables to compute present value. Rationality is bounded, and neither elders nor wrestlers can exactly pinpoint a share's present value because future revenues are unknown. Instead, elders and wrestlers make educated guesses based on available information and negotiate prices that are generally in the range of the calculated value of the shares.

Keeping share prices high by keeping salaries high further limits the field of potential purchasers to elders who can best increase the firm's revenues. Banks generally do not finance elder share purchases because association rules prohibit the posting of elder shares as collateral. Accordingly, wrestlers generally finance the purchase of their expensive shares in one of only two ways. First, some wrestlers pay with the victory-based earnings that they have accumulated over the course of their careers. Only the very top wrestlers, however, earn the funds needed to purchase a share. Second, some wrestlers receive at least part of the funds for purchasing a share from supporters.[44] Only popular wrestlers—those who as elders will continue to bring in funds—will receive such financial backing. As a result, although at any given time approximately fifty wrestlers may meet the association's eligibility criteria, only a small number of this

42. Compare Arase, Arase no Utchari Hōdan [Arase's Table Turning Straight Talk], 111 (1984) (more than ¥100 million in 1988), and Sharnoff, *supra* note 41, at 140 ("it is rumored that the stocks sold in 1986 and 1987 went for well over 100 million yen each") with Heisei Sumō Kenkyūkai, Ōzumō no Himitsu [The Secrets of Grand Sumo], 209 (1993) (¥300 million), Nase, *supra* note 27, at 149 (describing a "seller's market" in which shares may sell for ¥400 million), and Schilling, *supra* note 6, at 55 ("[¥]300 million or more").

43. Ōnaruto, *supra* note 11, at 18, 58–71.

44. These supporters surely would not agree to finance an ex-wrestler's alternative investment in, for instance, certificates of deposit. Accordingly, a wrestler may be able to pay a higher price for an elder share than he would be able to invest in a more traditional investment.

elite group have the financial resources to purchase a share. The rules allow a second-division wrestler to become an elder, but in practice, the majority of elders come from the upper echelon of the top division, and an elder who never competed in the top division is virtually unheard of.

Still, though exit is permanent, not all popular wrestlers remain. The foreign-born wrestler Konishiki, discussed below, left to pursue a career as an entertainer. Perhaps more significant, two very popular yokozuna, Wakanohana and Akebono, each left the association, marking the only voluntary yokozuna departures in its history. Wakanohana had many interests outside of sumo (including American football, race car driving, and sports commentating), had many disagreements with the association about restrictions, and in 2000, at age twenty-nine, left. Akebono left in 2003 at age thirty-four, in part because of disagreements with his stable master and in part because he wanted to pursue another lucrative interest: K-1 boxing. (The former yokozuna, at 6 feet 8 inches and 463 pounds, was soundly beaten in his 2003 New Year's Eve debut by the very popular former Minnesota Vikings offensive lineman Bob Sapp, at 6 feet 7 inches and 344 pounds.) In both cases, the association might stand to benefit because neither would have been a particularly efficient elder given the structural disagreements. But as sumo faces competition for its elder talent, rules and norms will need to evolve to ensure success.

RULES AND NORMS

The elder share regime is based largely on formal rules. But in practice, those rules interact with norms in four basic patterns: strict application of existing rules with no deference to norms, defection from rules to norms, application of a combination of rules and norms, and creation of new rules.

Strict Application of Existing Rules: Kirishima's Lament

Kirishima was a very popular and successful wrestler in the late 1980s and early 1990s. But his performance in the ring began to decline in 1992 as younger and faster wrestlers began to get the best of his thirty-three-year-old body. He slipped lower and lower in the ranks, finally falling to the bottom spot of the top division for the March 1996 tournament.[45] Most

45. Kirishima, Gen'eki Zokkō e [Kirishima to Continue], Asahi Shinbun, Jan. 22, 1996, at 19.

wrestlers who reach the top two ranks never fall to such depths; before their level of performance falls, they purchase an elder share and begin life as an elder. But despite rising to the top of the sport, Kirishima was unable to purchase a share.

He first attempted to purchase a share from within his stable. His stablemaster, Izutsu, controlled two shares: his own share (Izutsu) and Shikoroyama. But unfortunately for Kirishima, the Izutsu stablemaster also had two top-ranked, good-looking, and wildly popular sons, Sakahoko and Terao. Sakahoko retired to take the Izutsu share, and the Shikoroyama share was promised to Terao (he received it in 2002). Kirishima then tried to purchase a share on the open market. But the market price for shares reportedly was at its highest ever—$4 million—and out of Kirishima's range.[46]

Unable to purchase a share, Kirishima was forced to compete past his prime. After suffering a losing record in the last spot in the top division, Kirishima faced a choice: slip into the second division for the first time in twelve years or retire altogether from the association. The association's official stance remained as it had throughout the years: it would not bend its rules to award Kirishima a share, and Kirishima was not of the caliber necessary to receive a single-generation share. At the last moment, he was able to reach an agreement with the Izutsu stablemaster under which Kirishima rented the Shikoroyama share until Terao's retirement. His share in hand, Kirishima retired at the end of the March 1996 tournament. The deal was bittersweet, because Kirishima would be forced to look once again for an elder share when Terao retired.[47]

In fact, the deal turned out to be more bitter than expected. Kirishima eventually was able to purchase the Michinoku share for an estimated $3.3 million, leaving the Shikoroyama share to Terao. But at least in part because of the drain on his financial resources, he failed to pay taxes on more than $2.2 million worth of supporter income from 1993 to 1998. In addition to tax penalties, the association docked his elder pay by one-fifth for six months and publicly reprimanded him.

46. The increase is said to be due to efforts by the Futagoyama stable to secure shares for its numerous eligible and highly ranked wrestlers (seven are in the top division). See Kirishima wo Haigyō Ōikomu [Cornering Kirishima into Retirement], Shūkan Gendai, April 6, 1996, at 182.

47. See Kazuhiro Kirishima, Rikishi Jinsei Aisaiki (The Life of the Wrestler: A Diary of Love for a Wife), Bungei Shunjū 270, 277 (June 1996); see also Kirishima Intai, Sumō ni Maku [Kirishima Retires, Closing the Curtain on Sumo], Asahi Shinbun, Mar. 25, 1996, at 19.

How could the association have avoided the share issue in the 1990s? It could have amended its rules to allow more wrestlers, or even Kirishima alone, to become elders. Two factors tend to weigh against this course of action. First, elders who make association rules have little incentive to allow more wrestlers to become elders, because flooding the market with additional elder shares would serve only to devalue the shares that they hold. Second, making an exception for Kirishima would send a signal that the association would not enforce its rules fairly. As repeat players in transactions with wrestlers, the association's elders could not afford the loss of this reputation bond.[48]

Alternatively, the association could have chosen to govern situations such as Kirishima's by norms rather than rules. But three factors weigh against such a choice. First, to the ticket-buying public, application of norms rather than rules in a situation such as Kirishima's might seem arbitrary and cast the integrity of sumo into doubt. Second, strict enforcement of rules relieves the association of the potentially volatile norm-based process of choosing who should become an elder. Law firms and university faculties are forced to centralize the selection process and rely on norms because candidates' human capital must be evaluated on a broad range of factors. But in the association, the belief is that only successful wrestlers have enough popular appeal to increase sumo revenues and as such should be elders. Accordingly, the association can assign the task of "choosing" which wrestlers should become elders to the operation of eligibility rules and rule-created price barriers. Making an exception to the rules for Kirishima calls the rule into doubt and forces the association into a time-consuming exercise. Finally, the rules can harmonize whatever differences may exist among wrestlers, stables, or camps. In the absence of concrete rules, some elders might be willing to admit Kirishima; others would not. The existence of a concrete rule might prevent costly disputes from arising out of parochial differences.

Defection from Rules to Norms: The Rise of Chiyonofuji

As shown in table 3.2 (the names are a bit complicated), the Chiyonofuji story centers around three yokozuna and consecutive holders of the

---

48. The association has unwaveringly applied its rules against other wrestlers like Kirishima. See Yōjū Kawabata, Monogatari Nihon Sumōshi [The Tale of the History of Japanese Sumo], 185–86 (1993).

Table 3.2. Kokonoe Elders

Fighting name	Period of Kokonoe share ownership	Current name (2004)
Chiyonoyama	1959–1977	(Deceased)
Kitanofuji	1977–1991	(Retired as Jinmaku)
Chiyonofuji	1991–present	Kokonoe

Kokonoe share: Chiyonoyama, Kitanofuji, and Chiyonofuji. Chiyono-yama, a former yokozuna from the Dewanoumi stable who held the Koko-noe share, was promised by the seventh Dewanoumi stablemaster that Chiyonoyama eventually would take over the Dewanoumi share and the attendant stable. But when Chiyonoyama was squeezed out of position in a political coup d'état, he acted somewhat radically and announced that he wanted to form his own stable under the Kokonoe name.[49] The Dewa-noumi stable (the head stable of the Dewanoumi camp) traditionally did not allow its former wrestlers to start their own stables and was initially reluctant to let Chiyonoyama loose.[50] The stable's leadership finally granted its permission on the condition that the new stable be established *outside* the Dewanoumi camp. Chiyonoyama left in 1967, taking ten wrestlers with him to form the Kokonoe stable, which affiliated itself with the Taka-sago camp.

Among the wrestlers who accompanied Chiyonoyama to the new stable was Kitanofuji, a rising star who eventually became a yokozuna. On Chiyonoyama's death in 1977, Kitanofuji became the Kokonoe stable-

49. When Dewanoumi died suddenly in 1960, the stable's leadership felt that at age thirty-three, Chiyonoyama was too young to be stablemaster. Instead, the elder Musa-shigawa (the former wrestler Dewanohana) was given the Dewanoumi share and became interim stablemaster. While Chiyonoyama waited, Musashigawa, then the eighth Dewa-noumi elder, used his political and business savvy to elevate himself to the position of chair-man of the association's board of directors. At about the same time, yokozuna Sadanoyama married Dewanoumi's daughter and in so doing inherited the rights to the Musashigawa share. Shortly after the wedding, Sadanoyama suddenly announced his retirement, inher-ited the Musashigawa share, and promptly traded shares with Dewanoumi. With that trade Sadanoyama became the ninth Dewanoumi stablemaster, and Chiyonoyama saw his hopes of becoming the Dewanoumi stablemaster dashed.

50. Only wrestlers whose stables are approved by the association may compete, and the association is unlikely to approve the establishment of a stable in a camp that does not want the stable. Chiyonoyama was at a particular disadvantage because the Dewanoumi elder from whom he sought approval was also chairman of the association's board of directors.

master.[51] Under Kitanofuji's leadership the stable became extremely successful, largely as a result of yokozuna Chiyonofuji. Nicknamed "the Wolf" for his ferocity, Chiyonofuji was arguably the greatest wrestler of the postwar era, and certainly was one of the more popular.[52] He also had had a special bond with the late Chiyonoyama because Chiyonoyama had recruited him from their mutual hometown in rural Hokkaido.

While still an active yokozuna, Chiyonofuji purchased a share with the name Jinmaku from Shimanishiki, a wrestler from the Takasago stable (a stable in the same camp as Kokonoe). Chiyonofuji made an offer to acquire from Kitanofuji what he really wanted: the Kokonoe share and its attendant Kokonoe stable. Although Kitanofuji was still many years away from mandatory retirement, he nevertheless agreed to an exchange of shares at a lower-than-market price for a stable share, reportedly ¥50,000,000 ($500,000).[53] After the exchange, Chiyonofuji would become the Kokonoe stablemaster,[54] and Kitanofuji would remain in the association as Jinmaku, a share without the extra income that a stable mastership brings.

51. The transaction was a bit more complicated than this simple explanation suggests. As Kitanofuji waited to take over the Kokonoe stable, the Izutsu stable was having problems. The Izutsu stablemaster had passed away, and there was no logical successor to the share. Despite the fact that the Izutsu stable was affiliated with a different camp, the late Izutsu stablemaster's wife approached Kitanofuji to become stablemaster, and Kitanofuji subsequently purchased the Izutsu share and became the Izutsu stablemaster. But Kitanofuji had no real connection with the Izutsu stable, and he never felt comfortable as the Izutsu elder. Accordingly, when Chiyonoyama died, Kitanofuji was the logical choice to return to Kokonoe. Because the former Izutsu stablemaster's wife had also died, Kitanofuji had no real remaining commitment as Izutsu. He acquired the Kokonoe share, brought his wrestlers from the Izutsu stable to the Kokonoe stable, and traded his Izutsu share (but not the accompanying stable) to Kimigahama (the former wrestler Tsurugamine) in exchange for the Kimigahama share (but not its accompanying stable). The Kimigahama stable was renamed the Izutsu stable after the trade.

52. Chiyonofuji dominated sumo in the 1980s, winning 31 tournaments, 53 straight matches, and more total matches (1,045) and top division matches (807) than any wrestler in the history of sumo. See generally Mitsugu Chiyonofuji and Matsuhiko Sakisaka, Watakushi wa Kaku Tatakatta [I Fought Like This] (1991), an autobiography.

53. See Yokozuna Chiyonofuji no 2000 man en Yaochō Sumo [Yokozuna Chiyonofuji's ¥20,000,000 Fixed Match], Shūkan Posuto [Weekly Post], Mar. 8, 1996, at 233, 237.

54. In 1989, while Chiyonofuji was still an active wrestler and before the Kitanofuji exchange, the association offered him a "lifetime share" (see *supra* text at note 35) that would carry his own name. Chiyonofuji turned down the honor on the grounds that he wanted to be Kokonoe stablemaster. In that role, he would be entitled to larger income from support groups, and, with inter-stable support, would have a better chance at rising in the associa-

Kitanofuji's decision to sell to Chiyonofuji at a lower price than he could have received doesn't seem to make sense. But his altruism was widely viewed as "the right thing to do" within the association—and it paid off. Shortly after the sale, Kitanofuji became a board member, and his annual annuity increased from $84,000 to $154,000. He eventually became number three in the association; some insiders believe that the only reason he did not become chairman is that the Dewanoumi camp held a grudge against him based on Chiyonoyama's defection. But had Kitanofuji broken the association's loyalty norms and refused to sell to Chiyonofuji, it is unlikely that he would have been elected to the board. The Kokonoe stable's financial backers might have turned against him as well. This incentive structure ensured that by taking a short-term loss on the Chiyonofuji sale, Kitanofuji would receive long-term net gain.[55]

Combination of Rules and Norms: The Fall of Wajima

Wajima rose to the rank of yokozuna in grand style. As a young competitor, he permed his hair in gangster fashion. Throughout his career he never changed his name to a sumo name, becoming the first yokozuna to fight under his birth name. On sumo tours, he drove a Lincoln Continental and stayed in luxury hotels while his fellow wrestlers slept on the floor in Buddhist temples. He associated with nonmembers of the sumo family (notably *yakuza*, Japan's mafia) and stayed out late drinking often enough

---

tion's political hierarchy. But because elders may not receive annuities on more than one share, to realize gain he would have been forced to loan one share to a shareless elder. Because the Chiyonofuji lifetime share would have been nontransferable, the only share that he could have loaned out would have been the Kokonoe share. But under this arrangement Chiyonofuji could not become the Kokonoe stablemaster. If he nevertheless wanted to be a stablemaster using the Chiyonofuji share, he would have been forced to establish a new Chiyonofuji stable, which would entail significant start-up costs, and the stable would not have been transferable. The cheapest alternative was simply to decline the lifetime share. By contrast, Takanohana, the only wrestler after Chiyonofuji to be offered such a share, accepted, because his family-held stable was quite strong and needed all the shares it could get to support its many qualified wrestlers. He was able to deliver his already acquired Fujishima share to former stablemate Akinoshima.

55. Loyalty is not unique to sumo. In the National Basketball Association, for instance, players sometimes agree to lower salaries in order to allow their teams to acquire new players while staying within the team's league-imposed salary limit. The newly acquired players can improve the team's performance, and the martyred player receives extensive positive publicity, both of which may raise the market value of the player whose salary was cut.

to earn the title "Emperor of the Night." As if Wajima were not colorful enough, he also was known as the "Sumo Genius" because he was the first yokozuna to graduate from college.

But it was after his retirement from the ring that Wajima truly pushed the limits of the sumo system. He retired in 1981 to a comfortable position as the Hanakago stablemaster, a position he secured by marrying the former Hanakago elder's daughter, Satsuki. Shortly thereafter, Wajima's troubles began. In an attempt to help his sister's restaurant out of financial difficulty, he posted his elder share as collateral for a large loan. If Wajima defaulted, the creditors had rights neither to sell the share nor to receive Wajima's annuity. But holding Wajima's share created a powerful incentive for Wajima to repay: blackmail. If he refused to pay, the creditors could simply inform the association, which would, as later events proved, take remedial action. If creditors otherwise squeezed Wajima for payment, he could sell the share legitimately within the association, but without a share, he would be forced to leave the sumo world.

It is widely known, or at least widely believed, that Wajima's loan came from the yakuza. The amount of the loan is rumored to be somewhere between ¥5 and ¥10 million ($50,000 and $100,000); Wajima "did not recall" the amount.[56] The loan was soon repaid and the share recovered, but the restaurant soon went bankrupt, with ¥300 million ($3 million) in bad debts. After the restaurant filed for bankruptcy, a fish wholesaler brought suit against Wajima's sister for ¥4 million that was supposedly owed by the restaurant. Preliminary court proceedings brought to light Wajima's posting of the elder share as collateral.[57]

The association's formal rules state that "[a]n elder share may not be transferred or posted as collateral to an outside party who is not a qualified elder or wrestler" and that "all elders . . . must observe this rule." Restrictions against transfer and collateralization are also printed on each share certificate.[58] The association intends for these rules to protect it from exactly the sort of situation that Wajima created—the appearance of numerous stories in the media about reputed ties between the associa-

56. See Nase, *supra* note 27, at 142.

57. See Wajima Oyakata wo Chōkaimen [Disciplinary Dismissal for Elder Wajima], Asahi Shinbun, Dec. 21, 1985 (evening ed.), at 11.

58. Toshiyori Myōseki Tokusō Henkō ni Kansuru Kitei [Rules Regarding Changes in the Acquisition and Disposition of Elder Stock], arts. 3, 4, 6, in Zaidan Hōjin Nihon Sumō Kyōkai Kifu Kōi Shikō Saisoku Fuzoku Kitei [Special Provisions Attached to Detailed Rules Regarding the Enforcement of the Act of Endowment of the Japan Sumo Association], 43.

tion and outsiders of questionable reputation. Such stories can be very damaging to the revenues of an institution that the public expects to be a pillar of Japanese culture.

The media pounced on the story, and the Ministry of Education, as the association's supervising agency, began to call for action.[59] Association rules provide that the membership of an elder, wrestler, referee, or other employee who "does not understand the essence of sumo and takes action that damages the credit or name of the Association" may be revoked and that such persons may also be punished by "lowering of rank, reduction of salary, or formal reprimand."[60] But no remedial rule dictates the precise punishment for posting a share as collateral. Accordingly, the association reverted to applying remedial norms. Remedial norms dictated that Wajima's conduct was of such magnitude that the appropriate punishment was to revoke his share and banish him from the sport.[61] Wajima retired in disgrace to become a WWF-style professional wrestler.

Wajima was not the only elder who had broken the rules. At approximately the same time, the association discovered that the Nishonoseki stablemaster elder, the former wrestler Kongo, had similarly posted his share as collateral. But Kongo's share was not revoked; rather, the association simply lowered his rank from officer to "regular" elder.

Although the association's rules account for the punishment of both Wajima and Kongo, its norms account for the difference in severity of punishment. Two particular substantive norms interact with formal rules to account for these differences. First, the association holds higher standards for former yokozuna than it does for other retired wrestlers.[62] Yokozuna are expected to be the living embodiment of sumo rite and history and accordingly are very much in the public eye. A breach of a rule by a yokozuna is regarded as a greater infraction than a breach by a non-

59. See Nase, *supra* note 27, at 142.

60. Association Act Rules, *supra* note 8, arts. 93–94.

61. See Moto Yokozuna Wajima, Kakukai wo Saru [Former Yokozuna Wajima Departs from the Sumo World], Yomiuri Shinbun, Dec. 21, 1985 (evening ed.), at 11. By rule, banishment is for life. Association Act Rules, *supra* note 8, art. 95.

62. When the yokozuna Futahaguro breached this norm by pushing an elderly supporter and knocking his elder's wife against a post, he was permanently expelled from the sumo world. Hawaiian-born yokozuna Akebono caused quite a stir when he drank too much and broke some glass at a bar. He and his stable's elder immediately apologized. See Akebono, Yotte Ōabure [Akebono Gets Drunk and Causes Great Disturbance], Asahi Shinbun, Mar. 7, 1996, at 23.

yokozuna because such breaches are more public and can result in greater scandals, which in turn may result in reduced revenue for the association.

Second, association norms dictate stronger punishment for repeat offenders. Wajima had been in trouble before with the association, not only because of his outrageous lifestyle as a wrestler but because of an incident in which his wife attempted suicide, reportedly in response to Wajima's incessant philandering.[63] Kongo had no such history, and accordingly his punishment was not as severe.

The association could codify these norms into clear rules, such as "A yokozuna who mortgages his share shall be expelled" or "A repeat offender shall be expelled." Alternatively, if could rely on minute gradations of rule-based punishments. But such rules might unnecessarily expel elders whom the association needs to produce revenues. It has no way of predetermining which elders would violate such a rule. Relying on more flexible norms to punish offenders such as Wajima and Kongo more efficiently serves its interests. Norms are also superior to rules in the Wajima affair because of the value the association attaches to secrecy. Norms regarding the degree of punishment meted out to offenders such as Kongo may be preferable to written rules that may be snooped into by the media (not to mention academic researchers) and criticized for their severity or laxity.

Creation of New Rules: The Foreigner Question

With his first tournament victory in 1969, Hawaiian-born Takamiyama (born Jesse Kuhaulua) became the first non-Asian to achieve fame and fortune in sumo. But despite his popularity and success in the ring, when it became clear in the mid-seventies that Takamiyama had his eye on an elder share, the sumo community became nervous. Never before had a foreigner become an elder, and the insular association felt a need to ensure that the purely Japanese sport so steeped in religious ritual was not corrupted by foreigners who did not understand the soul of the endeavor. Nevertheless, although a social norm may have dictated that foreigners should not be elders, no rule to that effect existed, and especially in light of the public nature of the issues, the norm alone could not supersede an otherwise silent set of formal rules regarding transfer.

---

63. See Tensai Rikishi "Hikari to Kage" [The "Brightness and Darkness" of the Genius Wrestler], Yomiuri Shinbun, Dec. 21, 1985 (evening ed.), at 11. The marriage ended in divorce.

After much internal debate, the association in 1976 announced a formal rule that created an additional requirement for a wrestler who aspires to be an elder: only elders with Japanese citizenship are allowed to hold elder shares.[64] The decision initially met with public outcry and cries of discrimination. But Takamiyama eventually obtained Japanese citizenship, became an elder, and opened his own stable under the name Azumazeki. Since then, no matter how popular or successful a foreign wrestler had become—even if he becomes a yokozuna—he must obtain Japanese citizenship (which, at least in the case of U.S. wrestlers, means renouncing U.S. citizenship) to obtain an elder share. Elders told me that the rules send a powerful message to potential foreign recruits that professional sumo is not an exercise to be entered into lightly; "You can't just retire on your elder share back home in Hawaii by the beach."

The association faced a similar situation in 1992 when it was forced to consider for the first time the promotion of a foreign wrestler, Hawaiian-born Konishiki, to yokozuna. As a successful ōzeki (the rank immediately below yokozuna), Konishiki had established himself as a suitable candidate. Because yokozuna are expected to be the embodiment of sumo (and because they are guaranteed a role as an elder at least for five years after their retirement even if they cannot obtain an elder share), the association and the Yokozuna Deliberation Council were faced with a real challenge. After much discussion, Konishiki was not promoted, and the international diplomatic dispute that resulted made front-page headlines around the world.[65] Konishiki's performance in the ring slumped, and he was never again considered for promotion (perhaps indicating that the association, regardless of its motives, made the wealth-maximizing decision). On retirement, he purchased the Sanoyama share but eventually left to pursue a more lucrative trade: that of an entertainer.[66]

Two years after Konishiki was passed over, the association promoted another Hawaiian, Akebono, to yokozuna. Akebono's success in the ring clearly met the criteria for promotion. In 1999, Musashimaru, another

64. See Association Act Rules, *supra* note 8, art. 48.

65. See David E. Sanger, Big American Wins Big, and Sumo Is Akimbo, N.Y. Times, Mar. 23, 1992 at A1; see also David E. Sanger, American Sumo Star Denies Accusing the Japanese of Racism, N.Y. Times, April 24, 1992 at A11 (the Konishiki issue "moved quickly from the sports pages to Parliament").

66. The association did not permit Konishiki to use the Chinese characters for his sumo name in the entertainment business, despite the fact that it was his legal Japanese name. Instead, he uses the English all-caps nomenclature "KONISHIKI."

Hawaiian, was promoted, and in 2003, Asashoryu, a Mongolian, became the third of only five yokozuna promoted since 1993 (the remaining two are the highly successful and popular brothers, Takanohana and Wakanohana). As of 2003, sumo wrestlers hailed from Mongolia (thirty-two), Russia (four), Brazil (three), the United States (two), Tonga (two), and six other countries.[67]

Although decisions regarding foreign elders were decided by rules, the decisions regarding foreign yokozuna and wrestlers in general were decided by norms. Perhaps the difference is permanence. As an association director told me, "A wrestler's career ends when he gets old or is injured. After that, even if you were a yokozuna, without an elder share, you're a joke, you're a nothing." Foreign wrestlers, then, are promoted if they are "good enough" for the association, a label that presumably includes an income-generating component, but they are never good enough to be elders if they don't nationalize.

CONCLUSION

Much like Japan's lost-and-found regime, rules and norms in the Sumo Association interact in mutually reinforcing ways that help maintain control within the association. The law-based elder share regime forms the basis of the control structure, norms help determine its application, and norms, in some situations, are codified into new rules. Law, then, matters where you might not expect it to matter—sumo—but it is not the only player in the ring.

67. Nakajima, *supra* note 38, at 121.

CHAPTER FOUR

KARAOKE

"Rock and roll," as one heavy-metal anthem proclaims, "ain't noise pollution"[1]—unless you happen to be the Kono family.[2] In September 1974, the Konos moved into a two-story building in Sakai City. They opened a sign-making business on the ground floor and lived upstairs. Eight years later, Akemi Hidaka opened a "snack" bar on the ground floor of the building next door, the kind often frequented by businessmen in search of whiskey and water and the friendly ear of a (female) bartender. Like many such establishments, it had a nice English name, "Sunshine." Hidaka equipped the place with the latest fad: a karaoke machine with which customers could sing with prerecorded music. From seven in the evening until past midnight every day and occasionally until two in the morning, her customers belted out karaoke tunes. The noise found its way to the second floor next door, where the Konos, Taro and Hanako, lay sleeping on futons.

The bar closed only five months later, but not before taking its toll on Hanako. She developed a "neurosis" that, two days after the bar closed, left her crying in the corner of her room in the middle of the night. She was rushed to the hospital in an ambulance and spent a month away from work in a hospital bed (and spent ¥123,190, or about $527 in 1983, on medical bills). Hanako sued. The court found that the defendant's bar was not the cause of Hanako's medical problems; she had been "neurotic"

1. AC/DC, "Rock and Roll Ain't Noise Pollution," on *Back in Black* (WEA/Atlantic, 1980).

2. *Kōno v. Hidaka*, Osaka District Court, 1104 Hanrei Jihō 104 (Nov. 29, 1983).

before. But because of the disturbance to Hanako's household, it ordered Hidaka to pay Hanako ¥200,000 (about $850 at the time).

Hanako is not alone. A CD-ROM search of Japanese court cases that mention "karaoke" yields eighteen hits. Six of those cases explicitly deal with noise concerns like Hanako's;[3] most of the rest concern copyright issues. A similar computer search in a U.S. database of all state and federal cases that mention "karaoke" yields forty-seven hits. These forty-seven cases concern a wide variety of subjects, including four copyright cases, two contract cases, and fifteen criminal cases, including four murders, one incident of public lewdness with a prostitute,[4] and one assault with a microphone stand.[5] The computer database is not complete, but as far as I can tell, there is no published case in the United States concerning karaoke noise.

We might expect more karaoke noise incidents in Japan. Owing at least in part to a relative lack of private space and various social factors, karaoke is much more popular in Japan than in the United States. Inhabitable land is scarce, people live close together, and many houses have poor noise protection. It is little surprise that noise is sometimes problematic.

Of course, not every person who finds herself in a karaoke dispute, or any dispute, for that matter, sues. Some settle amicably, some fight endlessly, and some, as is often said in Japan, use social norms of harmony and community to limit conflict. As George Priest and Benjamin Klein put it, disputes filed in court, though often the focus of legal scholars, constitute "neither a random or a representative sample of the set of all disputes."[6]

In this chapter, I use karaoke noise disputes as a vehicle for examining dispute resolution in Japan. My analysis leads to two claims. The first is descriptive: karaoke noise disputes, like virtually all pollution disputes in Japan, are usually resolved *before* they reach the litigation stage using a bureaucratic pollution complaint resolution mechanism led by "pollution complaint counselors." More than one hundred thousand complaints per year, many of which might otherwise clog the court system, are made to counselors.

3. See, e.g., *Nishiyama v. Kinoshita*, Nagoya District Court, 1532 Hanrei Jihō 96 (Aug. 5, 1994).

4. *Luong v. Texas*, 1999 Tex. App. Lexis 8879 (Tex. Ct. App. 1999).

5. *Perez v. Lieu's Garden*, 1997 Wash. App. Lexis 1244 (Wash. Ct. App. 1997).

6. George L. Priest and Benjamin Klein, The Selection of Disputes for Litigation, 13 J. Legal Stud. 1 (1984).

Determining the roots of the mechanism's widespread usage is more difficult. Complaints might go to counselors because Japanese law shunts them away from the judiciary. But no rules prohibit the filing of karaoke complaints in court. Complaints might be resolved by counselors because they are granted strong, judgelike powers by the state. But they have relatively little coercive authority. Eliminating these obvious potential causes leads to a second claim: use of the pollution complaint mechanism appears to be a function of both self-interested, institutionally encouraged behavior and social factors. A truism? Perhaps. But consider the context in which it arises.

Discussions of Japanese litigiousness that took place a generation ago often began—and ended—with some version of Takeyoshi Kawashima's view that the Japanese lack of *hō-ishiki* (legal consciousness) led to a predetermined disposition against litigation.[7] In a groundbreaking 1978 article, John Haley offered an intriguing alternative: institutions, such as high filing fees and slow courts, discourage Japanese litigation.[8] A decade later, Mark Ramseyer argued that institutions are indeed the cause of low litigation levels, but with a different function: the predictability of Japanese legal institutions encourages settlement.[9]

With few exceptions, discussions of Japanese litigation, in the classroom and in the literature in Japan and the United States, continue to be characterized by a dichotomy of economics, institutions, and structure versus culture.[10] But as we have seen in regard to lost-and-found property and sumo, both play important roles in everyday Japan, and the dichotomized field has left the interesting details of the truism—how the two interact—unexplored.

As for institutions, formal legal proceedings are costly, but pollution complaint resolution usually involves no direct monetary costs. Low costs and lack of formal court proceedings might lead to a perception of the complaint mechanism as being something less than "distinctly legal."[11]

7. See Takeyoshi Kawashima, Nihonjin no Hō Ishiki (1967); see also Setsuo Miyazawa, Taking Kawashima Seriously: A Review of Japanese Research on Japanese Legal Consciousness and Disputing Behavior, 21 L. & Soc. Rev. 219 (1987).

8. John Owen Haley, The Myth of the Reluctant Litigant, 4 J. Japan. Stud. 359 (1978).

9. J. Mark Ramseyer and Minoru Nakazato, The Rational Litigation: Settlement Amounts and Verdict Rates in Japan, 18 J. Legal Stud. 263, 268 (1989).

10. See Watanabe Yasuo et al., Tekisutobukku Gendai Shihō [Modern Justice Textbook], 219–31 (4th ed. 2000).

11. Paul Bohannan, The Differing Realms of the Law, 67 Am. Anthropologist 33 (1965).

Interview and quantitative data suggest, however, that these disputes are brought to counselors instead of courts primarily because of cost differences.

But social factors are important as well.[12] In this chapter, I look particularly at social capital, borrowing Robert Putnam's now-standard definition of social capital as "features of social organization, such as networks, norms, and trust, that facilitate coordination and cooperation for mutual benefit."[13] In the karaoke dispute context, social capital helps explain why some disputants do not complain even when complaining is free, as well as why counselors often successfully resolve disputes despite their lack of coercive authority. I support these claims with interview data and with statistical analysis of some well-discussed measures of social capital.[14]

Although karaoke disputes are admittedly a little quirky, three factors make them particularly interesting and well suited for analysis. First, they make up an easily definable set of disputes with a surprisingly good set of data. In addition to official prefecture-level data, this chapter examines a set of seventy-eight karaoke complaint files that I call the "Kansai Files." By limiting the analysis to the karaoke data set, it may be possible to mitigate the influence of obvious factors for which I could not control with a broader variable. Other types of pollution, such as the fouling of air or water, have potentially more nebulous and messier issues of causation, and nonpollution disputes often are messier still.

Second, because karaoke pollution incidents tend to occur in residential areas, karaoke is a good subject for testing community enforcement, which is said to be widely present in Japan. If cultural norms of harmony are as important in Japan as some proponents suggest, we would expect to find their effects here.

Finally, karaoke disputes are familiar and allow glimpses of everyday

12. Lisa Bernstein, Opting out of the Legal System: Extralegal Contractual Relations in the Diamond Industry, 21 J. Legal Stud. 115 (1992); Robert Ellickson, Order without Law: How Neighbors Settle Disputes (1991).

13. Robert D. Putnam, Bowling Alone: America's Declining Social Capital, 6 J. Democracy, 65, 67 (January 1995).

14. See, e.g., James Coleman, Foundations of Social Theory (1990); Francis Fukuyama, Trust: The Social Virtues and the Creation of Prosperity (1995); Lawrence E. Harrison and Samuel P. Huntington, eds., Culture Matters: How Values Shape Human Progress (2000); Robert D. Putnam, Bowling Alone: The Collapse and Revival of American Community (2000); Robert D. Putnam, Making Democracy Work (1993); http://www.worldbank.org/povery/scapital/.

behavior of individuals in Japan. As for the familiar (allowing for some variations in volume, timing, and musical styles), loud music problems, and perhaps noise nuisances in general, are basically the same throughout the world. Even more broadly, neighborhood noise disputes share some basic similarities with numerous common-pool resource cases and community governance issues.

The chapter proceeds as follows. First, I discuss the karaoke phenomenon and the pollution complaint system. I then focus on findings gathered from the Kansai Files and formal and informal interviews of hundreds of complainants, judges, offenders, bar owners, industry representatives, neighbors, police, pollution counselors, and other administrative officials. I present evidence suggesting the importance of both cost and social norms. Finally, I examine how social capital variables affect a complaint variable using multiple regression analysis.

KARAOKE

Although the exact origins of karaoke are somewhat ambiguous,[15] many researchers place the start in 1970, when the musician Inoue Daisuke recorded on eight-track tapes his band's own musical performances without vocals as accompaniment for amateur singers.[16] Inoue had a hit. He made a few machines, and soon machines began to appear in bars and clubs in the Kansai region. It was not long before major record companies entered the business.

In the early 1980s, karaoke moved from tape to CD, then to video and laser disk. Digital karaoke machines can now be bought by anyone for home or business entertainment. Because of wider selection and lower cost, cable karaoke has become the mode of choice for business use. But with the ubiquity of karaoke came a problem. Because most Japanese houses are built close together and have poor soundproofing, karaoke from next door quickly found its way into neighbors' living rooms and bedrooms.

In response to noise problems, in 1980 the Environment Agency issued a circular (No. 136, October 30) encouraging local governments to limit

15. Bill Kelly, Japan's Empty Orchestras: Echoes of Japanese Culture in the Performance of Karaoke, in The Worlds of Japanese Popular Culture: Gender, Shifting Boundaries, and Global Cultures, 75, ed. D. P. Martinez (1998).

16. Tōru Mitsui, The Genesis of Karaoke, in Karaoke Around the World: Global Technology, Local Singing 31, 33–34, ed. Tōru Mitsui and Shōhei Hosokawa (1998).

noise from restaurants and bars from 11 P.M. to 6 A.M. and to base volume limits on limits established for construction noise.[17] Osaka enacted such regulations first in 1982. By 1997, the Environment Agency reported that forty-four of the forty-seven prefectures had enacted some sort of noise control regulation for late-night businesses, and every prefecture had such regulation for urban areas.[18] Karaoke noise that exceeds such limits is officially "noise pollution," and officials may close such establishments. In practice, however, identifying and controlling the large number of karaoke establishments has proved difficult.

As policymakers searched for effective ways to control noise, innovation yielded a partial solution: "karaoke boxes." In 1984, an entrepreneur in Okayama Prefecture transformed a freight car into a karaoke facility by insulating it, installing a machine, and providing a few basic furnishings. The converted freight car, which sat in the middle of a rice paddy, proved extremely popular. Karaoke boxes, karaoke rooms, and karaoke studios soon began to appear all over Japan. In 1999, 57.3 percent of karaoke facilities were found at roadside locations.[19]

The karaoke box introduced karaoke to a new segment of consumers. It had previously been limited mostly to bars, where drinking comes first, but karaoke boxes found a new audience in teenagers, older people, and others who would not have visited a bar to sing. Japanese pop-culture aficionado Mark Schilling explains: "Instead of peeling off ten thousand yen notes to buy a bottle of Johnny Walker, the company of a barely bilingual Thai hostess, and a chance to fight for a mike with a roomful of other salarymen, patrons could sing to their heart's content for a low hourly charge and bring their own cans of Asahi Dry beer."[20] Karaoke has now become so popular that it influences the popularity of commercial music; "one of the important elements for hit songs changed from 'good to listen to' to 'good to sing.'"[21]

The karaoke box system did not end complaints. In a tort suit filed in the Sapporo District Court in 1991, for instance, neighbors lodged a complaint against the owner of Karaokeland Do-re-mi-fa-don, a karaoke

17. *Nishiyama v. Kinoshita*, Nagoya District Court, 1532 Hanrei Jihō 96 (Aug. 5, 1994).

18. Kankyōchō, Kankyō Hakusho [White Paper on the Environment] (1999).

19. Zenkoku Karaoke Jigyōsha Kyōkai, Karaoke Hakusho [White Paper on Karaoke], 16 (Daijesutoban [digest version] 2000) (hereinafter Karaoke Hakusho).

20. Mark Schilling, The Encyclopedia of Japanese Pop Culture, 87 (1997).

21. Hiroshi Ogawa, The Effects of Karaoke on Music in Japan, in Mitsui and Hosokawa, *supra* note 16, p. 45.

"center" composed of ten boxes that catered to teenagers. The boxes were located 1.5 meters from residences and played music until 3 A.M. Three residents, who complained not only about karaoke noise but also about noise from cars of late-night customers, were awarded $7,000 by the court.[22]

Despite such incidents, in 1999 karaoke was the fourth most popular leisure activity in Japan, with more than fifty million participants. The only more popular leisure activities were eating out, driving, and sightseeing.[23] In most cases, the experience is more than simply the singing. Besides the obvious benefit of camaraderie, one survey finds that 95 percent of karaoke boxes serve alcohol.[24] For the karaoke experience, customers pay an average of $19, roughly the same cost as a movie; a 1999 survey of karaoke users found that users, who sing an average of 2.4 times per month, would be willing to pay an average of $64 each month for the experience.[25] Most users visit between the hours of 8 P.M. and midnight, but young adults provide a relatively strong customer base between the hours of midnight and 6 A.M. in boxes (including 27.6 percent of men over the age of forty and 21.6 percent of women aged twenty to twenty-four) as well as bars (29.2 percent of men aged twenty-five to twenty-nine and 26.5 percent of women under the age of twenty-four; the legal drinking age is twenty).[26]

In 2000, the *White Paper on Karaoke* reported nearly 300,000 karaoke facilities in Japan, including 270,095 drinking establishments, 15,426 hotels and inns, and 12,844 karaoke boxes. Drinking establishments tend to be located in concentrated zones, while boxes are ubiquitous and inns are less patterned. The industry claims revenues of $3.8 billion in bars (270,000 machines), $5.6 billion in karaoke boxes (148,000 machines), and $560 million in hotels, inns, wedding halls, restaurants, and tour buses (106,000 machines), for a total of about $10 billion.[27] Karaoke is said to result in average monthly revenues at karaoke boxes and rooms of $57,000 and of more than $100,000 at 10 percent of facilities.[28]

22. *Shindo v. U.S. Leisure K.K, supra* note 2.

23. Yoka Kaihatsu Sentā, Rejā Hakusho [White Paper on Leisure], 15 (2000).

24. Sasaki Akihito, Bunkakeizaigaku he no Shōtai [Introduction to Cultural Economics], 47 (1997).

25. Karaoke Hakusho, *supra* note 19, at 46–47.

26. Ibid. at 42.

27. Ibid. at 3, 8.

28. Rejā Hakusho, *supra* note 23, at 182.

Still, karaoke entrepreneurs face a variety of problems. First and perhaps foremost, the karaoke boom appears to have peaked. Although dramatic declines are not likely in the near future, the number of karaoke users has fallen slightly each year since 1994. Karaoke entrepreneurs now cite as their number one concern (61 percent) fierce competition from other karaoke entrepreneurs. Other concerns cited by owners include the seasonality of the business (51 percent), and, far down the list, at 3 percent, public regulation, including noise control provisions.[29]

In recent years, karaoke has become a focus of academic interest, especially among economists, sociologists, and anthropologists. Some see the phenomenon as evidence of particularly Japanese cultural traits such as group harmony.[30] Others focus on the adaptability of karaoke to various international contexts, and still others note that the karaoke experience, given differences in bars, hotels, and boxes, is not uniform even in Japan.[31]

I am more interested in exploring one fact: karaoke is often loud. In some situations, volume may not be problematic: karaoke in red-light districts is unlikely to elicit complaints from other red-light establishments. But karaoke facilities often arise in residential areas for two reasons. First, many karaoke machines are owned by private individuals for home use. It is not unusual for the midnight music to emanate from one's next-door neighbor's residence.

Second, and more important, as anyone familiar with Japanese urban geography can attest, Japanese law often results in notoriously messy mixed land use. The zoning process is relatively straightforward: the national government, via the City Planning Act (Toshi Keikaku Hō, law no. 100 of 1968), defines several categories of districts, and prefectural governments designate districts. Japanese land use law on the books, at least, is said to be more uniform and "top-down" than that of the United States.[32] But in part because of high land prices, a tax policy that penalizes

---

29. Ibid. at 183.

30. See, e.g., Thomas Rohlen, For Harmony and Strength (1974).

31. William Kelly, The Adaptability of Karaoke in the United Kingdom, in Mitsui and Hosokawa, *supra* note 16, at 83.

32. See David L. Callies, Urban Land Use and Control in the Japanese City: A Case Study of Hiroshima, Osaka, and Kyoto, in The Japanese City, 134, ed. P. P. Karan and Kristen Stapleton (1997); David Callies, Land Use Planning and Control in Japan, in Planning for Cities and Regions in Japan, 59, ed. Philip Shapira, Ian Masser, and David W. Edgington (1994).

transfer of ownership,[33] and "flexible implementation,"[34] actual application of the law is less systematic than in the United States and often results in loose categorization and crazy-quilt zoning.[35] Twelve types of zones exist, and residences are permitted in eleven. Zoning regulation is extremely lenient, overlay zones are common, and much land, even in cities, is unzoned.[36] It is thus not uncommon for all sorts of businesses, including karaoke facilities and especially karaoke boxes, to be located in the heart of largely residential areas. Zoning for bars, which, at least in cities, are frequently clustered together, is often better, but bars still pop up near residential areas.

POLLUTION DISPUTES

Japan has a lengthy history of dealing with pollution and related disputes. After a series of pollution disasters and highly contentious disputes in the 1960s, Japan launched an effort to prevent future mishaps and control what promised to be an onslaught of disputes. It did so with vigorous environmental cleanup and with three complementary measures to divert conflict from courts: the Law for the Resolution of Pollution Disputes (the Dispute Law, Kōgai Funsō Shori Hō, law no. 108 of 1970), the Law for the Compensation of Pollution-Related Health Injury (Kōgai Kenkō Higai Hoshō Hō, law no. 111 of 1973), and the introduction of citizen participation into development planning.[37]

Pollution Complaint Counselors

The Dispute Law established the Pollution Complaint Counselor system. As Julian Gresser, Koichiro Fujikura, and Akio Morishima explain:

33. Yukio Noguchi, Land Problems and Policies in Japan: Structural Aspects, in Land Issues in Japan: A Policy Failure?, 11, ed. John O. Haley and Kozo Yamamura (1992).

34. Kazuhiko Takeuchi et al., Land Prices and Japanese City Planning: Evaluating the Effects of Land Use Control, in Land Policy Problems in East Asia—Toward New Choices, 134, ed. Bruce Koppel and D. Young Kim (1993).

35. Kuniko Fujita and Richard Child Hill, Together and Equal: Place Stratification in Osaka, in Karan and Stapleton, *supra* note 32, at 115.

36. Callies, Urban Land Use and Control, *supra* note 32; Yuichi Fukukawa, Zo-ningu to Masutaa Puran [Zoning and Master Plans], 4–8 (1997).

37. I draw from Frank Upham's discussion in his classic Law and Social Change in Postwar Japan, 56–67 (1986).

Counselors consult with residents, investigate pollution incidents, and provide guidance and advice. They are required to notify the responsible agencies of pollution disputes, and they may undertake other measures considered necessary for their settlement. Counselors are mostly lower-ranking staff in local government; the highest official is usually on the level of section chief. Counselors are employed full-time and often work in close contact with pollution control offices of local governments.[38]

Although most counselors have no formal training in dispute resolution, many have undergraduate degrees in law, and all have passed a civil service examination that requires basic legal knowledge. They are strongly expected to follow legal norms, and, as one counselor explained to me with refreshing honesty, "Of course we follow the rules; we're local bureaucrats. We don't know how to do anything else."

The stated purpose of the Dispute Law, which, in addition to complaint counseling, also provides for mediation, conciliation, and arbitration,[39] was to provide a dispute resolution process for pollution claims that was more efficient than litigation. But the system was not necessarily created because of an antilitigation sentiment. As Frank Upham notes, "The development of the mediation system . . . was less the result of traditional values than of political will."[40] The approach was a compromise between the Federation of Economic Organizations and the Ministry of International Trade and Industry, as the former succeeded in deleting various strict liability provisions, and the latter succeeded in establishing the administrative alternative to the tort system.[41]

The mechanism appears to serve well the purpose for which it was

38. Julian Gresser, Koichiro Fujikura, and Akio Morishima, Environmental Law in Japan, 327 (1981).

39. Formal mediation, conciliation, and arbitration measures, though less expensive than litigation, are rare; since 1970, only 733 cases have been heard by the Environment Dispute Coordination Commission, which hears only "grave" cases involving health claims and damages of more than ¥500,000 and cases with nationwide impact such as noise from shinkansen trains. See http://www.soumu.go.jp/kouchoi/. Prefectural environmental dispute councils have likewise heard only 828 cases since 1970.

40. Upham, *supra* note 37, at 58.

41. The pollution dispute resolution system may also be viewed as a victory for bureaucrats in the removal of a large set of disputes from the judicial system. Upham, *supra* note 37, at 60. As plaintiff after plaintiff won in court, establishing precedents against government polluters, the government sought to reestablish control of the problem. Only by removing pollution litigation from the province of lawyers and judges and placing it in

designed. In 2002, 13,077 pollution complaint counselors heard 105,110 complaints (including 1,828 referred by police and administrative agencies), for a total caseload of only about eight new cases per counselor per year.[42] Although this caseload sounds light, counselors are busy nonetheless: they are full-time civil servants, but many are responsible for tasks other than complaint resolution.

Government literature states that most of these complaints are filed, or at least are expected to be filed, in the early stages of a dispute.[43] Filing usually is accomplished by a trip to city hall or a similar local government office and a half-hour conversation with a counselor. In most cases, counselors are able to solve the problem. They do so with a combination of threats of administrative penalties, police and other enforcement pressures, and occasionally mediated settlements, though they do not have the power to award damages. In 2002, they solved or at least "disposed of" 91,784 cases, or 87.3 percent, including the previous year's backlog, and sent only 2,173 cases to other administrative agencies.[44]

Complainants are not prohibited from filing suit in court at the same time that they file a complaint. But few do, perhaps because complainants wish to give the less expensive system a chance before suing.[45] In 2002, only forty-three of the hundred thousand or more pollution complaints were also filed in court, and only forty-six went to other formal dispute resolution mechanisms. Of the forty-three, fifteen were filed within one week of the filing of the complaint, nine were filed more than one year after the filing of the complaint, and the remainder sometime in between.[46]

Speed, flexibility, and cost are among the attractions of the complaint

---

the hands of the more easily controlled area of bureaucratic settlement could the government maintain control.

42. Kōgai tō Chōsei Iinkai, Heisei 14nendo Zenkoku no Kōgai Kujō no Gaikyō [2002 Outline of National Pollution Complaints], available at http://www.soumu.go.jp/kouchoi/knowledge/report/index.html (hereafter "Pollution Complaints").

43. Kōgai tō Chōsei Iinkai, Kōgai Funsō Shori Hakusho [White Paper on Disposition of Pollution Disputes], 17 (2000).

44. Pollution Complaints, *supra* note 42, at 57. An additional 3,850 cases are listed as "other."

45. Pollution victims who take advantage of the more formal mediation and conciliation provisions of the Dispute Law often file suit at the same time that they file pollution complaints. In such cases, courts usually work with the less formal dispute settlement system to encourage settlement. See Gresser, Fujikura, and Morishima, *supra* note 38, at 329. Very few karaoke cases reach this stage.

46. Kōgai Kujō, *supra* note 42.

system—the filing of a complaint is free, and counselors are almost as numerous as lawyers and vastly outnumber judges. In 2002, of the 84.7 percent of complaints that were disposed of directly by counselors, more than half were solved in a week, and two-thirds were solved in a month. About two-thirds were solved with some sort of a written formal prevention plan. In 81 percent of cases, counselors visited the site once or twice; in only 3.8 percent of cases was there no visit. About 85 percent of responding complainants expressed satisfaction with the system.[47]

Although the data about karaoke complaints are similar to these general pollution numbers, the 2002 data relating to karaoke complaints, which have recently averaged about a thousand per year, show some differences from other pollution complaints. First, in 80.3 percent of cases, the trouble, unsurprisingly, comes at night. Second, counselors apparently are not as active in karaoke cases as in other cases—in 62.3 percent of cases, they visit the site once or twice, and in 10.7 percent they never visit at all. Although the lack of site visits may indicate sloth, counselors suggested to me that in fact there is little need for multiple visits to karaoke sites, because the problem is usually more clear and obvious than in air, water, or ground pollution cases. Third, in no case was a karaoke complaint that was filed with a counselor also filed in court or with any other alternative dispute resolution mechanism.

Pollution Complaint Dynamics

Although not always successful, complaining is at least cheap, because it requires no fees. But other factors besides cost might affect complaint rates. The amount and degree of pollution might matter—all things being equal, we might expect more complaints to result from more pollution. Community norms might also dictate for or against complaint, and we might expect parties to attempt some private remedy before complaining to local officials. Still, high Japanese background noise levels—from the usual sources as well as from election sound trucks, hawking merchants, train-platform announcements, and the like—might also affect complaint rates one way or the other.

Recent survey data offer evidence of the amount of, role of, and responses to pollution. First, the data for pollution. In response to a 1996

47. Ibid.

survey by the Prime Minister's Office on pollution in everyday life,[48] 46.6 percent of polled adults answered that in the past "two to three years" they had not been bothered by "daily life" pollution. More than half said they had been bothered, including 35.9 percent disturbed by car and motorcycle noise,[49] 9.2 percent by construction, 7.0 percent by noises, vibrations, and smells from work, and 3.0 percent by neighbors' pianos, stereos, and air conditioners.

The same survey offers interesting evidence regarding the participants' response to pollution. Among other responses, 81.4 percent said they did nothing, 7.3 percent resorted to some local government resolution mechanism (the pollution complaint mechanism), 4.5 percent called the police, 4.4 percent negotiated with the offender, and 0.1 percent sued. Of those who took no action, 45.1 percent said they did so because the problem was not very severe, 13.0 percent said they thought they would develop a bad reputation among neighbors, 17.2 percent said resolution was simply too troublesome, and so on.

To some degree, the response depends on the source of the pollution. If a neighbor were the polluter, 53.5 percent said they would solve the problem as soon as possible, 36.0 percent said they would negotiate, 6.2 percent said they would use a third-party negotiator, 2.4 percent said they would do nothing, and 1.9 percent said they did not know. If the problem were a neighbor's loud piano playing or air conditioners and a complaint were made to the local government or administrative office, 52.8 percent thought the government should solve it, 16.2 percent felt the government should step back and let the parties fight it out in court, and 15.5 percent said the government should make rules regarding household noise.

Additional survey evidence comes from a 1999 survey of fifteen hundred residents of Tokyo's Nerima Ward.[50] Respondents were told that neighborhood noise incidents had been occurring with some regularity

48. Sōrifu Kōhōshitsu, Seikatsu Kankyō, Seikatsukei Kōgai ni Kansuru Seron Chōsa, [Survey Relating to Daily Pollution and Environment], available at http://www8.cao.go.jp/survey/kougai.html.

49. Besides ordinary traffic noise, many neighborhoods in Japan are plagued by the motorcycle melodies of *bōsōzoku*, or teenage gangs, who install custom header pipes to increase the engine's sound. See Ikuya Sato, Kamikaze Biker: Parody and Anomy in Affluent Japan, 41 (1991).

50. Nerimakumin Ishiki Ikō Chōsa [Poll of Nerima Residents], in Sōrifu, 1999 Seron Chōsa Nenkan [The Year in Surveys], 334, 338 (2000).

and were asked how the problem should be solved; 35.5 percent said that the parties should solve the conflict on their own, but the largest share, 39.6 percent, said that it should be solved by local administrative regulation and guidance. Only 2.7 percent said that the courts should be involved.

This survey evidence suggests two related points. First, noise pollution is ubiquitous. Second, there is no single universally accepted response to noise pollution. The next section begins to explore the various alternative response options.

Other Pollution Dispute Resolution Options

In addition to complaint, two likely public enforcement options for solving pollution disputes exist: courts and police. The available evidence suggests that these options are seldom used, unhelpful, or both.

Courts. Pollution victims may choose formal complaint, filing in summary court, or filing in district court. Although the complaint system may be used simultaneously with court action, disputants may choose only one court forum.

Cases go to summary court if the damages claimed are less than ¥900,000 ($9,000);[51] otherwise they go to district court. Because filing fees are calculated as a percentage of damages, filing fees are lower in summary court than in district court. A claim of ¥900,000 entails a fee of ¥7,800 ($78); a claim for ¥10 million costs ¥57,600 ($576). Cases are decided more quickly in summary courts. In 1998, 96.8 percent of summary court cases were decided in six months, but only 61.5 percent of district court cases were. About 4 in 10,000 summary court cases were pending for more than five years; the figure in district courts is about 110 in 10,000. Most plaintiffs argue in summary court pro se (without an attorney): in only 1.1 percent of cases are both parties represented by attorneys; in 91.7 percent, neither party is.[52] In district court, both parties are represented by attorneys in 41 percent of cases, and in only 21 percent, neither party is.[53]

---

51. Saibansho Hō, law no. 59 of 1947, art. 33. In 1947, the civil jurisdiction of summary courts was limited to claims of less than ¥5,000. The amount was increased to ¥30,000 in 1950, to ¥100,000 in 1954, to ¥300,000 in 1970, and to ¥900,000 in 1982.

52. Saikō Saibansho Jimusōkyoku, Shihō Tōkei Nenpō (Minji/gyōsei hen) [Annual Report of Judicial Statistics], 99 (1999).

53. Ibid. at 119.

Summary courts are located in small villages as well as large cities; district courts are located only in large cities. Because of all these factors, summary court cases account for about two-thirds of all civil cases.

In practice, disputes that lead to complaint differ from disputes that lead to suit in ways that are not reflected in the data. During the course of my research, I interviewed fifty pollution counselors throughout Japan. They stated that of the entire range of complaints that are brought, those based on karaoke noise are the only kind that routinely involve noise in excess of limits set in local ordinances. Counselors told me that some karaoke complaints concern noise that does not rise to the legal level of noise pollution, but most concern noise that does.

Of the remainder of complaints that citizens bring to counselors, 90 percent or more are not legally noise pollution, because most other types of pollution that lead to complaint are not limited by statute. Instead, most complaints, according to counselors and my review of records, are simply cases of feuding neighbors. As one counselor put it, "They come to us saying 'the TV is too loud' or 'the air conditioner next door disturbs my sleep,' but when we investigate, we find that noise isn't the central problem. They're fighting over a mailbox, or a parking space, or they just don't like each other. We're really just neighborhood mediators." According to another, "Very little of this stuff, aside from karaoke noise, is real pollution. If it's real pollution, like poison in the water, they would go to court."

Almost all karaoke cases—the only subset of cases that routinely involves pollution as defined by law—go to counselors, not courts. Unfortunately, but not surprisingly, courts keep no statistics on karaoke-based cases. To construct my own data set, I began with summary courts. Over a period of several months, I spoke briefly with thirty summary court judges about their dockets. Only two could remember ever hearing a karaoke case in their courtroom, and none had any such cases currently pending.

On the recommendation of some of these judges, an assistant and I contacted clerks and other administrative officials at summary courts across Japan. I first contacted officials at all 55 courts in the Tokyo metropolitan area (including the Tokyo, Yokohama, Urawa, and Chiba jurisdictions). I then contacted officials at five courts, chosen at random, for each of Japan's remaining seven regions (Osaka, Nagoya, Hiroshima, Fukuoka, Sendai, Sapporo, and Takamatsu). Adding these 35 courts to the 55 for the Tokyo region results in a total of 90 summary courts, or about one-fifth of all 438 summary courts. These courts exhibit substantial variation; one court in Tokyo hears nearly two-thirds of all new cases in Japan; another hears fewer than 20 in an average year.

Of the ninety courts I contacted, officials at only sixteen could recall a single karaoke noise suit in his career at the court, despite the fact that the average term of employment of interviewed clerks was a relatively high 14.6 years. Only four clerks knew of any such suits currently pending. Although skepticism regarding data from memory is warranted, these interviews at least tentatively suggest that karaoke noise suits at summary courts are rare.

Apparently few suits are filed in district courts as well. I found six district court cases in the CD-ROM database on karaoke complaints (compared to none in the United States), and plaintiffs' attorneys in two of the six cases told me they that were aware of no others. Attorney statements may not be the best measure of small-claims litigation, because plaintiffs can always file pro se. But for plaintiffs who desire representation, these attorneys offered another cost-based reason why suit may be difficult: one charged a fee of ¥500,000 ($5,000); the other would not tell me his bill but stated that it was more than that amount.[54] Both told me they would be very reluctant accept another such case, and other attorneys with whom I spoke said they would never accept one because the "human problems" are not worth the fee. Instead, they would refer potential plaintiffs to the complaint system.[55]

Finally, as noted above, dual filing of pollution complaints is rare; survey data show that only 5.7 in 10,000 pollution complaints are also filed in court, and only a quarter of those in the same week as the complaint is filed.

Enforcement by police. Police often deal with noise pollution issues.[56] Limited data are available for police enforcement. From 1988 to 1996, the

54. Fees are normally based on a percentage of damages claimed and damages received. See Mark D. West, Why Shareholders Sue: The Evidence from Japan, 30 J. Legal Stud. 351, 365–66 (2001).

55. David M. Engel, The Oven Bird's Song: Insiders, Outsiders, and Personal Injuries in an American Community, 18 L. & Soc. Rev. 565 (1984) (local bar seen as inhospitable to personal injury suits).

56. See Abe Yasutaka, Karaoke Jōrei [Karaoke Ordinances], 817 Jurisuto 40 (1984), at 40; Harada Naohiko, Kinrin Sōon no Kisei to Sono Genkai: Tōkyōtō Karaoke Jōrei ni Kanren Shite [The Status of Neighborhood Noise Regulation: The Case of Tokyo Karaoke Ordinances], 872 Jurisuto 42 (1986).

National Police Agency (NPA) maintained and published data relating to noise complaints. On average, police responded to 61,734 noise complaints each year, of which an average of 21,564 were karaoke-related.[57] These figures suggest that formal legal complaint to a pollution counselor is unlikely to be one's first line of attack. Still, the data are somewhat questionable. As the person in charge of data collection at the NPA explained to me, some areas of Japan do not use "check-the-box" forms and must rely on handwritten analyses, some police who walk the beat (*omawari-san*) do not fill out a form for every such minor incident, and multiple responses may lead to multiple reports, even reports of the same incident by more than one officer. With respect to each of these points, the pollution complaint system offers much more uniform and reliable data.

Again, because of the incomplete nature of the available quantitative data, I created an interview data set to attempt to determine what role police play in resolving karaoke noise disputes. I interviewed police in ten stations in seven different prefectures throughout Japan, including urban and rural areas. In all, I spoke with about fifty police officers. On three occasions, I was allowed to accompany police as they responded to noise complaints, two of which were caused by karaoke.

The data I gathered suggest that police enforcement is an incomplete substitute for suit or complaint. With few exceptions, police uniformly stated that they do not have the resources to patrol all potential noise pollution sites and accordingly refer complainants to pollution complaint counselors. They considered enforcement to be a one-time middle-of-the-night stopgap measure and not a substitute for formal action. On one karaoke call response that I observed, police told the offender to turn down the volume, instructed the complainant to file a formal noise pollution complaint at city offices, and left the scene. One officer subsequently told me that although they could have arrested the offender for violating city noise ordinances, they "don't think that that would solve the ongoing problem. Why should I berate the guy when I know he's just going to turn it up again? I can't keep coming back every hour. They have to reach a solution." That job, he said, belonged to noise pollution counselors, not police.[58]

57. Keisatsu Hakusho [White Paper on Police], various years.

58. Although many factors might explain why police appear to assign low priority to noise complaints, several officers confided that economic incentives matter. Fines collected from traffic violations are paid to the state, then redistributed to prefectures by the Ministry of Public Management, Home Affairs, Posts, and Telecommunications according to pre-

Table 4.1. Types of Interviewees

Category of interview	Approximate number of persons interviewed	Location
Complaint counselors	50	Throughout Japan
Complainants	75	Throughout Japan
Offenders	25	Throughout Japan; mostly Tokyo, Kansai
Karaoke establishment owners (no complaints)	70	Tokyo metropolitan area, Osaka metropolitan area, Kyoto, Hiroshima, Kyushu
Karaoke establishment neighbors (no complaints)	50	Tokyo metropolitan area, Osaka metropolitan area, Kyoto, Hiroshima, Kyushu
Industry representatives	5	Tokyo

KARAOKE DISPUTE SETTLEMENT

To get a better idea of how karaoke disputes are settled (and not settled), I turned to interviews of persons directly involved in such disputes. Table 4.1 lists the subjects and the nature of the interviews. The interviews, some of which were very brief, took place over a three-year period; some were in group settings, some one-on-one, some via email, and a few over the phone.

Some of the most revealing interviews were those of complainants. Although I found some individually, most interview subjects came from the files of a semiurban local government office in the Kansai area (Osaka, Kobe, and Kyoto). At this office, I was given what I believe to be complete access to all 78 karaoke complaints filed from 1991 to 2000. The Kansai Files contained a wealth of information about complaints, complainants, offenders, and counseling practice.[59]

---

fectural collection rates. See Dōro Kōtsū Hō (Road Traffic Act), law no. 105 of 1960, arts. 128–29. Those funds are then used for construction of traffic safety features such as g traffic signals, guardrails, and crosswalks; see http://www.mha.go.jp/news/980330-2.html (ministry homepage). Police told me that traffic violations often take priority over noise complaints because the latter generate no income for the prefecture. Some local police also have internal reward structures that favor income-generating activity.

59. Although the information in the files technically is publicly available, I was allowed to review the files and contact complainants only on the condition of confidentiality for both

These interviews offered important insights into three specific areas. I first outline the workings of the karaoke dispute resolution process in practice. Second, I examine the choice of complaint versus suit. I find that most disputants complain rather than sue primarily because of the cost difference but that the evidence is not definitive. Third, I examine the choice of complaint versus settlement. I find that social norms play a dominant role in encouraging settlement.

Resolution Process and Institutions

Most karaoke noise disputes follow a standard pattern. Almost all of the forty-nine people I interviewed recognized the noise issue as a problem quite early on. Four stated that they recognized the problem after one incident, twenty-three after two or three incidents, fourteen after four or five incidents, and eight after more than five incidents.

Most complaints, as the pollution survey data suggest, are filed only after days, weeks, or months of toleration and attempts at negotiation. In the Kansai Files, the average period from problem recognition to complaint filing was three months. In the vast majority of cases (and in forty-two of the Kansai Files), the problem is the location of a private residence adjacent to a business that features karaoke. This is not always so—in a handful of cases, complaints were against private residents who had karaoke machines in their homes—but by and large, it is only this sort of situation that leads to a formal complaint.

The Sumida family is typical of many of the complainants to whom I spoke. In 1992, the Sumidas moved into the ground floor of a fourteen-unit apartment building in a Tokyo suburb. Three months later, a pub opened next door. The first night, the karaoke revelry lasted until 4 A.M., but the Sumidas dismissed it as a temporary problem. When the problem recurred every Friday and Saturday night, they said, "We began to realize that we had a problem, and that it was not simply going to go away on its own."

---

the office and the complainants. Officials assisted in my initial contacts with complainants and reviewed my research but not did otherwise affect its development. All in all, I obtained forty-nine contacts among the complainants in these files, including thirty in-person conversations, twelve telephone conversations, and seven emails. Of the remaining twenty-nine files, I was unable to contact twenty persons, and nine persons declined my request for an interview.

Before the dispute reaches the complaint stage, most complainants—including the Sumidas—attempt some sort of negotiation. In the Kansai Files, forty-two of forty-nine complainants attempted to negotiate before filing complaint. In thirty-four of those forty-two cases, complainants attempted to negotiate on their own by approaching owners or managers of the offending business. In nine others, particularly those in which the business is seen as especially powerful, a third party was brought in to mediate the dispute. Rarely is the third party an expensive lawyer (this happened only once in the Kansai Files); often it is a community leader or a member or affiliate of an organized crime syndicate.[60]

The Sumidas tried a variety of settlement methods. Yōichi Sumida, the father, showed up at the pub for what he called a "man-to-man" drink. He asked the owner to turn down the volume and suggested that he purchase more insulation. The owner refused. Yōichi then sought the intervention of the owner of the convenience store next door. Yōichi reasoned, "Maybe I just couldn't say things the right way. But [the convenience store owner] is a business owner, too, so maybe he could say it better." The owner still refused. The Sumidas then considered seeking the counsel of the local branch of an organized crime syndicate but decided—largely because of the strong opinions of Yōichi's wife Kumiko—that such a move might lead to more "problems."

They suspected that their problems were exacerbated by the fact that they appeared to be the only neighbors affected. The Sumidas were the only family in the building with young children, and many other tenants appeared to spend little time at home at night. "If there were others," Kumiko said, "[the owner] might have realized what a burden they are to the neighborhood. But because it was just us, he felt no sense of obligation. He had no idea who we were and didn't seem to care."

With the help of a pollution complaint counselor who threatened administrative action, the Sumidas eventually negotiated a settlement. When parties negotiate, the discussion usually centers on hours of operation, volume, or the construction of noise-reducing structures. In sixty-two cases, including forty-four from the Kansai Files, complainants and offenders discussed with me the settlement of karaoke noise issues. The results are not easily summarized, but the basic dispute and settlement facts of six representative cases from the Tokyo area are listed in table 4.2.

60. In more than a few cases, establishments of the sort in which karaoke can be found (bars and so on) have "sponsors" from the world of organized crime.

Table 4.2. Characteristics of Disputes and Settlements

Noise source	Complainant	Duration of noise	Settlement method	Settlement
Bar	Homeowner	6 months	Ten local residents sought private settlement from bar owner	Bar owner agrees to noise limits, installs extra insulation, builds noise wall, sends small presents to residents
Bar	Homeowner	1 month	Hired professional third-party "negotiator" with connections to organized crime	Bar owner signs formal agreement accepting time limits, pays homeowner ¥1 million
Bar	Condominium residents	Sporadically for 3 years	Pollution complaint counselor	Bar owner agrees to noise and time limits
Karaoke box	Apartment residents	1 year	Pollution complaint counselor	Box owner agrees to noise and time limits, issues formal apology to residents, offers half-price service to residents, pays each ¥30,000
Karaoke box	Apartment residents	3–4 months	Pollution complaint counselor	Box owner signs formal agreement accepting noise and time limits, agrees to build noise wall or pay settlement; after failing to build, pays residents ¥1 million to build noise wall
Homeowner with karaoke system	Surrounding homeowners	3 months	Pollution complaint counselor	After refusing requests from neighbors and police, homeowner agrees to counselor's "noise plan"

These cases were not chosen randomly and do not reflect the distribution of settlements, but their similarity to the Kansai Files suggests regional homogeneity with regard to such issues.

I cannot vouch for the accuracy of each settlement with total confidence, and some interviewees were not willing to disclose settlement amounts. Still, the results may yield basic insights. Sometimes outright exchange of cash is the mode of settlement. In some cases, the payment is compensation for hardship; in others, it is intended to fund the construction of a noise-reducing structure or to cover the transaction costs of moving to another location. Sometimes these settlements are reached by the parties alone, sometimes they involve mediators, and sometimes those mediators are pollution counselors. In many cases, the parties sign a formal agreement, precedents for which can be found in do-it-yourself neighborhood-dispute-resolution books.[61]

Complaint versus Suit

Complaining is free, and suing entails monetary and other costs. Moreover, another possible difference might arise: the social meaning attached to the filing of a complaint might differ from that of filing suit. David Engel found such differences in social meaning in his study of personal injury suits in Sander County, Illinois. Although contract-based "business" suits were viewed with approval, Engel found that personal injury claims violated the "local value system," and those who brought such claims "were characterized by their fellow residents as 'very greedy,' as 'quick to sue,' as 'people looking for the easy buck,' and as those who just 'naturally sue and try to get something [for] . . . life's little accidents.'"[62] If the social meaning of complaint and suit similarly differs in Japan, cost might be an incomplete explanation for why most people complain instead of suing. The evidence I found is somewhat equivocal but tentatively suggests only minor differences.

One counselor I interviewed offered a preliminary assessment. As a matter of routine, the counselor usually sits down with the establishment's owner and discusses provisions of the municipality's noise control ordinance. He then explains the possible consequences of not turning down

61. See, e.g., Tonari Kinjō no Hōritsu Chishiki [Legal Knowledge for Neighborhoods], 242, ed. Jiyūminkokusha (2001).

62. Engel, *supra* note 55, at 553, 561.

the volume, including police action, civil litigation, and community boy-cott. When I asked the counselor how likely these actions were, he began with a cultural argument but concluded with an institutional explanation:

Counselor: To be honest, the police aren't so much of a threat. They occasionally shut down a place or two, but if you're careful, you can often get away with it. . . . Most bar owners know they won't be sued, either. Japanese people don't like to sue.

Q: Why?

Counselor: It doesn't suit the character of the Japanese people. We don't like law-suits.

Q: Why?

Counselor: For some people, it's the expense. But they're expensive because no-body wants to sue.

Q: Does complaint differ from suit?

Counselor: For most people, no. Complaining is a big step, just like suing. There is a "plaintiff" and a "defendant," sometimes it's very confrontational, and sometimes the settlements are just like those ordered in court. We counselors have a pretty good idea of how a court will decide a case, and we wouldn't want to stray too far from that. Once you subtract all the costs of suing from any dam-ages you might hope to get, it's cheaper to complain for free, whether or not you get any money out of it.

To this counselor, then, as well as to other counselors I interviewed, the complaint process simply replicates trial. Although counselors cannot order damages and do not routinely assist in monetary negotiations, they often encourage parties toward settlement, the details of which are worked out privately. By informing the parties of what their expectations should be, the counselor reduces the administrative costs of suit, result-ing in net social gain. If counselors are successful, complaint might be a complete substitute for trial.

But the complaint process might not equal the trial process on all lev-els for all persons. A bar owner offered a more ambiguous account of why there had been no further noise complaints after the first six months of operation:

Matsumoto: After a while, this group of people from next door asked us to turn it down, so we did. Not a lot; just enough so they wouldn't be upset. I didn't want to provoke anybody. But apparently it wasn't enough, and they eventually filed a complaint against us. Before I knew it we had civil servants all over the place. "You're the neighborhood nuisance," they'd say. At one point there was even a [signifies *yakuza* by "drawing" scar on face with hand] around here. We eventually put in some extra insulation and agreed to turn it off at one just to get everyone off our backs. It could have been worse, I guess . . . they could have sued us.

Q: Do you think they would have really sued you?

Matsumoto: Not really. Most of the time they don't really want to sue.

Q: Why not?

Matsumoto: It costs too much. Suing also ruins the neighborhood. I know you Americans sue over hot coffee at McDonald's, but Japan isn't like that. Going to court is the last resort; it just causes problems.

Q: Isn't filing a complaint like going to court?

Matsumoto: For most people, yeah. But for others, it's not such a big deal. You don't have to go to court, just to city hall. It's free. They make it too easy to go after guys like me. If it's free, you're stupid not to complain.

Perhaps unsurprisingly, for this business owner, cost is what matters. A primary complainant in that case, a stay-at-home mother named Michiko Iizuka, offered a different perspective:

Iizuka: At first I thought that I should just put up with the noise. So I endured it for a while. But then I heard that others were complaining, too. And everyone said to me, "What's the matter? You really should be complaining." So I went over and asked the owner if he could just turn it down a bit, at least while my son was taking his high school entrance exams. He actually did, but only for about a week, and then it was bam bam bam bam all over again. I had some neighbors go over with me, but who's going to listen to us? My husband said we couldn't sue; it would be too difficult and cost too much. So I filed a complaint.

Q: Because of the cost?

Iizuka: Mostly because of the cost, but it wasn't just the cost. I mean, suing is a really big step. You have to go to a lawyer and so on. What business do I have talking to a lawyer? I'm just a housewife. I don't want to cause problems.

Q: And a complaint would not cause problems?

Iizuka: Actually, it does. To most people, [complaining and suing are] about the same. But to me personally, it didn't seem so dramatic.

Look closely at what we have here. Iizuka starts with a social explanation; she didn't want to complain until her neighbors sanctioned it. She then turns to costs, meaning going "to a lawyer and so on." But her perceived relation to the lawyer adds complicated issues of social status that do not fit easily into a pure cost model: she's just a housewife.

Iizuka's statements were more ambiguous than those of most other complainants, who stated that complaint differed from suit only with regard to cost. I pressed such complainants by asking whether complaining might differ from suing because the stakes are comparatively lower. As one successful complainant explained:

I don't think so. The counselor helped me get the noise stopped, and [the noise-maker] gave me some money, so I'm happy. But in some ways, this is more important than a court case. Nobody cares about a business contract. That's what goes to court, you know—business contracts. But when you've been kept awake all night over and over, well, for me, anyway, the stakes were high. If the counselor hadn't worked, I would have moved, and that's expensive. Or I might have sued; I thought of suing anyway just to cause the guy trouble, but in the end, the settlement was sufficient.

Interestingly, this interviewee notes that suing might be qualitatively different from complaint, both in the inconvenience it may cause a defendant and, paradoxically, in the level of importance of the disputes handled by each mechanism. Note, however, that he does not make a distinction based on the monetary stakes that would regularly steer karaoke complaints away from the court system. In this case and others, karaoke complainants routinely told me that although the monetary damages were not high, karaoke noise is so annoying and persistent that its resolution was extremely important to them. Yet even in some of the most egregious cases, disputants complained instead of going to court.

The Kansai Files offer additional evidence. None of the forty-nine complainants filed suit. To attempt to determine their motivations, I asked a simple open-ended question: "Why did you not go to court?" In response, forty-two complainants cited institutional factors such as excessive monetary costs and time to judgment. Three stated that (for whatever reason) they did not think the problem worth suing over. Two gave answers that were nonresponsive or difficult to classify, and two cited norms against suing in Japanese society.

I then asked interviewees to respond to a more direct statement: "If the court could provide the same results with the same speed and ease as the complaint system for free, I would have been indifferent between suit and complaint." I then listed the standard Likert scale choices as responses: strongly agree, agree, neutral, disagree, strongly disagree. Thirty-three of the complainants strongly agreed, fourteen agreed, and two gave nonresponsive answers.

These cases offer slightly differing perspectives on the ability of the complaint system to replicate suit. Many counselors thought the system to be a near-perfect substitute and based their opinions on their ability to replicate court-ordered solutions using negotiated settlement. Complainants such as Iizuka usually stated that there was little difference in the social ramifications of complaint and suit, although the economics differed. The Kansai Files suggest a similar finding. Karaoke owners such as Matsumoto implied that complaint was different from suit in nonmonetary ways, and even he did so in ambiguous terms that suggest monetary differences. Although the ambiguity might be due to complexity, one possible interpretation is that the difference simply is not very large. I tentatively conclude that for most people, most of the time, the social meaning of complaint is more or less equal to that of suit, suggesting that the reasons people complain instead of suing are primarily tied to institutionally determined costs. Still, I acknowledge that for many persons, for reasons both idiosyncratic and structural (recall Iizuka, the reluctant housewife), the calculus is more complex.

Complaint versus Private Settlement

If suing is too expensive, disputants are left with the choice of complaint or private settlement (including nonsettlement). Because both are free or involve trivial monetary expenses, usage is unlikely to be a function of cost alone. My interviews suggest that differences in usage rates can be explained at least in part by social norms.

To examine the potential role of such norms, consider one extreme: karaoke establishment owners who receive *no* complaints. To find interview subjects, I looked for karaoke establishments located extraordinarily close to residences and knocked on doors of both establishments and residents. One such establishment that I found—ominously named "Volume Up"—belonged to Junji Hasegawa, a fifty-two-year-old character, slightly rough around the edges, who had been in business in a small town in Kyushu for fifteen years.

Q: Surely you must have a lot of noise complaints from the locals. I can't even walk in the alleyway between your building and the apartment next door.

Hasegawa: Never. Not one. If I did, I couldn't sleep at night. I've got two feet of insulation in these walls. My employees joke that this is a dangerous place; you could kill somebody in here; nobody would hear them scream [laughs].

Q: That's a lot of insulation.

Hasegawa: It's not just the insulation. I tell the guys behind the counter late at night to make absolutely certain that the doors are closed and that we turn off the sound at the right time. I also make sure that the bikers [*bōsōzoku*] who come around don't rev their engines too loudly. They can be a real nuisance. But they respect me.

Q: Why are you so careful?

Hasegawa: Everybody in this community knows everybody else. I see my neighbors at the grocery store. I play golf with the kindergarten principal next door. If I'm the neighborhood nuisance, who is going to respect that? Nobody would even talk to me.

Q: And business would suffer?

Hasegawa: Of course. But I would suffer personally, too.

Q: Do you think this community is special in this regard?

Hasegawa: No, there's a lot of places left like this in Japan. Just country people around here. . . . We don't fight much. No crime. Nothing much to do for fun but drink with your neighbors, gamble, and screw.

Hasegawa's neighbors confirmed his story. One elderly woman told me that Hasegawa would "never cause problems. If he did, everyone would complain, and what good would that do him?" Another neighbor, a thirty-five-year-old male computer programmer who was new to the area, said, "I was really nervous about moving into this building. I do a lot of work at home, and, well, it's right next door, right? But when I asked around, everyone said there would be no problem. The owner knows everybody and doesn't want to cause trouble. . . . About three weeks after we moved in, I saw him while I was taking out the garbage. He came right up to me and introduced himself."

Such responses were not unusual. When owners viewed themselves as part of the local community, they tended to receive few—if any—noise complaints, and those they did receive were easily settled. Although owners might settle for business reasons,[63] especially if locals form their client base, they uniformly stated their motivations to me in social terms. And owners who saw themselves as part of the local community were usually perceived as such by their neighbors as well, who often reported frequent, indeed daily, interaction. "[The owner] is in the PTA with me at my son's school," one woman told me. "If he didn't keep the noise down, he'd get in trouble with all of us." A relational web among the parties appears to have significant implications for the use of legal institutions.[64]

Although the Kansai Files, which consist entirely of complaints, may not be directly responsive to the question of why some people do not complain, they do offer insights into why some do. To attempt to assess the social connections among establishment owners and residents, I asked the forty-nine complainants whether they knew the name of the offender before the karaoke noise incident. Only three said yes, suggesting again that social interactions may reduce complaints.

Still, social norms may not necessarily lead to universally predictable outcomes. Attitudes about "community" may differ across regions or can be manipulated by parties. Consider the twist on tit-for-tat logic reported by one karaoke victim: the architect Yamada Mamoru "was not able to persuade his [karaoke bar] neighbors to soundproof their building or quit the karaoke business. 'I tell them that we should respect each other's privacy because we are living next to each other. Their logic is I should put up with the noise because we are neighbors and if I don't like it, I should leave,' Yamada said."[65] In this case, the owner used norm-like language as

---

63. With respect to issues such as crime control and protection of minors, the karaoke industry has chosen to self-regulate in some regions. Although some karaoke establishments do not opt in to these self-regulatory alliances, the rules are still said to be generally effective. See Nagai Yoshihiko, Fūzoku Eigyō Torishimari [Regulating the Entertainment Industry], 178–80 (2002).

64. See Stewart Macaulay, Non-contractual Relations in Business: A Preliminary Study, 28 Am. Soc. Rev. 55 (1963); Joel Sobel, Can We Trust Social Capital?, 40 J. Econ. Lit. 139 (2002).

65. Ginko Kobayashi, Sounding the Charge in the Battle against Everyday Noise Pollution, Daily Yomiuri, July 18, 2000, p. 7.

a method of encouraging compliance. But in my interviews, I found little evidence to suggest that this method is widespread. There is evidence of norms against noise production, but there is little evidence of norms against complaint.

Norms interweave with structural factors to encourage compliance. A visit or other formal contact from a complaint counselor may reinforce existing norms and embolden their enforcement. One karaoke box owner explained, "I didn't take anything seriously until the formal complaint was filed. But after that, it was as if the neighbors suddenly decided to band together. They showed up in groups, saying 'Did you see the complaint? We're serious about this stuff' and so on. I didn't realize the problem was causing them so much trouble. Or I guess I shouldn't say problem [*mondai*], but 'event' [*jiken*]." The owner explained to me that he had two separate worries: his standing in the community and the potential economic loss he would face from turning down the volume on his customers.

At the opposite end of the spectrum, some disputes continue with little hope of private settlement. Consider the case of Yoshinobu Nogawa.[66] Nogawa owned a thirteen-story, steel-reinforced concrete condominium building in Yokohama named "Rose." He rented out part of the first floor to Noriko Andō to run a "snack" bar called the Needs Pub O$_2$. Prefectural regulations required that the volume be turned down from six to eleven, that machines be turned off at eleven, and that the business close at midnight. Andō did not follow the regulations; her customers treated the neighborhood to singing on weekdays until 4 A.M. and on weekends until 5 A.M.

A few local residents filed a complaint, and the Yokohama Antipollution Plan Noise Control Section served Andō with a warning. Neighbors complained to Nogawa, who was unable to evict because of a landlord-tenant law that is exceedingly protective of tenants' rights.[67] He renegotiated the lease, and Andō promised to keep the noise down. She didn't. The police visited—twice. The Noise Control Section warned her again, to no effect. She told Nogawa that she couldn't help that her customers liked to sing past midnight. Nogawa had a friend named Yamaguchi (coincidentally or not, the same name as that of Japan's largest crime syndicate) come and attempt to negotiate, and the friend was successful in fur-

66. *Nogawa v. Iwamuro*, Yokohama District Court, 721 Hanrei Times 189 (Oct. 27, 1990).

67. See, e.g., J. Mark Ramseyer and Minoru Nakazato, Japanese Law: An Economic Approach, 38 (1999).

ther strengthening the conditions of the lease. Andō even sent a letter of apology. She built a sound wall. Two months later, her customers were again singing past 3 A.M., and another complaint was filed. She responded with singing on the weekends until five in the morning. Nogawa eventually evicted her and sued for the remaining rent under the lease. The court agreed that a breach of trust had occurred and awarded Nogawa damages.

The larger point in this context is what did *not* work. For all the complaints, police presence, and enforcement of noise control laws, some offenders in Japan, as elsewhere, refuse to follow the rules. Although many explanations are possible, in this case, it is at least clear that Andō had few local community ties, suggesting that social norms may have been difficult to enforce against her. Neighbors whom I interviewed about the case also suggested a social capital explanation: most of the bar's customers, I was told, were outsiders, and Andō identified more with them than with the locals. As for the locals, many were unwilling to complain against the noise, either because it did not seem problematic, because many were commuters to nearby Tokyo and had little interest in the situation, or, in a few influential cases, because they frequented the bar in question.

QUANTITATIVE ANALYSIS

Cost differences are relatively easy to document. Complaining is free, it is usually effective, and disputants state that cost matters. Whatever the informal costs are, they should be relatively uniform across prefectures. Social capital, however, though strongly suggested in my interviews, is not so easily quantified; in fact, I know of no study in Japanese law that attempts to quantify it. In this section I try to do just that; I estimate a multiple regression model to examine the effects of karaoke-specific and social-capital-independent variables on karaoke noise complaint rates.

Three caveats are in order. First, this is not a study of how individuals make decisions to complain; it is an examination of average characteristics. Scholarship, however, suggests that litigated disputes "seem to be selected because of unusual, rather than common, features such as high stakes, extreme uncertainty about the outcome, and reputational stakes of the parties."[68] These factors are difficult to quantify across a broad range

---

68. Samuel R. Gross and Kent D. Syverud, Don't Try: Civil Jury Verdicts in a System Geared to Settlement, 44 UCLA L. Rev. 1 (1996).

of cases, and there is no guarantee that any conclusions drawn from complaint data are necessarily universally applicable to other dispute resolution methods. But by defining the universe of disputes to include only those based on a particular type of nuisance—karaoke—and given our knowledge of how the system works, quantitative analysis should nonetheless be informative.

Second, the available data cannot provide a complete picture of several areas that would be useful to know in evaluating the effects of institutions and culture, including the frequency of initial disputes, the ratio of public harms to private, the amounts of negotiated settlements, or even (given the scarcity of published cases) average damage amounts. Nor do the data capture concepts that might be internalized without obvious external linkages (such as a belief that "only wimps complain"). Third, by necessity I use a relatively small sample of data from forty-seven prefectures.

These three caveats stated, it should now be apparent that my goal is quite limited: I simply want to estimate the effects of particular independent variables of interest on the dependent variable and to compare those effects with the interview data. I predict that the quantitative data will not conflict greatly with the interview data.

I examine data collected from each of Japan's prefectures. The dependent variable is the total number of karaoke complaints per one thousand persons for the period 2000–2002 in each prefecture.[69] The independent variables are as follows.

Karaoke-specific factors. I control for potential regional differences in karaoke popularity, and potentially for noise levels, by including variables that represent the number of karaoke facilities in a prefecture. I split the number of karaoke facilities into three categories as the data allow: bars and restaurants (*inshoku*), hotels and inns (*ryokan*), and boxes. The division is important in analyzing the location of complaints. Although bars and restaurants tend to be clustered together in karaoke "zones" from which we would expect few complaints to arise, boxes, which can be located anywhere, may lead to more residential complaints.

Social capital and community. The interview data suggest that social capital affects complaint rates. To test this hypothesis, I include four crude

69. Complaint data are taken from various issues of Kōgai Kujō, *supra* note 42.

measures of social capital. In his study of social capital in Japan, Takashi Inoguchi uses data from the People's Life Indicators (PLI) reported by the Social Policy Bureau of the Economic Planning Agency.[70] The PLI is composed of eight groups of statistics, one of which is an "association" index composed of sixteen variables. Although Inoguchi relies on the association index as a crude measure of social capital for simple regressions, most of the underlying variables are not relevant to this study[71] and are not normally viewed as measures of social capital. Accordingly, I disaggregate the index data and choose two potentially relevant measures that are discussed in the social capital literature: voluntary social participation and membership in senior clubs.[72] To these two measures I add two others identified in the social capital literature:[73] voter participation and property crime.[74]

I also include an additional social capital factor that is often cited in discussions of Japanese culture: foreign population. Cultural, racial, and ethnic homogeneity is often said to be one factor that creates harmony in Japan. In rural Illinois, David Engel found that newcomer "union members, southerners and southwesterners, blacks, and Latinos" who brought new "conceptions of injuries, rights, and obligations" threatened the existing sociolegal order.[75] To test whether outsiders might have a similar effect in Japan, I add a variable that measures the foreign population in

70. Takashi Inoguchi, Social Capital in Japan, 1 Japan. J. Pol. Sci. 73 (2000).

71. Inoguchi uses the 1997 index, which included measures such as the number of public halls per million people, the percentage of international marriages, and the ratio of persons who correspond with people overseas per ten thousand. Ibid. at 110.

72. Still, recent cross-country empirical work suggests that membership in formal groups is not associated with trust or improved economic performance. Stephen Knack and Philip Keefer, Does Social Capital Have an Economic Payoff? A Cross-Country Investigation, 112 Q. J. Econ. 1251 (1997). The experience of Toyama Prefecture further predicts correlations. Toyama has the lowest rates of total environmental complaints and karaoke-related complaints in Japan. In some years no karaoke complaints are recorded. Coincidentally or not, Toyama also has the highest income, club membership rates, and social participation rates in Japan.

73. See, e.g., Francis Fukuyama, The Great Disruption: Human Nature and the Reconstitution of Social Order (2000); Putnam, Bowling Alone, *supra* note 14.

74. I use property crime rates instead of overall crime rates that include violent crime, following Fukuyama's logic that such rates "are probably a better negative measure of social capital than violent crimes" because of their widespread nature. See Fukuyama, *supra* note 73, at 32.

75. Engel, *supra* note 55, at 555, 578.

each prefecture. Statistically, about half of this foreign population is Korean, and another 15 percent is Chinese. Americans account for about 3 percent. Though Koreans own lots of karaoke establishments, I do not expect ethnicity of ownership to be reflected in the data. The 5 percent of urban karaoke establishments that is said to be owned by Koreans seems too small to have significant impact.

Each of these social capital factors and its related contextual baggage may not necessarily be directly analogous to the same factors in the United States. Club membership in Japan often involves sustained commitment that is more akin to church membership in some U.S. communities (and Japan has no widespread concept of church membership), and "foreigner" is likely to have a different meaning in a relatively more homogenous society.[76] Still, each factor fits with both commonly held notions of social capital and Putnam's more formal definition (cited at the beginning of this chapter) and the related literature.

Other control variables. To estimate enforcement effects, I include a measure of pollution counselors. The counselors variable might be positively correlated, because more counselors means increased ease of complaint. It might also be negatively correlated, because counselors might deter noise-related incidents. I find it unlikely that the number of karaoke complaints would drive employment of counselors, because that subset of complaints accounts for a relatively small percentage of their time.

Finally, I include three control measures: income,[77] population density, and the total number of pollution complaints per capita.

76. See Alan S. Miller and Satoshi Kanazawa, Order by Accident: The Origins and Consequences of Conformity in Contemporary Japan (2000).

77. The effect of the income variable is more difficult to predict than that of population density. A recent survey of residents of Japanese city-owned housing (for low-income residents), "public" apartments (rent-controlled and available by lottery), and condominiums suggests that income may affect dispute resolution in Japan. The primary difference among the three types of housing is income; average income of surveyed residents for each category of housing was $39,420, $62,840, and $75,800, respectively. When asked how they would solve the problem of a new resident's karaoke party, a statistically significantly higher 58.2 percent of city-owned housing residents said they would solve the problem on their own, while a significantly higher 8.9 percent of apartment residents would seek resolution by an outside institution. See Takenaga Hideki, Nyū Taun no Jūtaku Kaisō Mondai [The Rebuilding Problem at New Town], in Daitoshi no Kyōdō Seikatsu: Manshon Danchi no Shakaigaku [Group Living in Big Cities: The Sociology of Condominiums], 103, 112–21, ed. Shin Kurasawa (1990).

Table 4.3. Correlates of Karaoke Noise Complaints

Variable	Standardized coefficient	t-stat
Demographics		
Income	.035	−.355
Population density	.174	1.158
Institutions		
Counselors	−.269	−2.038**
Total complaints	.203	1.887*
Karaoke-specific factors		
Bars	−.214	−1.044
Boxes	.144	.716
Inns	.153	1.200
Social capital		
Club membership	−.227	−1.993**
Crime	−.111	−.821
Foreigners	.306	2.241**
Social participation	−.260	−1.826*
Voting	.071	.662
Intercept		1.229
Adjusted R^2	.645	
Observations	47	

Sources: Bars, inns, and boxes: Zenkoku Karaoke Jigyōsha Kyōkai, Karaoke Hakusho (2002). Club membership: Kōseishō, Shakai Fukushi Gyōsei Gyōmu Hōkoku (2002). Counselors: "pollution complaints," *supra* note 42. Crime: Hanzai Tōkeisho, ed. Keisatsucho Keijikyoku (2002). Foreigners: Kokusei Chōsa Hōkoku, available in Sōmuchō Tōkeikyoku, Shakai Seikatsu Tōkei Shihyō, ed. Sōmuchō Tōkeikyoku (2002). Income: Sōmuchō Tōkeikyoku, Kakei Chōsa Nenpō (2000). Population density: Kokusei Chōsa Hōkoku (2002). Social participation: Sōmuchō Tōkeikyoku, Shakai Seikatsu Kihon Chōsa Hōkoku, available in Sōmuchō Tōkeikyoku, Shakai Seikatsu Tōkei Shihyō (2001). Total complaints: "pollution complaints," *supra* note 42. Voting : http://www.nifty.ne.jp/CM/Forum/fnetd/san18hi/index.html.

Note: Bars is the total number of bars and restaurants with karaoke facilities per 1,000 persons. *Boxes* is the total number of karaoke box facilities per 1,000 persons. *Club membership* is the percentage of persons over sixty belonging to clubs for seniors. *Counselors* is the number of pollution counselors per 1,000 persons. *Crime* is the number of known larceny offenses per 1,000 persons. *Foreigners* is the number of foreigners per 100,000 persons. *Income* is disposable income per capita. *Inns* is the total number of hotels and inns with karaoke facilities per 1,000 persons. *Population density* is the number of persons per square kilometer. *Social Participation* is the percentage of persons who participate in voluntary social service activities and receive no remuneration other than reimbursement of expenses. *Total complaints* is the total number of pollution complaints per 1,000 persons filed for the same period as the karaoke complaints, minus karaoke complaints. *Voting* is the voter participation rate in the 1998 House of Councillors' election.

* and ** indicate significance at the 90 and 95 percent levels, respectively.

Using these variables, I estimated a multiple regression model,[78] the results of which are reported in table 4.3. The results may be interpreted as follows:

For karaoke-specific factors, no variables were significantly correlated. But it is at least interesting that boxes, which tend to be clustered in areas in which there are few residents to complain, are negatively correlated, and bars and inns are positively correlated.

For institutions, the correlation to the number of counselors is negative and significant, suggesting that counselors deter complaints. The total complaint variable is positively correlated and marginally significant, suggesting that karaoke complaints are not a unique kind of complaint.

For social capital, some of the variables are significantly correlated to the complaint variable. The club membership and participation in voluntary social activities variables are significant, even when controlling for income and other demographic variables. Greater levels of participation in social activities in a region mean fewer complaints, as social fabric theorists might predict. Another possible interpretation is that club membership and social participation support underlying norms of harmony and reciprocity.[79] Under either interpretation, it appears that social capital, perhaps in the form of reputation bonds formed by social participation in clubs, leads to fewer complaints.

The variable representing the number of foreigners in a prefecture is significantly correlated and positive. In some ways, this result is surprising. I uncovered no evidence of complaints by or against foreigners, and most of the counselors I interviewed had never met a foreigner in their official capacities. As always, it is entirely possible that the correlation has some other meaning or is simply spurious; however, it is consistent with the claims of those who point to homogeneity in Japan as a source of social capital, and with the claims of economic theorists who find that often "heterogeneity of people is the underlying source of conflict."[80]

78. Regressions are ordinary least squares (OLS). In addition to dropping some of the independent variables, I experimented with several more complex models to limit heteroskedasticity, variable endogeneity, and possible heavy influence from Tokyo and Osaka. I observed no significant changes in results.

79. See Gary S. Becker and Kevin M. Murphy, Social Economics: Market Behavior in a Social Environment 23 (2001).

80. Ibid. Counselors showed a negative but insignificant correlation. The direction of correlation suggests that counselors have some modest deterrent effect on karaoke noise. Counselors are appointed locally to take care of many tasks. Karaoke dispute resolution is

Still, although the model shows correlations between social capital measures and complaint rates, it does not reveal the mechanism by which social capital functions. My control for the number of karaoke establishments in a prefecture is only a proxy for the number of complaints per violation, data that simply are unavailable. Absent these data, the regression results are inconclusive as to whether the social capital variables correlate negatively with the complaint variable because social capital (a) limits noise violations or (b) limits the proclivity of people to complain given a certain level of noise violations. The interview data strongly suggest that (a), on balance, is correct, but (b) might also play an important role. Still, under either explanation or some combination of the two, regression analysis is consistent with the interview data that suggest a role for societal factors in the resolution of karaoke disputes.

Of course, this study by no means proves conclusively the social capital relation; statistics are imperfect. The regression results are somewhat redundant vis-à-vis the interview evidence, but that is part of the point: the two methodologies produce complementary results, each of which is consistent with theory.

CONCLUSION

I have tried to unravel some of the causal forces that determine the everyday relations of law and individuals in Japan. The available evidence suggests that at least in this context, decisions to sue, complain, or settle are a function not of one single factor but of a complex calculus of institutionally determined costs and social capital. Interviews suggest that decisions to complain rather than sue appear to be based primarily, but by no means exclusively, on institutional and monetary factors, and social factors appear to influence greatly decisions to complain rather than settle. Multiple regression analysis further suggests a role for both sets of factors.

Such a model, even one backed by empirics, is messy and imprecise. Although it lacks simplicity, its grounding in everyday experience suggests that it may provide a richer and more accurate explanation of legal behavior in Japan.

---

usually one of the easiest problems; unlike, for instance, PCB pollution, the source of karaoke pollution is at least easy to locate and the causal chain is relatively clear. The data tentatively suggest that prefectures that take a tough stance across the board against pollution may at least be successful in controlling this form of pollution.

CHAPTER FIVE

EARTHQUAKES AND
CONDOMINIUMS

Readers who have been conditioned to view Japan as a nonlegalistic place where relationships reign supreme might find law's role in the everyday arenas of the previous three chapters surprising. After all, one would think that Japan could do without legal rules for the trivial (lost-and-found items), the amusing (karaoke), and close-knit groups (sumo). That law matters in these areas suggests a pervasive influence in everyday Japan.

Still, perhaps I have found law in places that are interesting but really don't matter that much. In everyday areas in which the outcome really matters, in which emotions run high and interests diverge, or in which people just don't get along very well, we might expect a lesser role for law. To examine this possibility, this brief chapter examines law's role in Japanese condominiums (*manshon*). In comparison to renters, condo owners in Japan tend to interact less and be on less familiar terms with their neighbors.[1] A 2003 government survey showed that 93 percent of Japanese condominium buildings had some kind of "trouble," the largest category of which, with 83.3 percent, was the failure of residents to observe rules and manners. About 8 percent of the "trouble" found its

---

1. Ichirō Ozaki, Toshi no Kōkyōsei to Hō: Manshon ni Okeru Seikatsu to Kanri [Urban Common Living and the Law: Daily Life in and Management of Condominiums], 113 Hōgaku Kyōkai Zasshi 1324, 1470–71 (in four parts, 1996); Hideki Takenaka, Nyū Taun no Jūtaku Kaisō Mondai [Problems in the New Town High Rise], in Daitoshi no Kyōdō Seikatsu: Manshon/Danchi no Shakaigaku [Group Life in Urban Condominiums: The Sociology of Condominiums and Housing], 103, 119–21, ed. Shin Kurasawa (1990).

way to civil litigation, and another 3 percent was formally mediated.[2] Japanese condominium life does not sound particularly harmonious.

I examine these contentious condominiums in an especially contentious—and increasingly "everyday"—context: the substantial repair of buildings when damaged because of disaster or age. If owners cannot agree on repairs, the buildings will remain or become uninhabitable, a particularly difficult circumstance for the 48.9 percent of condominium owners who say that they plan to stay in their condos for life. But agreeing requires both cooperation and a personal outlay of cash. My claim is simple: law helps structure these decisions to agree.

UNANIMITY IN CONDOMINIUM DECISIONS

Since the 1960s, one of the more ubiquitous and enduring features of modern Japanese urban life has been the high-rise condominium building. The Tokyo area contains about 104,000 "new" units; the Kansai area (Osaka, Kobe, and Kyoto) area and Nagoya account for another 41,000 and 10,000, respectively. With the inclusion of older condominiums in more rural areas, the national total comes to nearly four million units. By comparison, the United States, with twice Japan's population, contains roughly the same number of condominium units, with the highest proportion of condominiums to total housing units in Hawaii (21 percent), followed by Florida (15 percent) and Washington, DC (10 percent).[3]

Japanese condos are tiny and expensive. New condominiums in Tokyo grew from an average of 615 square feet in 1990 to 730 square feet in 1999, and the average price remains around $400,000. The market for condominiums, however, like virtually all real property in Japan, has fallen in the past decade, which has in turn exacerbated the problems faced by owners of aging condominiums. The Ministry of Land, Transport, and Industry reports that about one-third of condominium stock is more than thirty years old, and by 2010, one million units will have hit that

---

2. Kokudo Kōtsūshō, Heisei 15nen Manshon Sōgō Chōsa [2003 Condominium Comprehensive Survey], available at http://www.mlit.go.jp/kisha/kisha04/07/070225_.html.

3. For Japan, see Naohiro Yoshida, Manshon no Kanri to Tekiseika no Suishin ni Kansuru Hōritsu ni Tsuite [Regarding the Law to Improve Condominium Management], 1195 Jurisuto 64, 65 (2001) (citing Construction Ministry data that show 3.84 million units, up from fewer than one million in 1980). For the United States, see U.S. Census Bureau American Housing Survey, at http://www.census.gov/hhes/www/housing/ahs/99dtchrt/tab2-1.html.

mark.⁴ Thirty years might seem relatively young for any building, but some experts state that Japanese condominiums are not designed to survive more than thirty years; others claim that such buildings could last one hundred years with regular maintenance but that Japanese residents, for reasons systemic (relating to increases in the standard or living, perhaps) or otherwise, simply prefer rebuilding.⁵

In any case, two-thirds of these aging condominiums (about 22 percent of all condos) now struggle with the decision of disposition. Besides falling prices, a number of factors frustrate the decision-making process: building code changes, neighborhood opposition, and the fact that about half the residents of buildings that are more than twenty years old are themselves over the age of sixty.⁶ Disposition of these aging buildings is one of the more complex issues facing urban Japan in the twenty-first century, and it suffers primarily from a simple phenomenon: unit owners cannot agree.

Disposition usually takes place through rebuilding. From 1975 until 2002, with the exception of cases arising out of the 1995 Kobe earthquake, which I review below, sixty-nine rebuildings nationwide were undertaken. Two preliminary points arise. First, rebuilding *not* related to the earthquake remains rare; only sixty-nine total cases not involving the earthquake, and only 25 in the Kansai area have been identified—ever.⁷

4. Manshon Tatakae Enkatsuka Hōsaku Kentō Iinkai Hōkoku ni Tsuite [Report of the Committee to Investigate Plans for Condominium Reconstruction], Nov. 30, 2001, http://www.mlit.go.jp/kisha/kisha01/07/071130_2_.html.

5. Kazusuke Kobayashi and Yoshiaki Fujiki, Manshon: Anzen to Hozen no tameni [Condominiums: Safety and Security], 5–9 (2000). The average building's lifespan is said to be 140 years in Britain, 130 years in the United States, 86 years in France, and 79 years in Germany. Yasuko Shimamoto, Tōkai: Daishinsai de Jūtaku Ro-n ha Dou nattaka [Collapse: What Happened to the Earthquake Mortgages?], 122, 123 (1998) (quoting Tsuneo Kajiura). The average lifespan of a Japanese house is said to be twenty-six years, compared with forty-four years in the United States. Mark Magnier, Japan's Houses of Horror, L.A. Times, Mar. 6, 2002, at A1.

6. Nissai Sōgō Kenkyūjo, Nihon no Chika to Fudōsan, 172 (1996) (citing Construction Ministry data).

7. The data apply to the period through 2002. See Manshon Tatakae Enkatsuka Hōsaku Kentō Iinkai Hōkoku ni Tsuite [Report of Committee to Investigate Plans for Condominium Reconstruction], Nov. 30, 2001, http://www.mlit.go.jp/kisha/kisha01/07/071130_2_.html; see also Tsuneo Kajiura, Shinseiki no Manshon Kyojū [Condominium Residence in the New Century], 226–29 (2001) (citing only sixty-four cases): Kōrei Manshon 100mantōno Ureutsu [Problems of One Million Aging Condos], Nihon Keizai Shinbun, July 29, 2001, at 17 (sixty).

Table 5.1. Condominium Owners' Voting Patterns, 1975–2000

	Non-earthquake cases	Earthquake cases	Total cases
Number of rebuilt condominiums	69	108	177
Location	Nationwide	Kobe Area	Nationwide
Time Period	1975–2000	1996–2000	1975–2000
Unanimous decisions	69 (100%)	14 (12.9%)	81 (45%)

Second, the average age of buildings rebuilt for reasons *not* related to earthquake damage was 34.04 years. Assuming a thirty-year building lifespan, rebuilding unrelated to the quake most likely occurred in buildings that were in poor condition.

More striking are the data regarding decisionmaking. Until the Kobe earthquake, every single major condominium rebuilding in Japan was accomplished by a unanimous vote, despite a lower voting threshold (usually four-fifths) in the law. Table 5.1 compares the 69 non-Kobe cases with the 108 cases arising from the earthquake.

Here's an easy explanation for the differences in the data sets. Japan is said to be a place that values harmony and consensus. In normal cases, decisions will be unanimous, because no one wishes to step on neighbor Tanaka's toes. But the destructive Kobe quake caused major social upheaval, disrupting these patterns of consensus. Relations became contentious, and the number of unanimous decisions, accordingly, fell.

A plausible hypothesis, to be sure. But compare the condominium situation to that of karaoke complainants or pollution complainants generally. In those cases (and certainly in many others), Japan is not a model of consensus; it is historically a model of bitter, hard-fought, lengthy feuds. It would be surprising if decisions of whether to rebuild a person's home—in the "troubled" condominium context, no less—were any less contentious. Although the social-consensus explanation explains some of the difference, another identifiable source of the difference, as we shall see, is legal incentives.

KOBE CONDOMINIUMS

In the early morning hours of January 17, 1995, an earthquake measuring 7.2 on the Richter scale leveled the Japanese port city of Kobe and surrounding areas. More than 200 people died during the first wave of tremors, and another 6,000 died while trapped in rubble or resulting fires. The Great Hanshin Earthquake left an additional 14,000 thousand injured, more than 410,000 homeless, and damages of $100 billion.

Recovery was difficult. Although the Hanshin elevated highway and many major department stores recovered and reopened to the public with relative speed, by May 1996, 48,300 households still lived in temporary housing, and most had no concrete relocation plans. In 2001, 3,548 still remained there. By December 1996 seven of ten buildings were still damaged or in ruins, and one in five small retail businesses had not yet reopened. Alcoholism increased, and many elderly and ill persons died from exposure and neglect.

More than twenty-five hundred condominium complexes were damaged in the quake. Individual unit owners were forced by circumstance to make decisions regarding the disposition of their homes. Unlike owners of single-unit homes, they had to do so *jointly* with other unit owners.

Postquake condominium owners might be expected to have a particularly difficult time reaching agreement. In addition to the usual sociological, psychological, and financial problems of adjustment after a natural disaster, the Kobe owners faced four unique legal problems.

First and foremost, insurance funds were sorely lacking in Kobe. The typical Japanese earthquake insurance policy is a modified fire insurance policy that provides only 30 to 50 percent as much coverage. In total, insurance covered only 10 percent of all Kobe quake damage.[8] Many Japanese property owners sued their insurance companies when they discovered that their policies also contained "exceptions clauses" that denied coverage for fire damage caused or aggravated by earthquakes. Government recovery funds did not provide much recourse, for they went first to public facilities and infrastructure in order to stabilize the economy and foster commerce. Only afterward did remaining funds go to private recovery efforts.[9]

Second, a web of zoning regulations strictly controlled the construction of new buildings. Rebuilding condominiums, even to their original size, often would have violated regulations regarding sunlight exposure, height restrictions, or garages. Capacity restrictions (from which many

8. Laura A. Johnson, Kobe and Northridge Reconstruction: A Look at Outcomes of Varying Public and Private Housing Reconstruction Financing Models, Presented at the EuroConference on Global Change and Catastrophe Risk Management: Earthquake Risks in Europe, International Institute for Applied Systems Analysis, Laxenburge, Austria, July 8, 2000, at 5.

9. Kōbe Shinbun, Towazu ni Irarenai [Can't Help But Ask], 368 (1999).

previously had been exempt) were especially problematic. At least in part because the Ministry of Construction encouraged local governments to relax regulations, the city of Kobe and Hyogo Prefecture both reformulated their land usage rules, but uncertainty remained.

Third, most of the destroyed condominiums were mortgaged.[10] Financing reconstruction or repair with a second mortgage became difficult because the underlying collateral was destroyed in the earthquake. More significantly from a legal perspective, mortgage agreements often stipulated lender consent as a prerequisite to rebuilding.

Finally, many condominium owners rented their units to third parties, to whom Japanese lease laws give significant rights. In many instances, the law effectively forced unit owners to find substitute housing for their lessees, often at considerable expense, while disposition of the condominium unit was pending.[11]

DECISION MAKING UNDER JAPANESE LAW

If condominium unit owners unanimously agree, they can improve, dispose of, or terminate the property as they see fit, pursuant to the Japanese Civil Code. But in many cases, unanimity is unachievable. Accordingly, the Japanese Condominium Law[12] in effect at the time of the earthquake provided unit owners with two basic decision trees to channel resolutions: "restore" (*fukkō*, used if the damaged portion of the building accounts for less than half of the building's value) or "rebuild" (*tatekae*, used when maintaining or restoring the building because of deterioration, damage, or partial destruction involves "excessive cost"). Two months after the earthquake, the Japanese legislature, recognizing that the Con-

---

10. Shimamoto, *supra* note 5 (providing details of mortgage problems and the invention of the reverse mortgage in Japan). A 1999 Asahi Shinbun poll of one thousand residents of reconstructed Kobe condominiums found that 40 percent had two mortgages and that 5 percent had mortgages of more than $400,000. The average cost of reconstruction per unit was $217,000. Heikin 2170 man'en Hanshin Daishinsai Higai no Manshon Saiken Hiyō [Average Cost for Condominium Reconstruction Post-Quake of ¥21.7 million], Asahi Shinbun, Sept. 26, 1999, at 1.

11. The Law for Temporary Disposition of Rental Property in Disaster Areas allowed renters of destroyed properties to assert priority claims on the property up to two years after the quake. Risai Toshi Shakuchi Shakuya Rinji Shorihō, Law no. 13 of 1946, as implemented by Cabinet Order 16 of 1995.

12. Tatemono no Kubun Shoyū tō ni kansuru Hōritsu, Law no. 69 of 1962, as substantially amended by Law no. 51 of 1983.

dominium Law failed to address cases in which buildings were completely destroyed, passed a new law (the "Special Law")[13] to create a third legal option for specified disaster areas: "reconstruct" (saiken).[14]

As the summary of the provisions in table 5.2 illustrates, Japanese law employs very specific provisions to structure this decision-making process. The law uses two graduated mechanisms to reflect the extent and cost of various recovery measures. First, as the stakes of the decision grow, the applicable decision rule likewise grows: rebuilding and reconstruction require the agreement of a larger supermajority than major restoration, which in turns requires a higher level of agreement than minor restoration.

Second, the law incorporates buyout measures in the form of "put and call options." "Put options" first appear in the provisions governing restoration of buildings that have lost more than half their value: unit owners who oppose a winning restoration resolution may "put" their units by demanding that assenting owners purchase their units at the current market price.[15] If unit owners do not pass a restoration resolution within six months after the building is damaged, the law provides that *any* owner may demand that any other owner purchase his unit at the current market price (§61(8)). If a building becomes so damaged that demolition and rebuilding or reconstruction becomes an option, the law makes "call options" available. Two months after resolving to rebuild, supporters or their designees may demand the sale of units from dissenting owners. If the requisite demolition has not started within two years of the resolution (or if construction has been delayed for no reason for six months, §61(7)), dissenters may buy their units back at the price they were earlier paid.

---

13. Hisai Kubun Shoyū Tatemono no Saiken tō ni kansuru Tokubetsu Sochihō, Law no. 43 of 1995.

14. Special Law §2(1). The Kobe region was so designated pursuant to Hisai Kubun Shoyū Tatemono no Saiken tō ni kansuru Tokubetsu Sochihō Dainijō Ikkō no Saigai o Kimeru Hōrei, Order no. 81 of 1995. Without the Special Law, destruction of an entire building would destroy all owners' right of ownership as well, leaving them merely joint tenants of the underlying land and thus subject to the Civil Code's unanimity requirement before they can construct a building or make any other use of the property. Civil Code art. 251. See Akio Yamanome, Tatemono Kubun Shoyū no Kōzō to Dōtai [Structure and Change in Condominiums] 34–35 (1999); Hisai Manshonhō Q&A [Special Law Q&A], 16, ed. Hōmushō Minjikyoku Sanjikanshitsu (1995).

15. This is a provision interpreted by the Osaka District Court in the context of the earthquake to mean (a) the price of the unit before the quake minus (b) the costs of restoration. *Kōno v. Urban Life K.K.*, Osaka District Court, 1668 Hanji 112 (Aug. 25, 1998).

Table 5.2. Legal Provisions for Condominium Disposition

| | Restoration | | | | Civil code alternative in all |
	Minor	Major	Rebuilding	Reconstruction	circumstances
Circumstances	Damage of less than 50% of value	Damage of more than 50% of value	Due to deterioration, damage, or partial destruction, maintaining or restoring building entails "excessive cost"	Entire building in designated disaster area is destroyed (Special Law)	Any (including partition and sale, Civil Code art. 258)
Vote	Unilateral (§61(1)) or simple majority (§§61(3), 39(1)), but 3/4 if "excessively costly" (§17)*	3/4 (§61(5))	4/5 (§62)	4/5	Unanimous (Civil Code art. 251)
Minority rights	None	Put option (§61(7))	None	None	N/A
Majority rights	Pro rata reimbursement for repairs (§61(2))	None	Call option (§63(4))	Call option	N/A
No-action rights	None	Put option (§61(8))	Option to repurchase two years after resolution (§61(6))	Option to repurchase two years after resolution	N/A

* See *Nakatani v. Hirakata Kintetsu Hyakka K.K.*, Osaka District Court, 1351 Hanji 90 (May 31, 1990). Expenses are borne by the unit owners in proportion to their share or as otherwise specified in the agreement (§17).

The Condominium Law, the Special Law, and other related laws created two additional incentives and disincentives to reaching agreement. The first is *uniform terms.* With the exception of minor restoration, the statute is silent as to the ability of the owners to alter statutory voting requirements. Commentators generally agree, however, that the respective vote thresholds for major and minor restoration, rebuilding, and reconstruction are not default rules but mandatory minima and in this way effectively constitute safe harbor provisions; owners may raise vote requirements, but they may not lower them.[16] Still, there is an extremely high degree of uniformity among condominium agreements regarding this issue. None of the eighty-six Japanese condominium agreements that I examined deviate materially from the defaults of the law, and all appear to have followed with relative precision the government-led Housing and Building Advisory Committee's model agreement (first written in 1983 and revised 1997), which also adopts the law's requirements.

The second is *time pressures.* Japanese law created time constraints that encouraged quick agreement. If a repair resolution was not passed within one year (by March 23, 1996), all owners received a put option (Special Law §5). Lessees of destroyed properties had to submit notice of their assertions to priority claims on properties by February 5, 1997. Public funds from the Ministry of Health were available for demolition only to owners who achieved unanimous agreement and applied for funds by March 31, 1997. In addition to the provisions above, §4 of the Special Law also prohibited parties from exercising their right under the Civil Code to partition jointly owned property until March 23, 1998. Finally, to allow for planning and policy development, the national government imposed a two-month moratorium on reconstruction.

RECOVERY PATTERNS OVER TIME

The postquake decision process was relatively successful. I begin by examining data suggesting that, despite the various institutional and economic obstacles faced by condominium owners after the quake, the vast majority of them reached decisions regarding their complexes in a surprisingly rapid manner. Although I recognize that bad decisions can be

16. Yōnosuke Inamoto and Kuniki Kamano, Komentaaru Manshon Kubun Shoyūhō [Annotated Condominium Law] 169, 328 (4th printing 2001).

Table 5.3. Damages to Condominium Buildings

Damage level	Tokyo Kantei data	Hyogo Prefecture data	Reconstruction committee data
Large	83	172 more than half-destroyed *and*	122
Medium	108	consulted with Hyogo authorities	189
Small	353	—	544
Light	1,988	—	?
No damage	2,729	—	2,080
Unknown	N/A	—	9
Total	5,261	172	2,935

made quickly, in this setting I generally view timeliness as a virtue, for the prolonged loss of housing and infrastructure can be devastating to both the economic and the psychosocial well-being of any community.

Dispositions

I rely on the very comprehensive longitudinal and cross-sectional study of 5,261 buildings in Hyogo Prefecture from 1995 to 2000 by Tokyo Kantei, an independent real estate information service.[17] The data appear in table 5.3, along with two other sources for comparison. "Large" refers to buildings whose foundations sustained fatal damage, have little structural use, and are good candidates for reconstruction or rebuilding. "Medium" refers to buildings that may need rebuilding but may be usable after major restoration. "Small" refers to buildings that probably do not require reconstruction but are appropriate candidates for restoration.

The temporal data suggest that resolution and agreement were not automatic. Figures 5.1 and 5.2 show the development of agreements over time for buildings that sustained large and medium damage, respectively. The eighty-three condominium buildings that sustained large damage

17. Three separate and slightly different sources of data exist. One consists of the rather limited official statistics of Hyogo Prefecture, home to both the city of Kobe and epicenter of the quake. See Kōbe Shinbun, *supra* note 9, at 363. The second contains the more comprehensive results of a separate independent study conducted by academics and industry officials in the Great Hanshin Earthquake Special Committee on Reconstruction. See Kajiura, *supra* note 7, at 58–59. The third, from Tokyo Kantei Eye, uses a larger data set, corresponds to the legal categories, and is updated regularly. See Hisai Manshon no Fukkō Jōkyō [Recovery Conditions of Damaged Condominiums], 22 Kantei Eye, Dec. 1, 2000, at 7.

Figure 5.1. Dispositions of Large-Damage Buildings

Figure 5.2. Dispositions of Medium-Damage Buildings

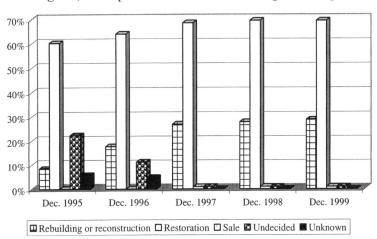

were the slowest off the mark. By the end of the first year, owners in only thirty-two of the eighty-three had reached agreement. Other data sources paint an even gloomier picture early on. The Great Hanshin Earthquake Special Committee on Reconstruction found that only 24 percent of large-damage buildings had obtained unit owner agreement eight months after the quake.[18] A year and a half after the quake, newspapers continued to

18. Kajiura, *supra* note 7, at 64–65.

headline disagreements preventing demolition of more than half of the 2,540 structures in need of rebuilding, including a significant number of condominium complexes.[19] Similarly, the Hyogo Prefecture's official (but more limited) data show that of the 123 condominium buildings that the prefecture determined to be in need of rebuilding, only eight had started the reconstruction process and ninety-six could not reach agreement one year after the quake.[20]

As the figures show, however, only a year after the quake, almost 70 percent of the medium-damage condominiums had at least decided what to do, and by the second year after the quake, this number had increased to well over 80 percent of the large- and the medium-damage buildings. Of course, in some cases, an agreement fell apart even after a formal decision was reached. Some unit owners changed their minds, and one survey of ninety-nine buildings found that of the thirty-eight that had unanimous votes for reconstruction, only eighteen actually had full participation when it came time to pay the bill, and sixty-four had more agreeing voters than participating voters.[21]

Nevertheless, by the end of the year 2000, condo owners had resolved most of their issues, at least tentatively suggesting success. As figure 5.3 shows, owners in sixty-five such buildings had voted to rebuild or reconstruct by this time, and all but four were completed. Another twelve of the buildings sustaining large damage had voted for restoration, and all were completed. Five buildings—or what remained of them—had been sold. In only one building did disputes prevent further developments.

A similar result obtained for the 108 buildings with medium damage shown in the figure. By December 1999, 31 buildings had voted to rebuild or reconstruct; ail but one project was completed. Of another 75 buildings that voted for restoration, all were completed. One building was sold; another remained in dispute. In total, only two buildings of the 191 that had sustained medium or large damage were in dispute five years after the quake. Six were sold, 87 had completed restoration, 91 had completed re-

19. Hanshin Daishinsai: Hassei kara 1-nenhan: Nao Kaitai Dekinai Tatemono 1413 [1,413 Condos Can't Rebuild One Year and a Half after the Quake], Mainichi Shinbun, July 16, 1996, at 1.

20. "Hassei ni Mukete" 9wari ga Tatekae Susumazu [90% Can't Rebuild], Kyodo News Service, July 19, 1996.

21. Tatekae Sansei kara Kokoro Kawari [Changing Minds after Reconstruction Agreement], Kyodo News Service, May 19, 1998.

Figure 5.3. Dispositions of Large-Damage Buildings, 2000

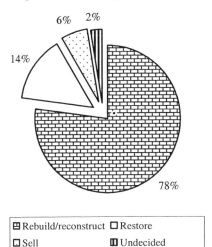

⊞ Rebuild/reconstruct	☐ Restore
☐ Sell	→ Undecided

building or reconstruction, and another 5 were in the process of reconstruction following a vote for such disposition. Among the buildings that sustained small or light damage, 99 percent (2,318) were restored, 20 were rebuilt, and only three of a total of 2,341 buildings were unable to reach resolution.

Sometimes owners used the call and put options to solve disputes; in other cases dissenters simply gave in. Interviews with quake victims and experts suggest that in a few cases bribes solved the problem as majority owners simply shouldered the recalcitrant owners' share of the costs rather than lose their desired resolution or face costly litigation. Still, I found little evidence of strategic holdouts; whether because of legal, social, or other incentives, all holdout situations of which I am aware were at least perceived to be genuine, even by those in the majority.

In four cases involving building disposition, the courts decided. In all four cases—by building name, Takarazuka, Tōwa Ashiya High Town, Higashiyama Corpo, and Rokkō Grand Palace Takabane—minority plaintiff owners brought suit to void resolutions to rebuild. Three suits were brought on the grounds that the "excessive cost" standard was not met; the fourth (Higashiyama Corpo) involved a split vote in which a rebuilding resolution was approved by 80.2 percent of voting interests (seventy-three of ninety-one approving) but only 79.5 percent of owners (seventy of eighty-eight).[22] The Kobe District Court voided the Higashiyama Corpo resolution in 2001, but in the "excessive cost" cases, the Supreme Court (in the Takarazuka case, 2003) and subsequently the Osaka High Court (in the Rokkō Grand Takabane case, 2004) upheld the resolutions. The parties in the Tōwa Ashiya High Town case settled in 2001 (they rebuilt).[23] In a fifth relevant case (the Ashiyagawa Urban Life case) not directly involving building disposition, the Kobe District Court in 2003 rejected arguments of a majority owner who claimed that the "market price" of the put options was too high (about $1.4 million) and that the owner was unfairly being singled out because it was the condominium development and sales office.[24] Five court cases stemming from a tragedy such as Kobe is minimal, if not trivial. Japan's slow judicial system notwithstanding, all five court cases were resolved by April 2004, and all dispositions were completed shortly thereafter.

Of course, law was not the sole factor in shaping decisions. I examined two building characteristics—age and number of units—among the 108 quake-damaged condominium buildings that Hyogo Prefecture identified as undergoing reconstruction or rebuilding by the end of 2000, data later used by the Ministry of Land, Transport and Industry. The result for building age was equivocal,[25] but the data suggest a negative rela-

22. See Tatekae Ketsugi Yūkō: Takarazuka Hisai Manshon Soshō [Rebuilding Resolution Upheld in Half-Destroyed Takarazuka Condominium], Kobe Shinbun, April 10, 2004, available at http://www.kobe-np.co.jp/kobenews/sougou04/0410ke23980.html; Tatekae Giketsu "Yūkō" [Rebuilding Resolution Upheld], Asahi Shinbun, Nov. 1, 2001, at 38.

23. Hanshin Daishinsai Hisai Manshon, Tatekae Meguri Hajime no Wakai—Kōsha, Tekichiken Kaitori [Public Housing Corporation Agrees to Purchase Property Rights in First Settled Case of Rebuilding: Condominiums Damaged in the Great Hanshin Earthquake], Nihon Keizai Shinbun, Oct. 26, 2001, at 43.

24. Shinsai Higai Manshon Soshō, "Kubun Shoyū, Hanbai Gaisha ga Kaitori wo" Hanketsu ["Real Estate Agent to Buy" Decision in Quake-Damaged Building Lawsuit], Nihon Keizai Shinbun, Jan. 20, 2003, at 18.

25. Although older buildings sustained heavier damage (Kazusuki Kobayashi and Yoshiaki Fujiki, Manshon: Anzen to Hozen no tameni [Condominiums: Safety and Security] 211 [2000]; Hidekazu Nishizawa and Yōsuke Enmanji, Jishin to Manshon [Earthquakes and Condominiums] 46–47 [2000]), the data for Hyogo Prefecture presented above show no obvious correlation between age and speed of resolution. The Tokyo Kantei data, however, show that of the eighty-three buildings deemed to have sustained "large" damage, the rate of rebuilding was 83.8 percent for those built before 1970, 78.6 percent for those built the in the 1970s, and only 50 percent for those built after 1980, while the rates of restoration were 6.5 percent, 14.3 percent, and 40 percent, respectively. Older buildings tended to be

tion between number of units and the speed with which agreement was reached.[26]

Comparison to Nonearthquake Cases

We can now compare the Kobe data with those of the nonearthquake cases seen in the beginning of the chapter. The earthquake cases pose a startling contrast. Excluding currently pending litigation, 91 of 108 reconstruction and rebuilding cases that arose after the Kobe tragedy were decided not by the unanimous consent required by the Civil Code but by the four-fifths rules of the Condominium Law and the Special Law. In another postquake survey of thirty-five reconstructions undertaken pursuant to the Special Law and twenty-three rebuildings done pursuant to the Condominium Law,[27] fourteen were decided by unanimous consent, and in another six cases owners achieved unanimity pursuant to the Civil Code. Table 5.4 breaks down the levels of agreement for the fifty-eight total cases decided pursuant to the two laws.

The Kobe earthquake cases are the first instances in the history of Japanese condominium law in which owners have reconstructed in the *absence* of unanimous consent—and most of them did.[28] These agree-

rebuilt; newer buildings, despite consistent categorization by independent parties as having "large" damage, were merely restored. Age also was a determining factor in the destruction of noncondominium buildings. Masatomi Tanba, Hanshin-Awaji Daishinsai ni okeru Jūtaku Higai to Hisaisha no Dōkō/ Fukkō he no Shiten [Multi-Dwelling Building Damages in the Great Hanshin-Awaji Earthquake and the Recovery of Victims], in Shinsai Chōsa no Rinri to Jissen [Practice and Theory of Disaster Surveys], 127, 131, ed. Kōbe Toshi Mondai Kenkyūjo (2001).

26. See Eiki Maruyama, Manshon no Tatekae to Hō [Condominium Reconstruction and the Law], 55 (2000). It is also worth noting that although early reconstruction usually kept the same number of units or fewer, later reconstruction often included the addition of new units. Because the data do not show any decrease in average floor space per unit, I interpret this result to reflect both relaxed capacity restrictions and a need for additional funding from new residents.

27. Manshon Tatekae Enbotsuka Hōsaku Kentō Iinkai, Manshon no Tatekae no Enkatsuka ni Mukete [Toward an Active Condo Reconstruction Market], Nov. 30, 2002, data appendix at 14, available as PDF file at http://www.mlit.go.jp/kisha/kisha01/07/ 071130_2_.html.

28. The data are from ibid., data appendix at 9, available as PDF file at http://www .mlit.go.jp/kisha/kisha01/07/071130_2_.html; and Kajiura, *supra* note 7, at 78, 226–33. See also Ozaki, *supra* note 1, at 113 Hōgaku Kyōkai Zasshi 1324, 1701 (discussing lack of unanimous decisions in reconstruction).

Table 5.4. Agreement Levels in 58 Kobe Condominiums

Agreement level	Number of buildings	Percentage of sample
80–85%	3	5.2
85–90%	9	15.5
90–95%	12	20.7
95–100%	16	27.6
100%	14	24.0
Unknown	4	6.9
Total	58	100

ment levels cannot be evaluated independent of the decision rule in place; we might see a different distribution under, for instance, a 70 percent supermajority rule. But the difference in the frequency of unanimity between earthquake and nonearthquake cases remains despite the underlying identity of available decision rules.

At least five reasons account for the unanimity norm in nonearthquake cases and its relative absence in the Kobe earthquake aftermath. The first three reasons might be specific to disaster. First, the earthquake may have created unique social dynamics. Second, it often left disparate damage patterns; some units were destroyed, while others in the same complex were untouched. The age-related damage in nonearthquake cases might be more evenly spread across units. By the same token, evenly distributed damage patterns may explain why some buildings that were totally destroyed in the quake were able to achieve unanimity. Third, many owners simply wanted to move elsewhere rather than reconstruct following the quake. Although unit owners unaffected by earthquakes might feel the same way, the earthquake destroyed entire neighborhoods and alerted residents to the presence of conditions that might wreak havoc again in the future.

The remaining two reasons are institutional. First, although postearthquake legislation attempted to encourage recovery by creating time periods that tolled several legal provisions, the effect of the legislation was to create deadlines for achieving agreement. Second, unit owners in nonearthquake cases often seek unanimous consent in order to obtain "equal exchange" (*tōka kōkan*) rebuilding, commonly known as "rebuilding for free."[29] Although an equal exchange is not actually free, it often

29. Kajiura, *supra* note 7, at 184.

requires owners to procure no additional cash. In such a transaction, a developer rebuilds in exchange for partial ownership of the property. This method of reconstruction was extremely popular through the 1980s and early 1990s, as rising property values provided incentives to developers and tax-related disincentives to sale by owners.[30] "Almost all" of non-earthquake-related reconstructions of condominiums are said to have relied on equal exchange for financing.[31]

Equal exchange was not available to owners of earthquake-damaged units; because capacity restrictions were already exceeded, there usually was no unused portion of the property to trade to developers in exchange for their services, and the Condominium Law allows neither the purchase of additional land nor conversion of use. But even if capacity restrictions were eliminated, low property values likely made such arrangements prohibitively expensive for developers.[32] The unavailability of equal exchange financing thus lessened incentives for achieving unanimity and could not help smooth over the differences in wealth among unit owners.

Still, Kobe condominium owners did not lack incentives to achieve unanimity, and as table 5.4 shows, many buildings, perhaps about one-third, did so. A dominant factor in explaining unanimity in the absence of equal-exchange transactions appears to be the Ministry of Health's policy that only buildings that achieved unanimous consent were eligible for national funds for demolition.[33]

In short, the levels of agreement seen in earthquake-related and non-earthquake-related condominium reconstruction cases suggest that despite some time lags and litigation, the Condominium Law and the Special Law were useful in structuring rapid agreement among unit owners.

30. Kikuo Iwata, Manshonhō to Keizai Bunseki [Economic Analysis of Condominium Law], in Jūtaku no Keizaigaku [The Economics of Residential Buildings] 53, 54, ed. Kikuo Iwata and Tatsuo Hatta (1997).

31. Manshon Tatakae Enkatsuka Hōsaku Kentō Iinkai Hōkoku ni Tsuite [Report of Committee to Investigate Plans for Condominium Reconstruction], Nov. 30, 2001, http://www.mlit.go.jp/kisha/kisha01/07/071130_2_.html. See also Kajiura, *supra* note 7, at 226–29 (51 of 64 cases). Ozaki reports that all reconstructions before 1995 were based on equal exchange. See Ozaki, *supra* note 1, at 113 Hōgaku Kyōkai Zasshi 1324, 1701. The remainder had similar incentives for unanimity such as eligibility for government aid under community redevelopment programs. See Iwata, *supra* note 30, at 60–61.

32. See Yasuo Kawawaki and Mitsuru Ota, The Influence of the Great Hanshin-Awaji Earthquake on the Local Housing Market, 8 Rev. Urban & Regional Development Stud. 220 (1996).

33. Kajiura, *supra* note 7, at 154.

Unit owners who could achieve unanimity did so. Those who could not abided by the four-fifths rule, sold, or managed instead to satisfy the lower-threshold requirements for restoration. The buyout measures of the law also encouraged agreement, either by forcing the choice or by allowing the majority to squeeze out the minority in the name of overcoming collective action problems. Law mattered.

Had institutional incentives been the same for earthquake and non-earthquake cases, I might have found less stark differences in agreement patterns. Still, given the dearth of comparative evidence, I cannot refute a claim that timely agreement in earthquake cases would have arisen in other legal regimes. But I can investigate a related claim: if the social fabric in Japan is as strong as the literature often suggests, timely agreement might have arisen even in the complete absence of a formal legal regime.

Self-enforcing norms and social capital are often said to thrive in Japan, which might make solutions to commons problems relatively easy. As difficult as it may be to discuss such factors with precision, it seems extremely likely that social factors played an important role in decision making and that these factors are important in explaining differences between Japan's system and other systems.

Still, the evidence for positive results from Japanese norms and social capital in this particular context is equivocal. Japanese sociologists, legal scholars, and lawyers note that condominium owners are often contentious with respect to a wide range of issues, and the sociological studies cited above suggest owner heterogeneity and a lack of owner interaction.[34] A survey of the way Kobe condominium owners formulated their votes suggests that social factors might not have been particularly important, at least in the owners' *perceptions* of their own behavior.[35]

Consultants, attorneys, bureaucrats, and unit owners involved in Kobe condominium dispute resolution told a similar story. As one consultant

---

34. See, e.g., Bengoshi Nakaseno Kinjō Funsō Kaiketsugaku [Study of Solutions to Neighborhood Disputes That Make Attorneys Cry], ed. Tokyo Bengoshikai (1998) (detailing disputes about sunlight, parking lots, pets, renovations, management, use of common space, and noise); Masaki Abe, Kisei Gyōsei to Funsō no Henyō: Kyōtōshi ni Okeru Manshon Kensetsu Funsō wo Sozai to shite [Regulation Administration and the Transfiguration of Disputes: Evidence from a Kyoto Condo Dispute], 40 Hōgaku Zasshi 1 (1993); Ozaki, *supra* note 1, at 113 Hōgaku Kyōkai Zasshi 1324.

35. The survey studies owners who switched their vote from yes to no to achieve agreement. When asked why they changed their vote, the three most-cited factors were "the construction methods and plans became clear" (41.2 percent), "we received information about

explained, "Most owners don't hate each other, and resident owners are usually fairly interconnected. But the quake was just beyond anyone's comprehension. If there had been no legal provisions in place, the situation would have been pure chaos." Or as one unit owner put it when I asked about the importance of social harmony, "If we ever had harmony, it ended in January 1995. After that, we needed law. . . . At some point in time, we might have reached a solution without the law, but I don't even want to think about how that process would have worked or how long that would have taken." Statements such as these from knowledgeable players suggest that social factors might not always lead to consensus, even in Japan.

CONCLUSION

Kobe condominium owners might have reached consensus—eventually—even without the law, and social norms surely played a role in achieving agreement. But when we compare the rapid consensus achieved concerning condominiums with the rancor that often surrounds other decision-making processes in Japan that historically have lacked clear rules, one factor that differentiates Kobe is the existence of clearly delineated legal rules regarding consensus. Those rules, and other supporting institutions, played a major role in structuring agreement.

---

financial support for rebuilding" (38.2 percent), and "we received information that showed that rebuilding would raise property values" (32.4 percent). Kajiura, *supra* note 7, at 153.

CHAPTER SIX

LOVE HOTELS

We now examine interpersonal relations in Japan in a context much more intimate than the usual condominium-owner relation: sex. In particular, let's peek at law's role in a place where people in everyday Japan have lots and lots of sex: love hotels. Although exact quantitative data are lacking, the Japanese love hotel industry plausibly calculates that couples make over half a *billion* trips to such establishments each year.[1] If that number is reasonably accurate, and if a recent survey of frequency of sex in Japan is also close to the truth, by my calculations, about half of all sex in Japan occurs in love hotels.[2]

Few enterprises amuse adult visitors to Japan more than these limited-purpose facilities—especially when the visitor inevitably mistakes one

1. Fuasshon Hoteru Yumekūkan [Tale of Fashion Hotel Dream Space], 104–5, ed. Futabasha (1999) (citing 576,076,762 couples); Yukari Suzuki, Rabu Hoteru no Chikara [Love Hotel Power], 148–49 (2002).

2. The 2001 Durex Global Sex Survey into Sexual Attitudes and Behavior (see www.durex.com) found that Japanese respondents between the ages of sixteen and fifty-five reported having sex an average of 36 times per year, last among surveyed countries. The Japanese population in that age range is approximately 70 million persons. If each such person is having sex 36 times per year, a total of about 1.26 billion acts of sexual intercourse are occurring ((70 million × 36)/2). Another study of sexual practices in Japan found that the average number of couplings is 7.0 per month for men and 2.1 for women. Futsū no Sekkusu Hakusho [White Paper on Regular Sex], Spa!, Mar. 5, 2002, at 48. Although this study is unscientific and based only on a limited age range of single persons (two hundred men aged 25–35 and two hundred women aged 22–32), it does suggest that the Durex numbers are not implausible.

for a more legitimate place to spend the night. Love hotels, or at least "adult hotels," exist in the United States as well, but they are often seedy, low-rent joints in the wrong parts of town. By contrast, Japanese love hotels, often enveloped in blazing neon and gaudy architecture in the style of such landmarks as the Disneyland castle and the Statue of Liberty, are situated so that couples can quickly dart in off the street without attracting attention. In other areas, they are often set back from the highway to allow inconspicuous entrance through rubber-curtained gates that close just in time to prevent passersby from glancing at one's license plate. In either setting, for about $50 for two hours or $100 for the entire night, a couple gets a fully furnished room, often with rotating beds, mirrored ceilings, glass bathtubs, and entertainment extras such as large-screen televisions and karaoke machines. For a little extra, theme rooms are available, featuring everything from traditional Japanese furnishings to Cinderella fantasies to medieval torture chambers.

Love hotels can't merely be about oversexed Japanese who can't wait to get home. The multinational survey data, though of questionable validity, place the Japanese, who apparently only get down to business 36 times a year, at the rock bottom of the chart (Americans, with 124 times per year, are number one).[3] So what else is going on here? In this chapter I explore the role of Japanese love hotel regulation in this phenomenon. Although law did not create love hotels, it influences significantly their numbers, location, and form. Because love hotel regulation is so integrally linked with social and historical notions of sex, sexuality, privacy, and the role of the state in a previously unexamined context, I can think of few topics in Japanese law that would arouse more natural curiosity. But for readers who might not approach the topic with the same inquisitiveness, allow me to advertise here that I in fact use love hotel regulation to explore two broader areas of law and legal theory.

First and perhaps most simply, love hotel regulation provides an interesting case study of the interrelation between social norms and law in Japan. This case shows how social change can give rise to legal change and how legal changes, in turn, can affect social and industry norms and practices. In this case, the latter is particularly interesting, because the love hotel case shows how state intrusion may affect behavior in non-obvious ways consistent with a rational-choice framework—even in Japan, where social norms are often said to trump law.

3. See *supra* note 2.

Second, this chapter examines how state regulation can create change in ways that may not be easily foreseeable. Until 1985, love hotels were regulated primarily by laws governing ordinary hotels and inns; there was no separate regulatory scheme for lodgings that were specifically for sexual activity. At least in part because of their ambiguous legal status, many people, I argue, saw love hotels as dark, seedy, and shameful. In 1985, in response to groups that noted various negative externalities (in moral, social, and environmental terms) that arose from love hotels, the Japanese government attempted to crack down on love hotels via legislation. The evidence presented in this chapter suggests that law led to an increase in love hotels (or at least did not lead to decrease), primarily because of a narrow statutory definition of what constitutes such an establishment.

The statute's narrowness had two related effects. The first was economic: law led to industry restructuring and consolidation. Some hotels failed, but in their place came many successful new ones. The second is social: the law appears to have destigmatized love hotels. This claim is impossible to quantify and somewhat difficult to support, but it at least appears that among many industry players and consumers, the perception that law changed people's minds about the love hotel industry is widely held. The change was not one that the industry could have undertaken on its own simply by cleaning up its act, because the legal status awarded to love hotels by the law played an important role in their legitimization.

I rely on several different data sources. I examine the Japanese secondary literature, which is sparse and recent,[4] as well as the relevant law, the Entertainment Law,[5] corresponding regulations, and several sources of quantitative data. I also rely on firsthand data. Over a period of about three years, I made (unaccompanied) visits to fifty love hotels of varying sizes in locations throughout Japan. In addition to spending many hours in observation, I conducted interviews with seventy-one persons at eighteen hotels and spoke more casually with employees at approximately thirty additional hotels about their enterprise. At each of the hotels where

4. Futabasha, *supra* note 1; Kazuhiko Hanada, Rabu Hoteru no Bunkashi [A Cultural History of Love Hotels] (1996); Shōichi Inoue, Ai no Kūkan [Love Space] (1999); Yoshikazu Nagai, Fūzoku Eigyō Torishimari [Controlling Leisure Industry] (2002); Suzuki, *supra* note 1; Isshō Yasuda, Rabu Hoteru Gaku Nyūmon [Introduction to the Study of Love Hotels] (1983). A photographic work is available as Satellite of Love: Rabu Hoteru Kieyuku Ai no Kūkangaku [The Vanishing Love Space of Love Hotels], ed. Kyoichi Tsuzuki (2001).

5. Fūzoku Eigyō tō no Kisei oyobi Gyōmu no Tekiseika tō ni Kansuru Hōritsu [Entertainment Law], Law no. 22 of 1948.

I conducted interviews, I spoke with at least one employee, and often more, mainly desk clerks (usually men) or cleaning persons (always women). At fifteen of them I also spoke with managers, and at seven I spoke with owners. I also gathered information from attendance at two industry conferences (at which I spoke informally with approximately thirty people); from interviews with love hotel consultants (five), industry executives (four), police and public safety commissioners (nineteen), workers, managers, and industry experts at ordinary hotels (twenty-five), antihotel campaigners (eight), and sex-industry insiders (nine); and from informal polls (an exaggeration; perhaps "locker-room conversations" is more appropriate) of long-term regular customers (approximately fifty over the course of several years).

LOVE HOTELS

In this section I describe love hotels and place them in sociohistorical context. I supply this information principally because it is essential to understanding changes in the legal scheme, but also because it is unavailable in English and not widely known even in Japan.

What Is a Love Hotel?

The primer has three basic lessons: facilities, clientele, and economics.

Facilities. Although urban legends of first-time visitors to Japan who stumble into the wrong inn are commonplace, to most observers, love hotels historically have been easily identifiable from the outside, with three or four clear characteristics. First, love hotels, especially those built in the 1980s, are often ablaze in neon and light. In general, the more urban the setting, the more neon; rural love hotels need little gaudiness to compete with surrounding rice paddies. Second, love hotels often have easily distinguishable architecture. Although some hotels have drab exteriors, many suggest a carnival-like atmosphere. Sometimes this can be accomplished simply by bright and colorful paints; other times the scheme is bolder, with architecture reminiscent of castles, Victorian mansions, or the *Queen Elizabeth*. Third, location often gives an indication of hotel type. In cities, love hotels are seldom built directly across from rail stations; although usually very close to mass transit, they are more likely to be slightly off the beaten path to assure greater customer anonymity. In

rural areas, the same is true; such hotels are likely to be set off the highway, with multiple signs from the highway to the front door. Finding a
love hotel is rarely difficult; if one cannot be located nearby easily, guide-
books are available, magazines (from lurid publications to weekly entertainment guides) publish pictures and descriptions of popular rooms, and
Internet directories abound.

Finally, love hotels have a distinctive nomenclature. They rarely have
names that one would expect for an ordinary hotel such as "Tokyo Hotel"
or "Oriental Hotel." Sometimes the names are silly and meaningless, such
as "1985," "21," or "The White House." In other cases, it seems that love
hotel operators are in competition to determine the most inventive, hu-
morous, or sexually suggestive name. The best-selling Japanese novelist
and columnist Haruki Murakami once held a contest to see which readers
could send in the best true love hotel names. The winners included "Human Relations" (*ningen kankei*), "Mendel's Law" (*menderu no hōsoku*),
and the meaningless yet oddly appealing "$\pi = 3.14$." Some of the more
creative submissions do not translate well to English, but they included
"Kōshien" (the name of a stadium famous for a high school baseball tournament), "Asoko"—a double entendre meaning either (a) a somewhat
ambiguous "over there," allowing a couple to say "let's go over there" or
(b) genitalia—and the characters for the flower hydrangea, which can be
read either "Ajisai" (the actual name of the flower) or "Shiyōka," meaning, roughly, "let's do it."[6]

Customers usually enter love hotels surreptitiously. Pedestrian entrances are covered, and auto entrances often feature direct access from the
garage to the rooms. In hotels with garages, a shield is available for the customer to hide his license plate once the car is parked. For security reasons,
an employee usually records the license plate number, and those records
are said to be reviewed by authorities only when investigating a crime.

Once inside the hotel, customers choose a room. At smaller and older
hotels, the decision may be made at a sort of "front desk" at which a clerk,
usually shielded from the waist up to avoid learning a customer's identity,
simply slides the customer the key to an available room. At most hotels,
however, the system is more sophisticated. On entering, customers are
faced with an array of photos of the hotel's rooms accompanied by a description of each room's amenities and the fee schedule. Available rooms

6. Haruki Murakami and Anzai Mizumaru, Murakami Asahidō ha Ikanishite Kitarere-
taka [Has Murakami's House of the Rising Sun Been Trained?], 222–23, 303 (1997).

are backlit. (If no room is available, as is often the case on weekends and holidays, many hotels have a clock that gives approximate waiting times, the determination of which is a science in and of itself.) To choose a room, a customer presses a button under the appropriate picture. The button triggers a trail of lights that direct the customer from the lobby to the appropriate room.

Although some hotels offer little more than a bath, a bed, and a few pornographic videos, most offer a full array of both sexual and nonsexual entertainment. As for the nonsexual, many offer room service, large-screen satellite television, piped-in karaoke music, massage chairs, and video games. A popular Osaka hotel named Rondchamps boasts a private glass elevator from the bath to the bedroom, with a slide from bedroom to bath (warning sticker: "Sliding while naked will result in dangerous speed; please wear a bathing suit, available for rental free of charge"); another room features a dance floor with automated dancing bears. As for the sexual, hotels offer such amenities as luxurious, oversized transparent baths, king-size beds that rotate, vibrate, or both, mirrors galore, and a separate room-service menu of sexual equipment. Some specialty hotels offer costumes that allow customers to depict a variety of scenarios, ranging from nurse-and-patient to knight-and-damsel to Mickey Mouse and Minnie Mouse.

When a couple has finished using the room, they either exit to pay the shielded employee or call the front desk on the house phone. In some hotels, an employee may conduct the payment transaction with the callers through a slot in or near the door. In others, a vending-machine-like apparatus accepts payment. In more sophisticated hotels, a pneumatic chute system is employed. Much like the drive-in window at a bank, the customer places payment in a plastic canister, presses a button, and the canister is vacuum-delivered to the front desk, where change is made and discount coupons for the next visit or membership cards are inserted.

Prices vary by location, size, and quality of the room. Smaller rural hotels might charge $30 for a two-hour "rest" and $70 for the night. Larger hotels may start at $50 for a rest and charge between $100 and $200 for the night. Still more luxurious hotels, or at least the most popular rooms in nicer hotels, may charge upwards of $250 for the night. In general, prices are roughly similar to, or slightly less than, those of ordinary hotels.

Clientele. Little research has been conducted on love hotels' clientele. Although such hotels are popular and the customer base is quite large, visits are not considered polite dinner conversation in many social circles. I was able to gather data only through interviews and observation. At eight hotels on ten separate occasions, I observed more than six hundred couples entering the establishment (it felt like spying, but the behavior is of course public). I initially attempted to categorize these couples with some precision, but that exercise proved fruitless, and accordingly I can only make general estimates of relative frequency. My observations, which correlate with the interview evidence, suggest that the clients usually belong to one of four types, in the following order of frequency.

First, there are lovers: "traditional" young dating couples. As one might expect, some dates end (and many surely begin) at love hotels, an unsurprising locale given the fact that many young people live at home until they marry.

But not all love hotel clients are young singles. At some hotels, the average customer appeared to be in his or her late thirties, and I saw customers carry in sleeping babies on four occasions. According to love hotel management and industry experts that I interviewed, a large number of clients—perhaps one-fourth—are said to be in the second category: married persons, or more accurately, persons married to each other. At some hotels, managers told me that married couples are the largest category of customers; at others (such as those located next to Tokyo nightclubs), the percentage was said to be significantly smaller.

Married couples might be expected to confine their sexual activity to their bedrooms, but people in Japan commonly cite three factors to explain marital love hotel visits. First, many married couples live with children or with their parents; more than a third of persons over the age of sixty-five live with their married adult children.[7] As one surveyor of Japanese sex explains, "With little privacy from growing children and/or the husband's widowed mother, the love hotel is for many Japanese virtually the only haven of sexual intimacy there is."[8] Second, houses in Japan are small and not particularly well soundproofed, a fact which, combined with the demographic arrangements, might lead some customers to love hotels. Third, the hotels, with their blatantly nonessential luxuries, might simply be more enjoyable than a couple's own home. To

7. Kōseishō Tōkei Jōhōbu, Kokumin Seikatsu Kihon Chōsa [Basic Survey of Citizen Life] (1995), available in Jinkō no Dōkō [Population Trends], 251, ed. Kōsei Tōkei Kyōkai (1999).

8. Nicholas Bornoff, Pink Samurai: Love, Marriage, and Sex in Contemporary Japan, 17 (1991).

summarize these three factors, as one long-time observer of Japan puts it, "The main reason for their popularity . . . is the lack of venue anywhere else."[9]

The third category, as one might expect, consists of couples engaged in extramarital affairs. It is difficult, of course, to find exact data on the topic; although I observed couples entering love hotels on several occasions that I suspected to be having affairs, I have no proof of such. Still, it is commonly assumed that love hotels are a popular destination for people who are cheating on their spouses or others. In fact, some hotels cater to such a crowd; five hotels that I visited had phone systems that play background sounds of offices, bars, or train stations (at the customer's choice) when customers place an outgoing call. The sounds are designed to mislead recipients of calls into believing that the caller is actually at such a location and not a love hotel.

Finally, there are prostitution-based visits. Prostitution has a long history in Japan, and it continues to thrive in various forms today. In the eighteenth and nineteenth centuries, prostitutes were licensed and often worked as indentured servants.[10] Although national regulation was attempted in the early twentieth century, the Prostitution Prevention Law (Baishun Bōshihō, Law no. 118 of 1956) was not passed until 1956. A 1948 survey shows one reason why: 70 percent of respondents (78 percent of men and 59 percent of women) thought organized houses of prostitution to be "socially necessary," and 52 percent of respondents (58 percent of men, 45 percent of women) opposed the law.[11]

Despite the law, prostitution is "a massive, well-established industry accepted by most Japanese, including the police, as a fact of life, and one major component of the pattern of leisure activity for many Japanese men."[12]

9. Donald Richie, The Donald Richie Reader: 50 Years of Writing on Japan, 194, ed. Arturo Silva (2001). The lack of usable public space appears to affect many aspects of life in Japan, where singles looking for time alone often sleep or read in their air-conditioned cars on less-traveled roads, and young persons spend much more time at fast-food restaurants than is required for a meal. See, e.g., Emiko Ohnuki-Tierny, McDonalds in Japan: Changing Manners and Etiquette, in Golden Arches East: McDonald's in East Asia, 161, ed. James L. Watson (1997).

10. J. Mark Ramseyer, Odd Markets in Japanese History: Law and Economic Growth, 109–34 (1996).

11. National Public Opinion Research Institute, The Japanese People Look at Prostitution (1952).

12. Stephan M. Salzberg, The Japanese Response to AIDS, 9 Boston Univ. Int'l L. Rev. 243, 258 (1991).

The Prostitution Prevention Law does relatively little to control the industry; although public solicitation, serving as a broker for prostitution, contracting to engage in prostitution, and furnishing a venue for prostitution are punishable acts, prostitution per se is not (hence "Prostitution Prevention Law," not "Prostitution Prohibition Law," a distinction that is equally clear in Japanese). Even with this structure, in a 1985 survey by the Prime Minister's Office, 76 percent of respondents stated that the prostitution law was not obeyed.[13]

There are no data available that directly illuminate the connection between prostitution and love hotels, but Tokyo police data offers clues. Of the 1,276 prostitution cases involving 185 persons (including 125 men) that the Tokyo Metropolitan Police sent to prosecutors in 2002, only two were working at love hotels. Those two were arrested for furnishing a venue.[14]

The statistics reflect both lack of enforcement and a vague legal (and perhaps social) concept of prostitution. As for enforcement, managers at several hotels told me that police consider love hotels to be "off limits" unless something obviously amiss was observed. But prostitution exists: in Tokyo and Osaka, I often observed prostitutes loitering near the seedier love hotels. These women are usually non-Japanese and are often southeast Asian. Police, hotel employees, and the women themselves told me that most such workers had overstayed their visas or had sexually transmitted diseases, and as such could not get hired at established legal sex shops. The only alternative, I was told, was to look for customers outside love hotels.[15] But even if the law were enforced more rigorously to eliminate street prostitution, other forms of the sex trade at love hotels would likely flourish. Outside of Tokyo and Osaka, I saw no obvious cases of street prostitutes loitering near such facilities. A woman who sells sex at a love hotel in such a manner, risks charges of public solicitation.

Still, some love hotels are widely used by pay-for-sex services, some of which violate prostitution laws and some of which do not. Hotel employees with whom I watched closed-circuit video of customers entering

13. Baishun Taisaku Shingikai, Baishun Taisaku no Genkyō [Status of Anti-Prostitution Measures], 93 (1986).

14. Keishichō, Heisei 14-nen Keishichō no Tōkei [2002 Police Statistics], 144–45 (2003).

15. Estimates of illegal profits from the sex industry in Japan attribute 92.9 percent of such income to established facilities, 4.9 percent to underage prostitution known as teenage "compensated dates" (enjō kōsai), and 2.3 percent to "foreign prostitutes." Takashi Kadokura, Nihon no Chika Keizai [Japan's Underground Economy], 136 (2002). Note that there is no category for free-lance Japanese prostitutes.

the hotel easily pointed out regular female customers who arrived with many different male companions. Some were employees of hostess bars and were providing illegal prostitution services. Others were working around the law. Mayumi Takeda, who worked in such a capacity in the late 1990s, discussed her experiences in her widely read autobiography. The "shop" at which Takeda was employed was a one-room condominium in the Dogenzaka section of Shibuya in Tokyo, adjacent to an area known as "Love Hotel Hill," home to about sixty such establishments. Customers came to the shop to purchase sexual favors: "The cost depends on the course, but a cheap course is 10,000 yen, and an expensive one was about 25,000. The shorter the time, the cheaper; the longer, the more expensive. Customers pay an extra 1,000 or so to pick their companion. A customer can extend his time by about 30 minutes, but he has to pay extra."[16]

Once paid, Takeda (like other women working in the industry) took her customer to a nearby love hotel, where "he pick[ed] the room, and then we start[ed] to play as planned." "Play" includes bathing, costume play, petting, and oral sex (all mutual), but the rules of the game, both in law and in industry practice, prohibit vaginal penetration. The perception in the industry is that sex would subject the shop to prostitution charges resulting from the brokerage, but the lack of a definition of "sex" makes this a gray area of the law.[17] Industry workers might have other motivations; in Takeda's words, "The reason I chose this [sex] shop was because of this 'can't go all the way' rule. I just really didn't want to do that. Going all the way would have made me no different than a prostitute."[18] At some love hotels, particularly in urban areas, these paid-for sexual encounters, which technically do not violate prostitution laws, are commonplace, but even at these hotels, such business is said to account for only a minor portion of revenues.

Economics. At sixteen of the eighteen hotels at which I conducted in-depth interviews, owners, managers, or management representatives spoke with relatively few inhibitions once they discovered that my purpose was aca-

16. Mayumi Takeda, Faito! [Fight!], 99 (2001).

17. The Prostitution Prevention Law contains no definition of prostitution or of sex. By contrast, the recently enacted Child Prostitution and Child Pornography Act (Jidō Kaishun, Jidō Poruno ni kakaru Kōi tō no Shobatsu oyobi Jidō no Hogo Tō ni Kansuru Hōritsu, Law no. 42 of 1999), specifically prohibits the touching of sexual organs, the anus, and the breasts (art. 2).

18. Takeda, *supra* note 16, at 98.

demic and that privacy was ensured. At two hotels, I was flatly rejected. In one of those cases, I was told of a connection with organized crime that inhibited candor; in the other, I simply couldn't get a response. In addition to making site visits, I spoke with other managers and owners at two industry conferences. Although love hotels are notorious for tax evasion,[19] I think that the data supplied to me are reasonably accurate, because owners said such things as, "Of course, I only reported half of that income," but I cannot be confident that everyone gave me true information.

The economic aspects of love hotel management appear not to differ significantly across Japan, and the variation that does exist principally reflects location. In Tokyo or Osaka, $10 to $15 million might be needed to start a love hotel; in smaller cities, $5 million is often sufficient. On average, to build a nice, modern hotel of twenty to thirty rooms requires approximately $10 million. Expenses quickly mount. Furnishing and construction costs account for the bulk of the $10 million; furnishing each room costs approximately $100,000 to $150,000, for a total cost of $2 to $3 million. Adding a black-light system might add $10,000 per room; a sauna, $15,000. A computerized check-in system adds $200,000, and a video karaoke system may add $100,000. In addition, to mitigate neighborhood opposition to construction, love hotel operators told me, it is wise to prepare about $100,000 for donations to politicians and neighborhood associations.

For large corporate owners such as Nomura Finance, which owns several establishments, foreign venture capital firms such as MHS Capital Partners,[20] or wealthy individuals (often executives at construction and real estate companies) using love hotels as part of tax avoidance schemes, $10 million might be a relatively small investment; for others, it is of course quite large. For entrepreneurs without independent wealth, the needed $10 million is usually procured with a bank loan, the terms of which require repayment at the rate of approximately $50,000 monthly. Assuming use by two to three couples per day and average room rates of $50 for a two-hour rest and $100 for a full night, a love hotel operator might receive an average of $200 per day per room.[21] For twenty rooms, the monthly gross

19. See Kadokura, *supra* note 15, at 39–45.

20. See Barney Jopson, Sheepish Investors Catching the Love Hotel Bug in Japan, Financial Times, May 7 2004, at 20.

21. The trade publication Kikan Reja-Hoteru [Leisure Hotel Quarterly] cites average sales of $5,303 per room per month, an average of 20.7 rooms per hotel, and an average occupancy rate of 258 percent. See Data, Kikan Reja-Hoteru, Aug. 2002, at 34.

revenues can reach $100,000 to $150,000, more than enough to repay the bank loan. Tokyo hotels that generate less than $5,000 per room usually do not survive, but at hotels in smaller cities such as Hiroshima, I was informed that a twenty-room hotel can generate about $50,000 to $70,000 per month; the busiest generate as much as $100,000.

From these revenues, hotel operators must pay staff, utility bills, and, occasionally, taxes. Staff expenses are high, because cleaning is an especially difficult task in a love hotel. Customers expect cleanliness, requiring special diligence on the part of cleaning personnel, whom I have seen change bed linens in seconds and use black-light technology to locate bodily fluid stains throughout the room. Utilities are not insubstantial; in addition to the large linen cleaning bills, the monthly water bill at a twenty-room hotel averages $4,000, at least in part because customers bathe before and after sex, and hotels are often designed to facilitate sex in the bathroom, which presumably sometimes occurs with the tap on. Taxes, though mandated, are notoriously difficult to collect from love hotels, in part because of the difficulty of monitoring income. According to one account (perhaps urban legend), tax inspectors identified tax-evading love hotels by comparing their water usage rates with their reported income.[22]

History

Love hotels have humble origins. In the Edo Period (1600–1868), the service was performed by *deaijaya*, literally, meeting tea-houses, with ten to fifteen small rooms of six tatami mats (about one hundred square feet) each. On arrival, a female employee secured customers' shoes and other possessions, not for safety but as a security deposit on the bill, which was paid on exit. She then escorted customers to a private room, served tea and cake, drew a bath, and left the couple to their own devices. At their peak, sixty such institutions functioned in the Sendagaya district of Tokyo alone, and every town was said to have five or six.[23]

In the early part of the twentieth century, a similar function was served by two types of establishments. First, *machiai* (literally, meeting places), small facilities with tatami mats for activity, were quite common, espe-

22. See James S. Henry, Noncompliance with U.S. Tax Law—Evidence on Size, Growth, and Composition, 37 Tax Law 1 (Fall 1983).

23. Hanada, *supra* note 4, at 22; Yasuda, *supra* note 4, at 64.

Table 6.1. Number of Machiai, 1926

Location	Number of Machiai
Tokyo	3,251
Kanagawa Prefecture (Yokohama)	330
Aichi Prefecture (Nagoya)	129
Gifu Prefecture	121
Hiroshima Prefecture	91
Tokushima Prefecture	59
Miyagi Prefecture	47
Kyoto Prefecture	45
Ibaraki Prefecture	42
Osaka Prefecture	33

Source: Naimushō, Keisatsu Tōkei Hōkoku, Daiikkai [First Police Statistics Report] (1926).

cially in Tokyo, as seen in table 6.1. Second, sexual liaisons occurred in a rather unlikely location: noodle restaurants (sobaya). At the beginning of the twentieth century, it was common knowledge that noodle restaurants rented upstairs rooms for short periods of time for sex. In fact, it was such common knowledge in some areas that restaurants that served noodles but had no rooms for rent were forced to write "REAL noodle restaurant" on their outdoor signs in order to enable clients to distinguish them from locations used for sex.[24]

Machiai and noodle shops were not for amateur couples but for pros. Both types of locations were widely used as prostitution centers; male customers met geisha and other paid companions there for sexual services. This use was not exclusive, but the "professional" atmosphere and stigma were said to be so strong in most such establishments that they drove away amateur customers.

So if machiai and noodle shops were mostly used by pros, where did the "amateurs" go? The available evidence points to one primary location: outdoor. As Shōichi Inoue explains in his thorough history of Japanese "love space": "At the beginning of the Twentieth Century, many couples made love outside. In fact, the general movement of male-female inter-action from outdoors to indoors is said to be an extremely recent development."[25] Even as late as 1973, the novelist Aiko Gotō, in an interview re-

24. Inoue, supra note 4, at 132–140, 169.
25. Ibid. at 68.

garding a recent increase in the number of love hotels, responded: "Sex was originally something to be done while bathed in sunlight in the middle of a field. The need to seek stimulation behind closed doors shows how weak people have become. Young people don't need stimulation like that; young people should be doing it in the park. It's much more pleasant."[26]

And do it in the park young people apparently did. A 1916 news report noted that park benches and fields were full of amateurs in the evenings, including "doctors and nurses, office workers and female assistants, manual laborers, cooks and their girlfriends, reporters and their contacts, bank workers and female apprentices."[27] The practice continued well into the U.S. occupation, when "as the sun set, lovers gathered in places like the Imperial Palace grounds and Inokashira Park, and the next morning the grass was full of paper scraps and condoms."[28]

With all the doctors and nurses and so on, you'd think the whole town was there. But note the missing actor in outdoor sex: prostitutes. The territorial distinction was said to be clear: amateurs have sex outdoors, professionals have sex indoors. It was not until the 1930s that the market provided amateurs with indoor facilities suitable for them in the form of *enshuku,* the first true predecessor of the modern love hotel. *Enshuku* literally means "one-yen dwelling," and customers paid one yen per person to rent a room by the hour. Enshuku, unlike ordinary hotels and other facilities, marketed what was then quite exotic: rooms with Western furnishings, double beds (so scandalous that they could not be pictured in print ads), and locking doors.

From the 1930s until the late 1960s or 1970s, enshuku, and to a lesser extent bathhouses (including the inappropriately named "family baths," which are said to allow a "family" to "bathe" in privacy, away from other bathers), were said to be the primary locations for indoor amateur sex. But at some time in the late 1960s, and the details are far from clear, the love hotel was born, bringing many couples in from the cold.

The most famous of these early love hotels is the Meguro Emperor hotel, designed with architecture similar to that of the Disneyland castle,

26. Interview in Shūkan Posuto, Oct. 5, 1973, quoted in Inoue, *supra* note 4, at 61–62.

27. Kōen no Benchi ya Sōgen wo Shitonetoshi: Hanjūteki Kōi [Enjoying Themselves on Park Benches and Fields: Half-Beast Activities], Chūō Shinbun, Aug. 12, 1916, quoted in Inoue, *supra* note 4, at 51–52.

28. Yasuda, *supra* note 4, at 60; see also Shōichi Inoue, Rabuhoteru no Jidai [The Age of Love Hotels], in Fūzoku no Shakaigaku [Sociology of Leisure Industry], 185, 186, ed. Shun Inoue (1987).

which opened in Tokyo in 1973. But before 1973, love hotels had begun to make their way into the vernacular. In "A Misstepping of Virtue" (*Bitoku to Yoromeki*, 1957), author Yukio Mishima has a character speak of an "*avec* hotel*" ("*avec*" is the Japanized French for "couple"). Contemporaneous weekly magazine articles reveal a host of different labels, including yellow hotels (1967), couple hotels (1970), and love hotels (1973).[29] Whatever the name, these early love hotels were set apart from their enshuku predecessors by two primary features: "elegant," "gorgeous," or "royal" architecture and furnishings (ostensibly designed to appeal to female customers) and large-scale sex-related playthings, including electric beds, mirrored ceilings, foam-filled bathrooms, and see-through bath mirrors (visible from the bedroom).

In the early days, the relation of love hotels to professional sex was not clear-cut. Love hotels were designed to appeal to amateurs, but part of the excitement is said to have been that indoor sex was traditionally the domain of professionals.[30] Professionals remained indoors as well; at many love hotels, a male customer could order a prostitute by calling down to the front desk.[31] Although the Prostitution Prevention Law effectively closed centuries-old red-light districts, workers from previously legal prostitutions houses simply resumed their trade in less conspicuous love hotels.

Many forms of adult entertainment were not unregulated; they were covered by the Entertainment Law, promulgated in 1948 under considerable influence from authorities of the American occupation. Despite several subsequent revisions, the 1948 law was ill-equipped to deal with these new enterprises. The Entertainment Law had always regulated machiai, and it was revised in 1972 to regulate motels.[32] But love hotels, which could not easily be distinguished from ordinary hotels, remained regulated only by the Inn Law, which covered both sex-related and non-sex-related types of establishments, and other related laws not specific to the trade. No law contained any mechanism by which love hotels could be distinguished from ordinary hotels.

As the number of love hotels increased, so, too, did perceived problems

29. See Inoue, *supra* note 4, at 304.

30. Ibid. at 336, 350.

31. Yasuda, *supra* note 4, at 44.

32. Fūzoku Eigyō Torishimarihō no Ichibu wo Kaisei Suru Hōritsu, Law no. 116 of 1972. See also *Nakasako v. Aichi Ken Kōan Iinkai,* Nagoya District Court, 320 Hanrei Times 131 (April 14, 1975), *aff'd,* Nagoya High Court, Oct. 20, 1977, 355 Hanrei Times 207 (finding local assembly restriction on motels, based on national law, valid and reasonable).

associated with them. As we saw in chapter 4's discussion of karaoke, Japan's loose zoning scheme permits residences in eleven of twelve types of zones. Of those eleven residential zones, "hotels" are permitted in six, including some of the most ubiquitous zones.[33] Thus, hotels, including love hotels, operated not only in red-light districts but also next door to the retirement home, across the street from the school, and in the space where a backyard would be if Japanese urban dwellings had such luxuries. Accordingly, the problems cited by antihotel campaigners were quite visible.

Opponents of love hotels, a group led largely by grass-roots citizens' movements (including NIMBY groups and children's rights groups) but also including small businesses with ties to the ruling Liberal Democratic Party (LDP), generally noted four areas of concern. First, they often cited the social and moral concerns of having a sex-oriented business on daily public display. The constant exposure to sex was said to affect not only children but also the general population.

Second, crime often accompanied the appearance of love hotels.[34] In some areas, the crime was prostitution. In others, love hotels and related businesses had ties to organized crime, which until 1992 was unregulated as a specific type of crime. In still others, the privacy afforded by love hotels led to a wide range of criminal acts, from extortion schemes to property crimes to sensational murders.[35]

Third, practical cost-related issues arose as well. Love hotels often raised issues of traffic safety, annoying neon signs, and water runoff.[36]

Finally, and most centrally for many opponents of love hotels and sup-

---

33. Kenchiku Kijun Hō [Building Standards Act], Law no. 201 of 1950, arts. 27, 48, Beppyō Daini (chart no. 2).

34. Similar arguments made in the United States about crime related to adult businesses seem misplaced. See Daniel Linz et al., An Examination of the Assumption That Adult Businesses Are Associated with Crime in Surrounding Areas: A Secondary Effects Study in Charlotte, North Carolina, 38 Law & Soc. Rev. 69 (2004).

35. As for extortion, in one widespread scheme, blackmailers filmed couples entering hotels, traced their license plate numbers, and blackmailed them with the videos. Furin Kyōkatsu: Rabuhoteru Mae de Bideo Satsue, 4nin Taiho [Adultery Blackmail: 4 Arrested after Filming Love Hotels], Mainichi Shinbun, Oct. 22, 2002, available at http://www.mainichi.co.jp/women/news/200210/22-4.html. As for property crimes, in one case, a woman lured her male victims to love hotels, drugged them, and robbed them. Seductress Dopes, Robs Horny Men, Mainichi Daily News, May 21, 2002, at 1. For murder, see, e.g., Suzuki, *supra* note 1, at 82–84.

36. Hiroku Kume, Mo-teru Shisetsu no Kisei ni Tsuite [Regarding Motel Regulation], 542 Hanrei Times, 68 (1985).

porters of legislation to restrict them,[37] minors were not legally banned from love hotels, and they often used hotels for smoking, sniffing thinner, and illegal sexual activity.[38] These four factors led to cries for regulation.

Although love hotels could have self-regulated to avoid government intervention, at least two factors made self-regulation unlikely. First, although many hotel entrepreneurs expected regulation, they did not expect any new legal scheme to be too terribly onerous. Many leisure facilities that had functioned well under the 1948 Entertainment Law (motels, for instance), experienced few problems when they were regulated by 1972 amendments to the Entertainment Law. Second, the barriers to collective action were significant. Although industry associations existed at the time, the love hotel industry was fragmented among elite knock-offs of the Meguro Emperor run by legitimate business interests, small-town bed-and-breakfast-type inns run by Mom-and-Pop family businesses, and low-rent facilities that encouraged prostitution, many of which are said to have had connections to organized crime. There were obvious difficulties involved in the coalescence of these varied groups, but in addition, industry officials told me that they considered the source of most love-hotel-related social problems to be the low-rent facilities. The owners of these facilities had the least desire to self-regulate and were least able to understand the consequences of not doing so. They may also have been concerned that industry-sponsored self-regulation would affect their business negatively.

Faced with apparent social problems and no solutions from industry or national legislation, in the late 1970s, several local municipalities attempted to regulate these establishments on their own.[39] In the most famous court case arising from such regulation, the village of Iimori (population 8,451) in southern Nagasaki Prefecture passed an ordinance requiring the approval of the mayor for the building of any hotel or inn. When on November 9, 1978, Toyoki Torii, the owner of a local supermarket, applied to the mayor for permission to build a love hotel within

37. Tsuyoshi Furuyama, Fūzoku Eigyō tō Torishimarihō Ichibu Kaisei no Gaiyō [Outline of Revision of a Portion of the Entertainment Law], 823 Jurisuto 13 (1984).

38. Ayako Uchiyama, Fūzoku Kankyō to Shonen Hikō [Leisure Environment and Juvenile Misconduct], 57 Hōritsu Jihō 13, 14 (1985). "Illegal sexual activity" was often a code word for prostitution by underage girls.

39. See, e.g., Tasuke Masago, Akihiro Minamikawa, and Hisashi Hiraoka, Ryokan Kenchiku Kisei Jōrei ni Tsuite [Regarding Inn Construction Regulations], 34 Hō to Seiji 229 (1983).

seven hundred meters of a junior high school, he was flatly rejected a week later and was informed of the decision the following January. Torii sued. The Nagasaki District Court and the Fukuoka High Court found for Torii, holding that a local municipality needs a rational basis to enforce a test stricter than that of the national Inn Law,[40] which required no such approval. In this case, the local regulation had no such basis and thus interfered with the plaintiff's constitutionally guaranteed freedom of occupation.[41]

LEGAL ANALYSIS: THE 1985 LEGISLATION

In the wake of the Iimori case, in addition to the problems of crime, juveniles, and residential environmental problems, love-hotel opponents now had an additional banner—the search for a constitutionally permitted regulatory scheme to assist municipalities such as Iimori in maintaining their local autonomy. In response to these concerns, the Diet in 1984 undertook a major revision of the Entertainment Law that became effective in 1985 (the "1985 revisions").[42]

The 1985 revisions were the Japanese government's first attempt to regulate love hotels directly. Before looking at the details of the regulatory scheme, it is useful to examine the choice set that was available to Japanese policymakers. To do so, I first consider some alternative approaches.

Alternative Approaches

Japan could have employed any number of tactics to combat the problems associated with love hotels. One possible solution might have been to enact a comprehensive zoning plan in which hotels of all sorts, or at least all hotels of a certain size, are zoned out of residential neighborhoods. Although this approach may have done little to combat crime and juvenile problems, it would likely have had some impact on neighborhood environments. But given the state of Japan's zoning at the time (as now), such a comprehensive rezoning would have required a near-complete reorgan-

40. Ryokangyōhō, Law no. 138 of 1948.

41. *Torii v. Mayor of Iimori,* Nagasaki District Court, 978 Hanji 24 (Nov. 19, 1980); *aff'd,* Fukuoka High Court, 1083 Hanji 58 (Mar. 7, 1983). In a later case, the Nagoya District Court held that a local government may not inordinately delay approval of an application to build a love hotel. *See Marui K.K. v. Aichi Prefecture,* 156 Hanrei Chihō Jichi 78 (Jan. 31, 1996).

42. Fūzoku Eigyō tō Torishimarihō no Ichibu wo Kaisei suru Hōritsu, Law no. 76 of 1984.

ization of urban and suburban Japan, including the removal of many long-established hotels and surrounding businesses that cater to hotel guests. Such a drastic change would have been impractical, would have opened the debate about the zoning system to all sorts of unrelated and potentially difficult issues, and, given the support of small businesses for the ruling LDP, would likely have also been politically impossible.

Japan might also have tried attacking directly the social problems raised by love hotels. Increased police presence might have mitigated prostitution and juvenile usage issues. The latter might have been further reduced by introducing some sort of identification check. Neighborhood environmental problems might have been mitigated by requiring hotels to deal with traffic and water issues as a condition of licensing and by limiting explicit advertising.

It is unclear why Japan did not choose this path. Although representatives to the Diet repeated the social problems mentioned above as bases for love hotel regulation,[43] alternative legislative or regulatory approaches are not mentioned in any of the legislative records or related committee histories. Determining legislative intent with precision is impossible, but three possibilities seem likely: path-dependent legal culture, politics, and love-hotel usage patterns. As for legal culture, the Entertainment Law presented a familiar preexisting framework for regulating such industries. Simply adding love hotels to that law's definitional and registration scheme (then forty years old) was simpler than (and perhaps superior to) some of the more direct solutions listed above. Lawmakers were used to acting in this way; when the field of regulated industries was expanded in 1959 to include tea houses, bars, and nightclubs, again in 1966 to include baths with separate attached rooms, and again in 1972 to include motels, the Entertainment Law was simply amended to add the new categories to the list. Given this history, apparently there was little thought in 1985 of doing otherwise; hotel industry officials and antihotel campaigners alike told me that they never even imagined other alternatives.

Two political factors seem important. First, love hotel operators, like other small businesses, supported the LDP. Industry representatives told me that some large-hotel operators, who made regular donations to the LDP, publicly opposed any sort of regulation. Although there is no direct evidence of intense lobbying by these entrepreneurs, their support may

---

43. See, e.g., Minutes of Sangiin Honkaigi [House of Councillors], no. 21, July 11, 1984, at 1 (statement of Minister of Home Affairs Seiichi Tagawa).

have been a consideration when the LDP addressed the problem. Second, some operators suggested to me that the legislative scheme might have reflected the bureaucracy's desire to widen its jurisdiction.

Finally, love hotel usage patterns might have played a role in the process. Then as now, it was common knowledge that many upstanding citizens regularly used the hotels for purposes that, though perhaps embarrassing, were neither dangerous nor socially unacceptable. With the exception of serious opponents, love hotel visits, as a political insider of the time told me, "usually provoke giggles and red faces, not scorn and outrage." Accordingly, it might have been difficult for lawmakers seriously to consider stricter proposals.

Whatever the precise causal mix that led to the approach, Japan opted to regulate love hotels directly under the Entertainment Law. Before examining the specific provisions, consider the approaches adopted by legislatures in the United States that, like Japan, attempt to regulate adult motels directly.[44] Approaches to regulating adult-oriented businesses in the United States usually include obscenity, zoning, licensing, or nuisance laws. In the case of adult (love) hotels, obscenity is seldom an option, and only in extreme cases could nuisance be useful. When adult hotels are part of the regulatory scheme—and they typically are not—they usually are regulated as part of comprehensive statutes that govern other adult-oriented businesses as well, such as strip clubs, escort agencies, and adult bookstores. Local governments usually rely on licensing or zoning approaches. As a whole, the jurisdictions that regulate the trade do not appear to favor one approach rather than the other.

The particular approach taken—licensing or zoning—often is not as controversial as the underlying statutory definition of adult hotels that determines what businesses may be regulated. One method of definition,

44. There is no direct analogue in the United States. The most direct analogue to Japanese love hotels outside of Japan appears to be the Korean love hotel, which may have more in common with the Japanese love hotel industry of the 1970s and 1980s. Korean love hotels are said to be "seedy" and used only by "illicit lovers" and are said to have increased in recent years. Cho Se-hyon, Many Splendored Things, Korea Herald, Nov. 7, 2000, available at http://www.koreaherald.co.kr/SITE/data/html_dir/20000/11/07/200011070040.asp. As in Japan, one problem of Korean love hotels appears to be that the owners "seem to have a knack of finding places near primary schools or in residential areas to build their love hotels." Ibid. Opposition groups have filed lawsuits, which have produced conflicting rulings. See Joon Hyung Hong, Rule of Law in Korea: Recent Development and Trends [2002], at 22–25.

upheld by the Supreme Court in *FW/PBS, Inc. v. Dallas* in 1990, is to define the hotel in terms of visual amenities or usage periods. The Dallas ordinance in question defined "adult motel" in the following manner:

ADULT MOTEL means a hotel, motel or similar commercial establishment which:

(A) offers accommodations to the public for any form of consideration; provides patrons with closed-circuit television transmissions, films, motion pictures, video cassettes, slides, or other photographic reproductions which are characterized by the depiction or description of "specified sexual activities" or "specified anatomical areas" [each as defined] and has a sign visible from the public right of way which advertises the availability of this adult type of photographic reproductions; or

(B) offers a sleeping room for rent for a period of time that is less than 10 hours; or

(C) allows a tenant or occupant of a sleeping room to subrent the room for a period of time that is less than 10 hours.[45]

The Court stated, among other things, that the ten-hour rule did not violate plaintiffs' right to due process, at least in part because the legislature based its judgment on a 1977 study of Los Angeles that found increased prostitution and other negative effects for neighborhoods containing such short-term-stay hotels. Nor did it violate the right to freedom of association, the Court stated, because any "personal bonds" formed by the use of a motel room for fewer than ten hours are not those that have "played a critical role in the culture and traditions of the Nation by cultivating and transmitting shared ideals and beliefs."[46]

The Court did not consider section (A) of the ordinance, which defined adult motels as those that offer certain video services. Although some courts have upheld such provisions,[47] others have found them to be impermissible. Some courts disallowed them because they were unsupported by factual findings that these hotels, as distinct form other sex-oriented businesses, contribute to neighborhood deterioration.[48] Other

---

45. Dallas City Code, ch. 41A, Sexually Oriented Businesses §41A-2(19) (1986). Kansas has a similar provision; see Kan. Stat. Ann. §12-770(a)(5) (1999).

46. *FW/PBS, Inc. v. Dallas*, 493 U.S. 215, 237 (1990).

47. See *Redner v. Dean*, 29 F.3d 1495 (11th Cir. 1994).

48. *Patel and Patel v. City of South San Francisco*, 606 F. Supp. 666 (N.D. Cal. 1985).

courts have found such provisions to be overbroad, noting, for instance, that "some of Atlanta's finest hotels" offer similar adult programming.[49]

Neither of the above schemes would be entirely effective in regulating love hotels in Japan, because neither definition would adequately distinguish love hotels from ordinary hotels. A wide variety of hotels, from small business hotels to the country's finest, offer the same video programming that can be seen in love hotels (including the Imperial Hotel, often considered the finest in Japan, where until recently it was known by the euphemism "videography"). Moreover, most love hotels in Japan do not advertise the availability of videos with sexual content; their existence is assumed. And unlike adult motels in the United States, the Japanese versions, while offering hourly rates, also serve many customers that stay all night, perhaps because of hotel expenses, perhaps because they feel safer than the U.S. equivalent. And in Japan, where physical privacy is scarce and transportation is often by trains that stop running at midnight, other establishments offer private rooms by the hour for purposes other than sex. Accordingly, in Japan it was necessary to employ a more complex definitional scheme.

The Japanese Approach

The Japanese Entertainment Law regulates a wide variety of leisure establishments, from sex-related facilities to game centers and pachinko parlors. In the case of love hotels, it relies primarily on two elements: zoning and definitional restrictions.

Zoning. The Entertainment Law, as modified slightly by post-1985 revisions, creates five basic categories of immovable sex-related establishments:[50] soaplands (bathhouses that often offer "full service"),[51] fashion health establishments (massage parlors that usually offer oral sex), strip

49. *Purple Onion, Inc. v. Jackson,* 511 F. Supp. 1207, 1220 (N.D. Ga. 1981); see also *Patel and Patel, supra* note 55, at 672 and n. 9.

50. The law also designates two categories of movable sex-related establishments: pornographic video delivery services and "delivery fashion health" (*deriheru*), a thriving home-delivery version of the "fashion health" stores described above.

51. "Full service" (*honban*) is in fact illegal, but some soapland operators and customers attempt to legitimize the arrangement by having customers pay the front desk clerk for the "bath" but having customers pay the woman individually for the "full service," thus supposedly creating no legal liability for the soapland (which is facilitating a bath, not prosti-

clubs, motels and love hotels, and adult goods shops. A business that falls in one of these categories may not operate within two hundred meters of schools, libraries, and similar institutions. Minors are prohibited from entering.

The law assigns most of the control of these enterprises and enforcement of the law to local governments. Every love hotel must register with the local government, which regulates advertising, hours, and location and may suspend business or close the establishment if it does not comply with the law.[52] To start a love hotel, an entrepreneur must give notice and a detailed business plan to the local prefectural public safety commission. If the commission grants approval to build, the plan is forwarded to the police, who work with prefectural officials to supervise construction and operation.

The reliance on zoning by local prefectural governments is a key element of the statutory scheme. As Michael Young and Frank Upham have each shown in the contexts of sunlight law and large retail store regulation, community involvement is one of the hallmarks of Japanese regulation.[53] Although in this case the government did not resort, to use Upham's phrase, to "privatized regulation," the reliance on prefectures to regulate the sex industry pursuant to local community mores and concerns involves some similar issues, because in each case local groups are able to exert influence over the location of neighborhood undesirables. In some cases, influence takes the form of bribery of local officials, as reflected in the "political contributions" line of the budgets of startup hotels.

Legislators created a significant exception to the zoning scheme: hotels existing before 1985 were grandfathered out (article 28(3)). In a nod to

---

tution) or the woman (who, by not soliciting publicly, is not covered by the law). Although it might seem to be a violation of the law, the law in this legal gray area is seldom enforced, and many soaplands thrive.

52. Articles 2, 27, 28, 30, 31. In 2000, Japanese police reported five violations of the law for love hotels (three operating without a license and two operating in restricted areas) and three violations for motels (including two operating without a license and two additionally operating in restricted areas). See Keisatsuchō, Heisei 12-nen no Hanzai [2000 Crimes], http://www.npa.go.jp/toukei/keiji4/hon290.pdf.

53. Frank Upham, Privatizing Regulation: The Implementation of the Large-Scale Retail Stores Law, in Political Dynamics in Contemporary Japan, 264, ed. Gary D. Allison and Yasunori Sone (1993); Michael K. Young, Judicial Review of Administrative Guidance: Governmentally Encouraged Consensual Dispute Resolution in Japan, 84 Columbia L. Rev. 923 (1984).

local interests, a constitutionally guaranteed freedom of choice of occupation, and the principle against ex post facto legislation, such hotels were free to maintain their location, whether those locations were otherwise counter to the national scheme (next to schools, for example) or the local scheme (in neighborhoods not zoned for love hotels).[54] In some cases, entire neighborhoods full of love hotels were grandfathered. Still, the clause has a catch: *any* love hotel—grandfathered or not—that rebuilds, renovates, or changes its facilities must re-register with local authorities (article 9). The requirement of new registration allows the prefecture to consider the love hotel in the same way it would any nongrandfathered love hotel, thus allowing closure if the hotel's location is prohibited by national or local rules.

The definitional scheme. Definitional approaches to sex-shop zoning regulation are notoriously troublesome.[55] As one Diet member expressed it in a 1984 House of Councillors Finance Committee meeting, "[L]ove hotels where I come from don't put 'love hotel' on their signs, so you can't tell what's a love hotel, what's an inn (*ryokan*) and what's just a simple place to spend the night."[56] Still, once the decision was made to include love hotels under the 1948 Entertainment Law's scheme instead of seeking more creative solutions, such definition became necessary.

The 1985 revisions to the law define love hotels simply as establishments designed specifically for staying all night or rest by customers of opposite sexes, the structure, facilities, and equipment of which are to be decided "by [government enforcement] order." Under this definition alone, of course, love hotels cannot be distinguished from ordinary hotels. The teeth of the statute lie in the accompanying enforcement order,

54. See generally *Sumiyoshi K.K. v. Japan*, Supreme Court, Case No. 120 of 1968 (April 30, 1975) (geographical restrictions on pharmacy location unnecessarily and unreasonably restrict plaintiff's freedom of choice of occupation).

55. When New York City attempted to regulate business that devoted a "substantial portion" of its inventory and space to adult business, enterprises responded by stocking kung fu videos and serving sushi. Dan Barry, With John Wayne and Sushi, New York Sex Shops Survive, N.Y. Times, Jan. 1, 2001, at A1. Because New York's Jazz-Age cabaret law prohibits dancing in bars that do not hold special licenses, bar owners often switch from dance music to the undanceable ("Eleanor Rigby") when inspectors arrive. Michael Cooper, Cabaret Law, Decades Old, Faces Repeal, N.Y. Times, Nov. 20, 2003, at A27.

56. Minutes of Sangiin Ōkuraiinkai [House of Councillors Finance Committee], no. 12, April 7, 1984, at 17 (statement of Shigeru Aoki).

which defines the relevant structure, facilities, and equipment.[57] Article
3(1) specifies that love hotel facilities have (a) rental rooms for rest by
members of opposite sexes[58] and (b) either no lobbies and restaurants or
lobbies and restaurants of small size only. For hotels that can accommo-
date thirty customers or fewer, the lobby and restaurant (neither of which
may be divided into separate rooms) must be more than thirty square meters each to avoid classification and regulation as a love hotel; a greater
number of customers increases the required floor space. Merely building
a space and calling it a lobby is insufficient; a "lobby" technically must be
a place in which customers meet employees face-to-face, sign a guest register, pay for rooms, and receive a room key.

Article 3(2) specifies the structure of a love hotel. If a hotel has (1) separate garages for each car or cars separated by walls or curtains, (2) parking spaces specified by room number, or (3) hallways that lead directly
from parking space to room, it's a love hotel. Article 3(3) specifies love
hotel equipment. If a hotel has (1) revolving beds, mirrors larger than one
square meter on the ceiling, wall, or attached to the bed, or other device
to arouse "sexual curiosity" or (2) vending machines selling sexually ex-
citing products (separately defined to include nude pictures, albums,
movies, tapes, disks, CD-ROMs, or other sexual products), it's a love
hotel.

Finally, the vagaries of the enforcement order are defined in the Standard Commentaries, a legal reference used by police officials enforcing
the law. Police are the primary means of enforcement in the institutional
scheme and frequently are consulted by love hotel operators to determine
the legality of their operations. Accordingly, the Commentaries are relied
on by hotel operators as a safe harbor.[59] The Commentaries state that
equipment includes "transparent bath tubs, sadomasochistic goods, and

57. Fūzoku Eigyō tō ni Kisei oyobi Gyōmu no Tekiseika tō ni Kansuru Hōritsu Sekōrei,
Order no. 319 of 1984.

58. Love hotels catering to a gay clientele would be legal under this definition. But same-
sex customers do not comprise a large segment of love hotel guests. Although there are a
handful of gay-friendly love hotels, employees at most love hotels who spot same-sex
couples on closed-circuit cameras often deny entry, citing security and safety concerns potentially too large for a small working staff. See Suzuki, *supra* note 1, at 185–88.

59. Keisatsuchō Seikatsu Anzen Kyoku, Fūzoku Eigyō tō no Kisei Oyobi Gyōmu no tekiseika Tō ni kansuru Hōritsu nō to Kaishaku Kijun [Standard Commentary on the Entertainment Law], Feb. 1999.

video camera equipment with which to film persons in a reclining position."[60] And according to the Commentaries, a mirror over a sink—even a big one—doth not a love hotel make.[61]

EFFECTS

The 1985 revision of the Entertainment Law had two primary effects. First, it gave power to local boards, which means that the location of hotels within a prefecture is predetermined. Second, despite the potential death knell that prefectural governments could have rung for hotels using this power, the legislation ushered in a new era of prosperity and growth for them.

Location

Soon after the adoption of the new regulatory regime for love hotels in 1984, each of Japan's forty-seven prefectures revised its local ordinance system to regulate love hotels. Before revising their zoning codes, most prefectures held public meetings or formed study groups that included community leaders. Based at least in part on these meetings, many prefectures restricted the areas in which love hotels could advertise. In a move with potentially more significant ramifications, every prefecture, in almost every case relying on existing zoning regulations for the formal framework, restricted the areas in which love hotels could function. The result is that they are often grouped closely together in zones, and some neighborhoods seem awash in neon.

The granting to prefectural governments of the power to regulate love hotels doomed potential owners like Torii, the builder in the small town of Iimori, discussed above. Torii's victory in the High Court came in March 1983. But unfortunately for him, the revised Entertainment Law was passed in 1984. In December of that year, before Torii could build his hotel, Nagasaki Prefecture, under the authority of the revised law, passed its own public morals regulations. Those regulations included a provision allowing love hotels only in designated zones. With the prefecture's provision firmly in place, Iimori abolished its permission ordinance, mooting the pending Supreme Court appeal. Thus, Torii lost the battle, and I am

60. Ibid., article 5, subsections 4, 17.
61. Ibid., subsection 16.

told by his lawyer that the land on which his love hotel was supposed to be built now sits vacant.[62]

Although grandfathered hotels had few qualms about the placement rules, those rules played a role in determining location for potential new entrants into the market, which were forced either to change location or change their business plan. The following section illuminates their choices.

Prosperity and Growth

A dramatic restructuring of the entire hotel industry occurred after 1985. The changes can be seen in three hotel categories, for which some terms of art are necessary: (1) hotels that fit the 1985 statutory definition of love hotels ("statutory love hotels"), (2) hotels that do not fit the statutory definition of love hotels but nevertheless clearly function as love hotels ("extralegal love hotels"), and (3) those that are not love hotels, at which businesspeople, singles, and families are welcome ("ordinary hotels"). Categories two and three sometimes overlap. Because the data allow it, I further divide ordinary hotels into large hotels (full-service Western-style hotels) and inns (smaller hotels that include some business hotels, some city hotels, and all Japanese-style *ryokan*).

I first attempt to determine the extent of industry change in these categories. I then argue that industry changes were caused primarily by the law and that one mechanism by which the law effected change was social legitimization. Finally, I discuss alternative explanations for the observed changes.

I rely primarily on two types of evidence: available quantitative data, including publicly available data and data obtained from anonymous sources, and interviews of persons in the business. In a few cases I present interview data collected by Japanese scholars. Such data, though sparse, mesh remarkably well with the data that I personally collected, suggesting that my sample is not unrepresentative. In all cases, of course, the evidence is imperfect, but given that parts of my claim concern infor-

---

62. *Torii v. Mayor of Iimori*, Supreme Court, 19 Hanrei Chihō Jichi 60 (June 6, 1985). See also Fūzoku Eigyō tō no Kisei oyobi Gyōmu no Tekiseika tō ni Kansuru Hōritsu Sekō Jōrei, Nagasaki Ordinance 42, Dec. 25, 1984 (regulation); Iimorichō Ryokan Kenchiku no Kisei ni Kansuru Jōrei wo Haishi suru Jōrei [Order to Abolish Order Relating to Iimori Inn Construction Rules], 36 Gyōsei Jiken Saiban Renshū 131. A few local governments still maintain provisions like that of Nagasaki and require mayoral consent for love hotel construction; see, e.g., http://www.city.sakai.osaka.jp/reiki/honbun/s0000382041310101.html.

mation held by insiders and the perception of love hotels in Japanese society, it seems appropriate to include it.

Post-1985 change. Figure 6.1 shows the changes in the number of statutory love hotels from 1985 to 2002.[63] As the figure shows, the total number of statutory love hotels nationwide declined from about eleven thousand to less than seven thousand during this period.

The figure shows that the traditional love hotel *as defined by the statute*, with rotating beds, mirrored ceilings, and sex toys, is in decline. Interview data complement the quantitative evidence and suggest that the decline is not temporary. Although national data concerning new love hotel registrations are not publicly available, hotel industry executives and public safety commissioners uniformly told me that to their knowledge, there have been *no* new registrations since 1985. In other words, the decline is solely the result of pre-1985 hotels closing their doors.

But a silver lining for the industry exists in the form of extralegal love hotels. The total number of statutory love hotels, as seen in figure 6.1, is a little less than seven thousand.[64] But no one with even a passing familiarity with the industry seriously believes that this is the true number of hotels in Japan that exist primarily for sex. Industry data are quite specific: there are 37,417 love hotels, with an average of 16.87 rooms, supporting 576 million couples and generating ¥4.32 trillion ($43 billion) in annual revenue.[65] Another author, citing no specific data source, says that the figure is thirty-five thousand,[66] and the *Tokyo Journal*, relying on an older love hotel guidebook, says that it is thirty thousand.[67] Whatever the actual figure, the statutory love hotels form only the official, regulated portion of this larger group; the rest are extralegal love hotels.

To become the owner of an extralegal love hotel, an entrepreneur need only avoid the narrow definitional provisions of the Entertainment Law. A hotel that has a lobby and a restaurant and has no rotating beds, large mirrors, or sex toys is not a statutory love hotel. It still must register—all

63. White Papers from before 1984 list only the number of motels and are thus incompatible. The data for motels alone suggest that the number of facilities increased steadily until 1984.

64. Keisatsuchō, Keisatsu Hakusho [White Paper on Police] (2003).

65. Futabasha, *supra* note 1, at 104–5.

66. Yasuda, *supra* note 4, at 8.

67. Andreas Stuhlmann, Love Hotels: Between a Rock and a Soft Place, Tokyo Journal, April 2000, available at http://www.tokyo.to/backissues/apr00/tj0400p6-10/.

Figure 6.1. Number of Statutory Love Hotels, 1985–2002

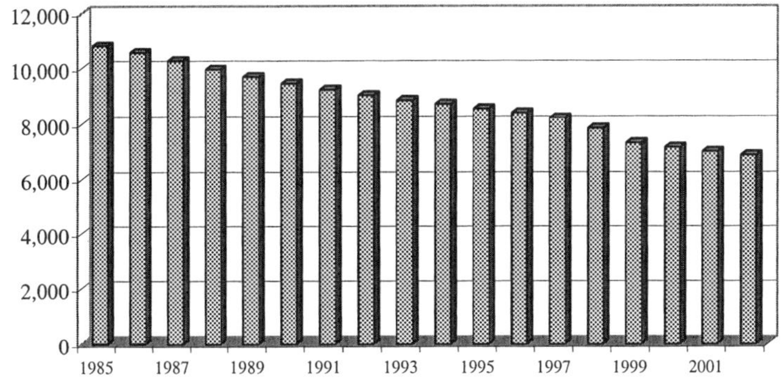

Source: Keisatsuchō, Keisatsu Hakusho [White Paper on Police], various years.

types of hotels, from luxury hotels to small inns, are required to register with prefectural authorities—but it registers as an ordinary hotel, not as a love hotel. Because of the smaller size of extralegal love hotels, they usually register as inns and not as large hotels.

Determining precisely the number of extralegal love hotels is difficult. The combined total of registered large hotels and inns fell from 84,328 in 1985 to 73,051 in 2000, while the number of rooms rose from 1.28 million to 1.57 million.[68] The decline in hotels and inns comes from the inn component; as the number of big luxury hotels increased over the period from 3,332 to 8,220, the number of smaller inns decreased from 80,996 to 64,831. But these statistics do not tell us how many of those hotels—especially inns—and rooms are actually extralegal love hotels, and each is of course affected by the specifics of the Japanese leisure and travel industry. Industry insiders and experts whom I interviewed estimated that the total number of extralegal love hotels rose from a handful in 1985 to approximately 30,000 today. This figure of course lacks scientific precision, but it is not inconsistent with the industry's gross figures for love hotels.

Extralegal love hotels arose from three sources to create the "Big Bang" in love hotels.[69] First, new market entries chose the vehicle. This option thus helps explain the lack of new love hotel applications; it seems unlikely that an entrepreneur would purposely subject himself to increased policy scrutiny by furnishing rooms with mirrors and rotating beds when

68. Kōseishō Hōkoku [Statistical Report on Health Administration Services], various years.

69. Inoue, *supra* note 4, at 399.

in fact he could omit these amenities, replace them with others, and register as an ordinary hotel or inn.

Second, many pre-1985 love hotels that converted to the extralegal form often had good reasons to avoid the new statutory love hotel classification; in addition to placement restrictions, many wanted to avoid excessive consultation with police and other state officials. To evade scrutiny, many love hotels made cosmetic changes such as the addition of dining rooms. But to the surprise of their managers, customers actually began to *use* the dining facilities in the same way that they might use such facilities at an ordinary hotel. As one long-term cleaning person told me: "[The boss] tore out a stairwell to make space for a dining room. I thought he was crazy; what does he think a love hotel is for? But apparently he had to do that to avoid getting shut down. I couldn't imagine that anyone would use such a thing. I occasionally made simple things for room service, but that was a pretty short menu—eggs, toast, rice balls. When people actually came and sat at the table to order stuff, I was really surprised! It's like all of a sudden we were the Prince Hotel or something; it was such an exaggeration [ōgesa]."

Third and finally, some extralegal love hotels initially were very ordinary hotels. As statutory love hotels decreased in number and became more expensive, many customers chose ordinary hotels for liaisons in their place.[70] Ordinary hotels in Japan traditionally made about 70 percent of their revenues from wedding parties; room rentals were a relatively small part of the business. But with the new influx of customers, ordinary hotels began to introduce hourly rates for "day use" in order to capture the love hotel crowd. Although these day-use plans were not explicitly advertised as sexual, usage patterns were quite similar, and these establishments thus became extralegal love hotels.

As love hotels and ordinary hotels evolved toward a common model, distinguishing the two became more difficult. Hotels with models of King Kong on the roof are extremely likely to be love hotels, but not all cases are so clear-cut, because with some modification, both types fit in the category of extralegal love hotels. And with only slightly more modification—adding a big mirror or two or providing hardcore sexual paraphernalia when the police are not looking—they can easily function illegally as "true" love hotels.

The distinction between love hotels and ordinary hotels is based

---

70. See, e.g., Inoue, *supra* note 4, at 365.

largely on factors not mentioned in the statute but known to most Japanese adults. For instance, love hotels, whether statutory or extralegal, often hang a curtainlike divider in the driveway (except those in prefectures that prohibit the practice), but ordinary hotels do not. Love hotels have a "vacancy/no vacancy" sign, but most ordinary hotels do not. Love hotels post rates for short-term stays, but ordinary hotels do not. And for the former, excessive neon remains a giveaway.

Although most extralegal love hotels are identifiable as love hotels from the outside, many ordinary big hotels also run a sex-related business that was either not available or seldom used before 1985. Insiders such as Shiroo Kimura, the representative director of real estate developer Tachibana Corporation, which owns many love hotels, offers the following estimates of ordinary hotel usage patterns:

When we recruit new employees and ask them about their prior employment, more than half of them come from big ordinary hotels in cities. From interviews of those recruits, we learn that more than half of those big hotels are actually love hotels. When they go to clean the rooms, the evidence is all over the place. Rooms without the "evidence" are a slim minority. . . . The only difference between the big ordinary hotels and love hotels is the process. . . . These estimates don't just spring from my head; they come from years of interviewing people who actually work in such places.[71]

The phenomenon about which Kimura speaks is not the conversion of inns into extralegal love hotels but the use of big luxury hotels as romantic getaways, often for the noon crowd. Kimura's comments suggest that about four thousand of the eight thousand ordinary big hotels function to some extent as extralegal love hotels. My interviewees, including those from ordinary hotels, made similar statements, and observation—including noon rates at the Kyoto Holiday Inn, of all places—tends to confirm them.

Although it might not sound unusual for couples to use luxury hotels for sex, before 1985 they were seldom viewed as an avenue for that purpose. Big hotels were primarily for weddings, banquets, family trips, vacations, and foreigners, not for romantic getaways. One industry expert whom I interviewed was particularly forthcoming about the change: "Do you think that the Hotel Nikko Tokyo and all those other hotels out that

71. Hanada, *supra* note 4, at 159.

way [by the coast and Disneyland] are just for schoolgirls who want to see Disneyland? Those places couldn't survive without sex. It's only a quick jump on the train from the city, and [the man] gets big points for taking his girl there." At the aforementioned Hotel Nikko Tokyo, which indeed has a reputation as a romantic spot, I was told: "We most certainly are not a love hotel. . . . Our customers are very discriminating people with good taste, and we strive to please all elements of our broad customer base. . . . It is true that we make special advertisements to couples at romantic holidays such as Christmas, but that is only one small element of this hotel's service . . . we also hold many weddings, host foreign dignitaries, and hold musical and other special events." Again, this particular usage pattern may not be unusual by American standards; hotels in the United States similarly advertise weekend getaways, cater to "nooners," and host parties and other social events that may lead to sex in its rooms. In this respect, Japanese luxury hotels are more akin to their American counterparts than to Japanese love hotels, and I do not with to exaggerate the importance of these four thousand Japanese establishments. The point is not luxury hotels' share of the love hotel market but the fact that usage patterns changed after 1985.

Combining the available quantitative evidence and the estimates gleaned from my interviews allows us to construct a rough (perhaps *very* rough) picture of the changes that occurred from 1985 to 2000. Figures 6.2 and 6.3 estimate hotel population for each of those dates.[72]

Figure 6.2, which relies on official registration data for all but the love hotel estimate, shows that inns comprised the bulk of the hotel industry in 1985. Love hotels, which were regulated at the time only by the Inn Law, numbered only about thirty thousand establishments, and large luxury hotels comprised only a tiny share of total establishments.

Figure 6.3 uses official registration data for statutory love hotels and the total numbers of ordinary inns and ordinary large hotels but relies on estimates from interviews for the breakdown of the other two categories. As the figure shows, inns have now effectively split into two separate categories: ordinary inns and inns functioning as extralegal love hotels. Statutory love hotels comprise only a small category, because extralegal love hotels largely fulfill that function. Ordinary big hotels have doubled in number, and about half are said to serve a sex-based clientele.

---

72. I omit from each figure a few minor establishments such as bed-and-breakfasts and public facilities that house school groups.

Figure 6.2. Hotel Distribution, 1985

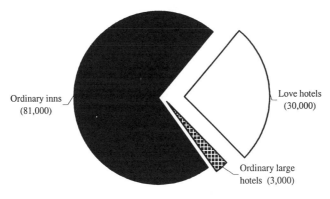

Ordinary inns
(81,000)

Love hotels
(30,000)

Ordinary large
hotels (3,000)

Figure 6.3. Hotel Distribution, 2000

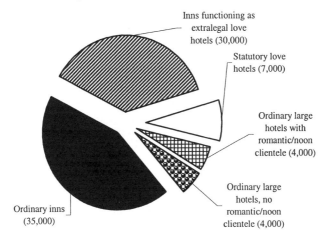

Inns functioning as
extralegal love
hotels (30,000)

Statutory love
hotels (7,000)

Ordinary large
hotels with
romantic/noon
clientele (4,000)

Ordinary large
hotels, no
romantic/noon
clientele (4,000)

Ordinary inns
(35,000)

Allowing substantial leeway for the imprecision of the above estimates, establishments similar to love hotels appear to have increased by
about one-third during the fifteen-year period. The data are even more
imprecise with respect to issues such as customers and profits; the available time-series estimates typically assume maximum usage rates and
simply multiply the number of establishments or rooms by estimated
room charges and turnover rates. Inevitably, these estimates show increases in both customers and profits. Still, all interviewees to whom I
spoke firmly stated that each increased substantially during the period,
and this trend indeed appears to have been the experience at the hotels
that I visited. It is of course possible that interviewees are inaccurately

extrapolating their personal experiences or unintentionally exaggerating industry health, but I see little systemic reason to doubt the interviewees' veracity.

I was unable to obtain precise customer and profit data for the period for the industry as a whole, but the evidence that I was able to compile suggests increases for some establishments even in what is arguably the weakest segment of the industry: the shrinking market for statutory love hotels. Those that chose *not* to convert to extralegal, less sex-oriented facilities after the 1985 revisions faced two possibilities: closure or survival as statutory love hotels. As the data in figure 6.1 suggest, closure was likely. Statutory love hotels that did well before the regulation could not survive the intense competition from extralegal hotels that faced less police scrutiny. More damning for many hotels were the renovation provisions: renovation meant new registration, and new registration for grandfathered hotels in otherwise prohibited areas meant closure (or conversion to extralegal love hotels). Hotels that never renovate lose customers as they deteriorate.

But for a few statutory love hotels, the 1985 legislation signaled prosperity. The new legal scheme effected at least two economic trends. First, and perhaps most obviously, it eliminated competition from certain areas by granting grandfathered hotels a monopoly over business in prohibited areas. Second, the law indirectly segmented the market between statutory love hotels, extralegal love hotels, and ordinary hotels, allowing consumers to differentiate among them more easily. As a result of these two trends, the new limits placed on statutory love hotels, to the dismay of their critics,[73] actually increased the prominence and profits of survivors. Although the data about usage are more difficult to ascertain, industry officials claim, and private data also suggest, increased usage in the unregulated period.

I examined financial data supplied to me on the condition of anonymity from ten statutory love hotels. Seven have been in business since before 1984. Seven is admittedly not a large number, and this evidence is by no means definitive. Perhaps most obviously, and most potentially problematic, these data are subject to survivorship bias: firms that are still around for me to interview did well enough in the 1980s to remain in business. To supplement these data, then, I obtained financial information from three

73. See Hanada, *supra* note 4, at 209.

additional statutory love hotels: one that closed in 1986, one that closed in 1990, and that closed one in 1991.

Of the seven existing hotels, two (both, coincidentally, in Kyushu) kept detailed customer records. One hotel showed a customer increase of nearly 75 percent in 1985; the other, an increase of 24 percent. One raised rates in 1985; the other, in 1986. All seven had general data about profits and losses on at least an annual basis. All seven recorded an increase in net profits in 1985, the year the law took effect, and six of the seven recorded further increases in 1986. Because of promises of anonymity and questions regarding precisely how each hotel kept its books, it would be both inappropriate and misleading to report here the financial data for each particular hotel. But taken as an aggregate, and with the requisite caveat about the accounting standards of love hotel operators, the average increase in net profits for the seven hotels in 1985 and 1986 was 27.8 percent.

Data from the three now-defunct hotels show an unexpectedly similar story. Those that closed in 1990 and 1991, their owners told me, did so because of insufficient revenue, which they attributed to (a) an inability to renovate without facing closure and (b) a lack of viability of extralegal love hotels among their customer base. The owner of the Tokyo-area hotel that closed in 1986 gave me a panoply of reasons why his "family-run" hotel was forced to close, including the following: "I was tired of dealing with the police," "the girls [prostitutes] wanted more money," "we couldn't keep up with the competition," "I wanted more time for fishing," and "we wouldn't pay dues to the [yakuza]." None of the three hotels had solid customer data, but all three owners stated that their business *increased* after the law's passage. The hotels that closed in 1990 and 1991 experienced increased profits of 5.6 percent and 8.2 percent, respectively, in 1985; it was not until 1989 that profits began to fall. Somewhat surprisingly, even the hotel that closed at the end of 1986 performed slightly better in 1985 than in 1984.

Cause of change. The previous section suggests a restructuring of Japan's hotel industry in the mid- to late 1980s, the creation of a new love hotel sector with no apparent decrease in overall numbers, and an increase in profits for (some) surviving statutory love hotels. Although we can never be certain about causation, interview data strongly suggest that the law was a dominant factor.

Love hotel operators, love hotel design and management consultants, regular customers, city hotel operators, love hotel industry representatives, antihotel campaign leaders, and police in charge of enforcing the Entertainment Law all told me of vast increases in profits, customers, and reputation—and all attributed that result to the revisions. Note that these interviewees were not all success stories; some actually failed in the restructuring and made "comebacks" in other roles. Although each person told the causal story with different nuances and from a different perspective, among interviewees, the vote for law as a causal factor was virtually unanimous. For instance, one Tokyo-area consultant and owner told me: "The law was supposed to break our back. For some of the old-style love hotels, it did; those guys have a really hard time. But for the rest of us, the law just poured money right into our pockets. We just ate up all the love hotel business, and started more new business at the new hotels than the older generation could have ever dreamed. About all we did at most places was take out the rotating beds, take down the mirrors, and write 'sex' in English instead of Japanese, but that was enough." Tatsuo Koyama, the president of Aine System Group, a corporation that owns and operates 129 hotels with 2,743 rooms from Hokkaido in the north to Kagoshima in the south, expressed similar sentiments to a Japanese interviewer:

After the new Entertainment Law, as long as you followed the rules for building—not for building a love hotel, but for building an *ordinary* hotel—you could build anywhere you wanted. Financial institutions were lending money more freely than in the past. The outside changed to look like a "business" hotel but the inside was just a love hotel. . . . To put it simply, it made our business a lot easier. The essence of a love hotel is a place for men and women to have fun; a place may look like a "business hotel," but inside it's really a love hotel. On top of this, the new Entertainment Law wiped out our old dark image; rather than being a minus, the law was a real plus.[74]

Koyama's reference to financial institutions is interesting. On one hand, it might refer to the booming late-eighties economy in which many financial institutions lent more freely to all players. On the other hand, it might refer independently to increased confidence on the part of banks in the security of their lending transactions. If the latter, the confidence might have been created or bolstered by the Entertainment Law, which

---

74. Tatsuo Koyama, interview, in Hanada, *supra* note 4, at 205.

gave lenders who cared some assurance of the legality of the enterprise. Although I was unable to speak with lending agents who regularly loaned to love hotels, the borrowers (love hotel operators) told me that they believed that both were factors, with greater emphasis on the latter.

Love hotel owners also cite the law as a primary reason why the number of statutory love hotels is decreasing despite the profits that we observed shortly after 1985. When I asked why more owners do not cater to the rotating-bed crowd, owners cited zoning restrictions. Permissible locales for statutory love hotels are limited. Many of these permissible zones are red-light districts that attract a questionable clientele and therefore police attention. It's simpler, owners said, to offer other amenities instead, and only a small, "nostalgic" customer base seems to care that the amenities are not the ones specified by law.

Similarly, both of the Kyushu hotel owners discussed above (whose records reflected profits after 1985) told me that they attributed their success directly to the law. One said that the law put their primary competition, which had previously been only five hundred meters away but across the prefectural border, out of business. The other attributed to the law the fact that his customer base increased to include more "regular people." Suzuki (a pseudonym), the owner of the hotel that closed at the end of 1986, told a similar story:

Suzuki: [My hotel] went under, but that's not really the law's fault. Every love hotel in Japan should have a statue in the lobby of whatever idiot politician came up with that law. As long as you're not running a brothel with naked people running in the streets next to a school, everything is fine. And if you've been around a while you wouldn't even have to close if you were next to the school.

Q: But you couldn't build anything new next to a school, right?

Suzuki: Sure, but who wants to do that anyway? For most hotels, you just have to decide what kind of business you're going to run and stick to the law. As long as they did that, customers came more after the law than before the law.

Compare these comments to those of a manager at a large ordinary hotel:

We had a hard time expanding our business. The Japanese hotel industry is really competitive, and the only way we can compete in our price range is location. Before the law, we wouldn't have dreamed of competing with the love hotels.

Those places were too far removed from what we do; they were the "underside" (*ura*) of the hotel industry, like a black market. But when they became regulated, we decided to change our business to compete with them for two reasons. . . . First . . . we knew what the limits were now, because the law defined them. Second, the public now knew the limits as well, and they started to come to hotels in droves.

The latter comments echo those of others who suggested that the postrevision trends would not have occurred in the absence of the law. Managers and owners of ordinary hotels, including both the former inns operating as extralegal love hotels and luxury hotels whose clientele includes a similar crowd, had feared that entry into the love hotel market would be risky, tarnish their image, and might be illegal. And though some love hotels could have attempted to make their services appear more legitimate (and some did before 1985) to attract more customers, such efforts alone, I was told, were insufficient to change public perception.

Interestingly, campaigners against love hotels expressed similar views about causation, but with a more negative slant. Although they might be expected to be pleased with the cleaner and more upscale love hotel market, many blame the law for the increase in population:

Opponent: Many of us viewed the 1985 law as a victory. There had been no law to control the industry, and now there was. What we didn't realize was that by defining love hotels, the law was actually defining what a love hotel is not. If you don't want to be treated as a love hotel, all you have to do is create a "non-love-hotel" love hotel, and of course that's what everybody did.

Q: But isn't that success? Some "dirtier" establishments appear to have gone out of business.

Opponent: I wouldn't call it a complete failure. For instance, there now is regulatory authorization for local governments to keep the more dangerous elements out of some neighborhoods. But the old hotels, even though they're dying off, are still right there, and even the more decent hotels still cause the sorts of problems that we were worried about 20 years ago. . . . There is no check of identification, so anyone who looks 18 to somebody watching the [outdoor or hallway] video feed can get in, and they're not going to stop anyone anyway. There still are crimes committed behind these closed doors that I can't even imagine . . . prostitution is just the obvious one. And of course, there [are] always the children.

Q: What does this have to do with children?

Opponent: Kids see this stuff all around them. Lots of kids can't even walk to school without passing a few love hotels.

Q: What do you see as the danger in that? . . .

Opponent: Most Japanese think that it's not a problem; that's why it's allowed. They just think that sex is part of life, like filling your car with gas. Actually, I think the same, but you don't have a first-grader take your car to the service station. . . . Think about how [the love hotel regulatory scheme] would work for service stations. It's like saying, "If you look like a candy store, kids can buy gas there." That's essentially what the Entertainment Law did for love hotels; it made them all try to look like candy stores.

Finally, some entrepreneurs who work exclusively with statutory love hotels lament their demise as result of the law. As love hotel "planner" Shin Amii (a stage name; Amii's designs are copied throughout Japan) puts it: "Young people don't know real love hotels. The revised Entertainment Law made it harder to do my job, but if you'll just try one of my rooms, you'll never go back. I don't try to be like an ordinary hotel or be cute. My thinking might be juvenile, but I like to put things in the room that move. For instance, things like a tree swing with a built-in vibrator."[75]

Mechanism of legal change. The quantitative and interview data hint at two complementary mechanisms that may underlie the ability of the 1985 revisions to effect industry change. The first, market segmentation and monopolization, has been discussed, but the second possibility is more difficult to prove but also more intriguing: the law legitimized love hotels in the minds of consumers.

As discussed above, some people in Japan traditionally view indoor sex establishments as seedy locales that were not for amateurs: inside is for pros. Though love hotels began to change the norm, it remained prevalent for many ordinary couples. With regulation, however, the state unwittingly legitimized the love hotel industry in three specific and related ways. First, as discussed above, *ordinary* hotels turned to the love hotel clientele. In so doing, the overall love hotel market actually became more

75. Hanada, *supra* note 4, at 165–66.

legitimate, at least in the sense that hotels were cleaner, more open, and less overtly sex-oriented.

Second, the 1985 legislation increased incentives for love hotels to be less obviously intended for sex in order to avoid regulation or to build in nonexcluded areas. To avoid having their establishments classified and regulated as love hotels, owners, in addition to building dining rooms, removed the more explicit sexual paraphernalia from rooms. Gone were rotating beds, see-through bathrooms, and large mirrors specified in the regulations;[76] in their place, they added saunas, video games, tanning beds, massage chairs, and the like. The gaudy royal palace motifs of the 1970s gave way to more muted architecture, the "gorgeous" was replaced by the "cute," and love hotels began advertising themselves as "fashion" hotels.

To avoid the increased police scrutiny that accompanied the legislation, most love hotels, statutory or otherwise, stopped serving directly as liaisons between customers and prostitutes. To some extent, competition had already begun this trend; prostitutes found that they could avoid paying liaison fees to hotels by advertising directly to customers, and customers began negotiating directly with prostitutes for hotel-based services. Most hotels now post signs banning male customers from entering alone, a policy designed to end the practice of hotel-arranged prostitution. The net result of these changes is that although many love hotels can still be identified from the exterior as such, the interiors of many establishments look very similar to those of ordinary hotels. And unless the establishment is a statutory hotel or is a site for obviously illegal activity, police scrutiny is light.

Third, many statutory love hotels in fact changed their business and marketing little if at all, but the mere fact of regulation, accompanied by spillover effects from the newly legitimate hotels, may have legitimized them as well. The legal revisions were well publicized, and many customers knew of them. Industry officials and hotel operators told me the same story that I heard informally from the customers themselves: some customers apparently interpreted regulation as a latent form of approval. One operator, who first became a customer in 1985 and then entered the industry as a manager in 1996, turned the conversation from business to personal matters:

76. See Yasutaka Abe, Rabuhoteru Gekitaisaku [Anti-Love-Hotel Measures], 430 Hō-gaku Seminaa 68 (1990).

Customer: I was just a stupid kid then from the countryside. We didn't have fancy things like love hotels, and the girls were so naïve that they probably wouldn't have gone if we had. . . . So when I came to Osaka and saw love hotels [in the early 1980s] I was really curious but at the same time scared. The girls were scared of these places too, at least the nice ones. So anytime I got a girl we just went back to my room, which was pretty small. Only four-and-a-half tatami mats, you know! But I was working as a taxi driver then, and taxi drivers don't have anything to talk about but roads, sumo, baseball, and sex, and I remember hearing from them that these gaudy places had now had government approval. Well, it must be OK then, I thought, so I went.

Q: And how was it?

Customer: It depends on where you went. Some places were really nice; others were just complete dumps. But even the dumps didn't seem so bad. I always figured, "If these places were *really* awful, the cops would have shut them down." They might have been dumps, but the law made them *official* dumps.

Suzuki, the owner of the hotel closed in 1986, continuing the conversation quoted above, complemented these sentiments:

Q: Why did customers increase after the law was passed?

Suzuki: They stopped worrying that the police would haul them off to the pokey, or that the rooms would have dirty sheets. But most importantly, they stopped thinking that they were dirty people for going there. This was especially important for the women—the men usually propose the sex, so women want to at least have some say over the location.

Q: But even today, hotels hide license plate numbers in the garage, so somebody must still find this stuff a little embarrassing, at least, no?

Suzuki: A lot of people are just embarrassed about the person that they're going *with*, not the fact that they're going. "Doing it" is only natural. . . . . Some people are still a little embarrassed, but it's not enough to keep them away anymore.

Q: But your hotel failed, right? Why was the law unable to give you enough extra unembarrassed customers to keep you in business?

Suzuki: In the beginning, it did. If it weren't for the law, I would have closed in 1984. I just lost out because I wouldn't play all the extra games. Cops showing up all the time and so on. Plus my little joint couldn't compete with the big new fancy hotels; it was just my wife and me running the place.

Finally, consider the statements of a successful female love hotel "advisor" who regularly helps owners with issues relating to facilities and décor. She was among my more colorful and helpful subjects, and when I asked her how a person becomes involved in the love hotel industry, she volunteered a spicy personal tale worth recounting in detail:

Advisor: I became a hostess [in 1983] at 18. . . . I wasn't one of those tramps that sleeps with the customers, but I was a sucker for good-looking guys, so when somebody tried to pick me up, I often said OK. They used to try to take me to love hotels, and I was curious, but my girlfriends had told me to avoid those places . . . there was something dirty about them, with all that "sexually suggestive" (*yarashii*) neon. I know that must sound funny coming from a hostess, but that's the way I felt. . . . I went a couple of times when there was nowhere else to go but it was never my first choice. . . . But one of my boyfriends was really persistent; he was always pressuring me to go. I guess he liked that stuff, or maybe he just didn't like my apartment. We couldn't use his place because his wife would have objected. Ha! . . . When I kept saying no, one time he said, "Don't you know? Those places are legal now."

Q: Did you think that they were illegal before?

Advisor: I had no clue. I mean, everybody went there, so I guess I thought that they weren't really illegal, but people were always worried that something bad would happen if you went there. I don't know what; hidden cameras or con men or murders or something. But my boyfriend said they were legal, and I checked with my boss, who told me the same thing, so I thought maybe those places aren't not so bad after all. I started going, and I liked all that stuff. Ha! Do I look like someone who would enjoy mirrors on the ceiling?[77]

Q: So the legal revision made you a customer?

Advisor: I guess that's right. Without the law, I might never have become a regular customer; it was just too scary. But what has that got to do with my liking mirrors on the ceiling? Ha! Actually it wasn't so much the mirrors-on-the-ceiling places as it was the nicer hotels that tried to wink at you and pretend that they weren't about sex, but what else are you going to do there on your lunch hour for 5,000 yen an hour? Ha! . . . Those are the places that I liked. But I saw lots of things from a woman's perspective that needed improving, so I decided then that someday I would run my own hotel.

77. Yes.

I cannot postulate with any confidence that regulation created legitimacy equally among all hotels or all customers. Many consumers were unaware of the law and may have been responding more to economic changes than to legitimizing forces, and it seems unlikely that the seediest of love hotels would have been legitimized simply by legal action. Still, I heard enough similar stories in enough interviews, and heard few enough competing explanations, to suggest that for some love hotels, and some customers, it mattered.

Alternative explanations. In the preceding sections, I have attempted to show that the 1985 Entertainment Law revitalized the Japanese love hotel industry. But law, as we have seen, does not operate in a social or economic vacuum, and these factors may play significant causal roles as well. Three contemporaneous and potential causes seem most relevant.

I have already hinted at the first possible co-explanation: the timing of the love hotel industry's restructuring is contemporaneous not only with the passage of the legal revisions but also with Japan's economic boom, or the "bubble years" that caused huge increases in wealth. Although the bulk of the evidence points to law as a dominant causal factor, law might not have had the same force were it not for support of the hotel and leisure industry by freely lending bankers and freely borrowing consumers.

The second co-explanation relies on social phenomena. Perhaps, because of social changes (and internal market forces), industry changes were already coming, and the law was merely a reflection of these changes. Evidence that supports such an explanation exists; a few love hotels switched to more mainstream, "simple" themes in the early 1980s, *before* the legislation was passed.[78] Maybe customers had already grown tired of the rotating-bed scene, which would also suggest a reason why statutory love hotel numbers continue to decline. Moreover, as shown above, social factors clearly played a role before 1985, as well as in the events that led to the passage of the revisions, and there is little reason to suspect that they ceased with the Entertainment Law revisions.

Still, it is difficult to determine *which* social factors might have contributed to the changes and in which direction; plausible arguments can be made that Japan is becoming both more liberal and more conservative regarding sex. Consider three examples. First, "telephone clubs" that allowed men to meet teenage girls for "compensated dates" (*enjō kōsai*)

78. See Inoue, *supra* note 4, at 364–65.

began to appear in the 1980s, and the problem of compensated dates was prominent in the early 1990s.[79] But though such relations were said to have occurred long before telephone clubs came about, it was only in the 1990s that social outrage, as well as legal counterattacks, followed. Second, Viagra and a low-dose contraceptive pill were legalized in the 1990s (the approval of Viagra took six months; approval of the pill required thirty years), but contraception is still not mentioned in the sex education classroom, and AIDS is taught as a "disease of others."[80] Finally, administrative rules that prohibited the showing of female pubic hair in Japanese media were removed in the early 1990s. But the showing of male pubic hair or the genitals of either sex is still off-limits, and social groups that were nonexistent two decades ago now protest sexually violent comic books. These potentially opposing social forces complicate analysis.

Third, other demographic factors do not unequivocally point toward success or failure in the love hotel industry. Japanese society is aging, and this factor might reduce the number of love hotel guests. But more youth now are sexually active, and more have independent income to pay for the rooms. As we'll see in chapter 7, Japanese workers are working fewer hours, and thus might have more free time, but the post-1990 recession might reduce their economic options. Japanese young people are marrying and having children later, but this trend would not automatically lead to either an increase or a decrease in love hotel usage patterns.

Persons connected with the trade do not mention such demographic factors, rarely mention social factors, and only occasionally mention the macroeconomy in their explanations of industry change. Instead, they routinely cite the law as the basis for the changes. Their statements, if nothing else, show that there is at least a very strong *perception* that law matters. The evidence presented in the preceding sections suggests that the law did more than change perceptions; the removal of mirrored ceilings and addition of restaurant space was clearly undertaken in direct response to the statute. But such evidence by no means rules out alternative or correlating explanations, and it is likely that some of the forces that led to the law's revision affected the industry independently as well.

79. Andrew D. Morrison, Note, Teen Prostitution in Japan: Regulation of Telephone Clubs, 31 Vand. J. Trans. L. 457, 478 (1998).

80. Sabine Frühstück, Colonizing Sex: Sexology and Social Control in Modern Japan, 186–93 (2003).

CONCLUSION

Sex and sexuality in Japan are different things than in America. This chapter does not argue otherwise, and such Japanese merchandise as explicit comic books (to be read on trains) and used underwear (sold in vending machines), not to mention drastically differing gender roles, suggests that it would be foolish to do so. But in this chapter, I have attempted to show that at least one often-noted peculiarity of Japanese sexual practices—venue—can be better appreciated, if not fully understood, by analyzing it in its historical, social, and legal context.

The 1985 revision of the Entertainment Law led to a reduction in numbers of "real" love hotels but ushered in an era of prosperity for hotels that did not fit the definition of love hotel in the statute but nevertheless provided a similar service. The net effect of the legislation and the social changes that fostered the regulatory change was a healthier overall market for love hotels. Whether that is a plus or a minus is hard to say, even for initial supporters of the law, but the evidence suggests that one important cause of the trend was the law.

CHAPTER SEVEN

WORKING HOURS

We now turn from play to work. For most of the past half-century, Japanese workers have put in far more hours than their counterparts in other industrialized countries.[1] Although long working hours may help explain Japanese economic success, they also are an inescapable part of the fabric of Japanese society (as any other), affecting such basic choices as domicile, marriage, childbirth, and children's education and development.

Several theories have been offered to explain why Japanese workers appear to work so hard. Some scholars claim that this "lust for labor" is a "unique aspect of Japanese culture."[2] This work ethic, as the story goes, is firmly embedded in Japanese society. Hierarchical relations and loyalty, grounded in Confucianism or feudalism, make people work harder for their bosses and not question transfers. Japanese "groupism" discourages individual workers from selfishly leaving early and encourages the drawing of a stark line between "permanent" and "non-permanent" employees.[3] In addition, some studies note that the relatively large number of family-owned businesses in Japan can explain long hours or that long working hours are a tradeoff for early retirement.[4]

1. See, e.g., Organization for Economic Cooperation and Development, OECD Employment Outlook 2000, ch. 5 (2000).

2. Bruce E. Kaufman, The Economics of Labor Markets and Labor Relations (2d ed. 1986).

3. See, e.g., James Abegglen, The Japanese Factory (1958); Masayuki Nomiyama, Rōdō Jikan: Sono Dōkō to Kadai [Trends and Issues of Working Hours], 86 (1989).

4. See, e.g., Kazuo Koike, Understanding Industrial Relations in Modern Japan, 61 (1988); Carl Mosk, Competition and Cooperation in Japanese Labour Markets, 194 (1995).

More anecdotally, anyone who has spent time working for or with Japanese companies knows the amazing ability that many firms have to create daytime busy work. Whether due to organizational structure, accepted decision-making practices, or some inexplicable residue labeled as "culture," the workday at many firms seems to be filled with time-consuming meetings, briefings, and approval processes that accomplish little and require employees to work their hardest after sundown. The serious do work at night, and many of the slackers stick around because it's socially appropriate.

Each theory and anecdote is a plausible explanation for long working hours in some cases. In this chapter, I want to explore an *additional* variable that can, in conjunction with some of these social factors, offer a much richer account of Japanese working life. And unlike some of the other explanations, this institutional variable can be altered in ways that might improve everyday Japanese life.

I hypothesize that Japanese labor law plays an indirect but important role in determining how much people work, especially at the large firms that are the focus of this chapter, but not always in obvious ways. Beginning with a series of cases that arose in the 1950s, Japanese courts regulated the employment market to such an extent that it became practically impossible for most businesses, or at least large ones, to fire workers. As a consequence, large Japanese firms hired a smaller number of workers than were necessary. Large employers rely on the working hours of this undersized cadre of workers, carefully screened to rule out the slothful, as a buffer. In bad times, the size of the workforce makes dismissal unnecessary. In good times, workers are forced to work long hours. These practices kept working hours high for most of the postwar period.

In contrast to these decisions, recent labor statutes helped *reduce* working hours. In the late 1980s and 1990s, interest groups pressed the government for solutions to the working-hour problem. The government responded by passing legislation directly limiting working hours. At the same time, the legislature liberalized rules regarding temporary employees, allowing those persons to take up the slack. The result is a model in which Japanese workers now work less than their U.S. counterparts.

Labor law is by no means the only causal factor. The institutions that I discuss in this chapter are a product of union demands, social and economic forces, international pressure, and many other factors, some of which are idiosyncratic (think of the reasons why *you* work when and where you do). But labor law, in the form of cases and statutes, played an important role in mandating results and in homogenizing throughout Japan an otherwise heterogeneous set of working conditions. As Chiaki Moriguchi explains, law "legitimized the practices and consolidated the expectations as social norms."[5] In so doing, the social forces that led to legal change used law to buttress those same social forces even further.

Recent legal scholarship has examined the relation between institutions and lifetime employment. Dan Foote provides a probing historical account of the judiciary's formulation of a "no-dismissal" policy.[6] Ron Gilson and Mark Roe also mention the role of the judiciary and argue that human capital investment in Japan is better understood using an analysis of the complementary "no-poaching rule" that closed Japan's external labor market.[7] I turn the focus away from the legal origins of "big" lifetime employment to the subsidiary effects of the law in employment markets and, by extension, in low-stakes, everyday Japan. The extent to which the background institutions that I describe influence basic aspects of working life strongly suggests a need for more nuanced examination of employment law structures.

A warning: I did not conduct extensive interviews in this case, as I did for previous chapters, in part because data sets already exist, in part because interviews would not be as helpful in this broad context, and in part because it's likely that even if you know nothing about love hotels or sumo, you know a thing or two about work. The theory that I offer, which attempts to elaborate on what cultural norms matter and why, is a plausible and more empirically grounded alternative to accounts that rely on "culture" alone. The theory is informed by many casual conversations with Japanese workers, managers, lawyers, and judges that I do not cite directly.

DATA ABOUT WORKING HOURS

Long working hours and grueling conditions were commonplace in prewar Japan. At the turn of the century, twelve-hour-a-day, six-day-a-week

5. Chiaki Moriguchi, The Evolution of Employment Relations in U.S. and Japanese Manufacturing Firms, 1900–1960: A Comparative Historical and Institutional Analysis, NBER Working Paper 7939, at 65.

6. Daniel H. Foote, Judicial Creation of Norms in Japanese Labor Law: Activism in the Service of—Stability?, 43 UCLA L. Rev. 635 (1996); see also David Kettler and Charles T. Tackney, Light from a Dead Sun: The Japanese Lifetime Employment System and Weimar Labor Law, 19 Comp. Labor L.J. 1 (1997).

7. Ronald J. Gilson and Mark J. Roe, Lifetime Employment: Labor Peace and the Evolution of Japanese Corporate Governance, 88 Colum. L. Rev. 508 (1999).

194 CHAPTER SEVEN

schedules were common. Many workers, especially women, lived in dormitories that were often compared to prisons, resulting in annual turnover rates of 60 percent at some factories.[8]

Beginning in 1911, the Factory Law regulated working hours. This law limited the maximum time worked each day for women and children to twelve hours, with two days' rest each month, a schedule that could allow more than four thousand working hours per year.[9] It contained no restrictions on working hours for adult males.

By the 1930s, the number of hours worked decreased slightly. In the mining industry in 1930, an average working day was nine hours, seven minutes, a figure that varies by no more than ten minutes over the course of the decade.[10] Nationwide figures are similar. The Bank of Japan and the Ministry of Labor collected survey data on daily working hours and number of days worked each month for workers at manufacturing firms with more than thirty employees. As table 7.1 shows, the number of working hours for the period 1923–1939 is quite large.[11]

By comparison, in the iron and steel industry in the United States in 1920, with about two-thirds of blast-furnace workers and about three-fourths of Bessemer mill workers having twelve-hour shifts, these employees worked an average of 3,270 hours annually, roughly equivalent to the Japanese numbers. But by 1926, working hours in that sector had fallen to 2,860 annually, a figure higher than the U.S. manufacturing average but still far below the Japanese numbers for the period.[12]

During the occupation following World War II, the Japanese work regime was substantially revised by the 1947 Labor Standards Act (Rōdō Kijunhō, Law no. 49 of 1947, the LSA). The LSA established a six-day, forty-eight-hour work week and provided six days' vacation for workers with one year of employment (arts. 32, 32(1), 39(1)). Employers could as-

8. Nōshōmushō Shōkōkyoku, Shokkō Jijō [Work Conditions], 78–79 (1902, reprint, 1971).
9. Kōjōhō, Law no. 46 of 1911.
10. Nihon Tōkei Nenpō 292 (1949). Average industrial working hours during World War II were even higher; an average working day in 1945 is said to have been 11 hours, 14 minutes. Ibid. at 705.
11. I annualized the daily hours by multiplying average daily hours by days worked per month and multiplying by twelve. Japanese economists use similar procedures. See, e.g., Kōji Ishii, Rōdō Jikan to Nihon Keizai [Working Hours and the Japanese Economy], 17 (1982).
12. Martha Ellen Shells, Collective Choice of Working Conditions: Hours in British and U.S. Iron and Steel, 1890–1923, 50 J. Econ. Hist. 379 (1990).

Table 7.1. Annual Hours Worked, 1923–1939

Year	Hours
1923	3,252
1924	3,286
1925	3,231
1926	3,205
1927	3,168
1928	3,196
1929	3,169
1930	3,058
1931	3,037
1932	3,087
1933	3,147
1934	3,186
1935	3,191
1936	3,203
1937	3,219
1938	3,236
1939	3,224

Sources: Rōdōshō, Rōdō Tōkei Chingin Maitsuki Chōsa [Monthly Labor Survey]; Nichigin, Rōdō Tōkei [Labor Statistics], various years.

sign overtime work at the rate of time-and-a-quarter so long as they entered into a so-called "Article 36 agreement" on overtime with a majority of workers.

Compared to the grueling hours of the pre-war era, postwar hours were more reasonable, but they still remained quite high. Two official sources of data about postwar working hours are available. The Ministry of Labor's Monthly Labor Survey polls 16,700 establishments with more than thirty workers, chosen at random. These figures are usually cited as the authoritative and official numbers, but because survey respondents are businesses and not individuals, the figures may understate the total number of hours worked, especially the total number of unpaid and uncounted "service" overtime hours, which are estimated to account for one hundred to two hundred hours per year per worker in Japan.[13]

13. Kōji Morioka, Zangyō oyobi Saabiusu Zangyō no Jittai to Rōkihō Kaisei no Hitsuyōsei [Overtime and Service Overtime: The Need for Revision of Working Hour Legislation], 71 Keizai Kagaku Tsūshin 14, 14–15 (Nov. 1992).

Figure 7.1. Annual Hours Worked, 1948–2001

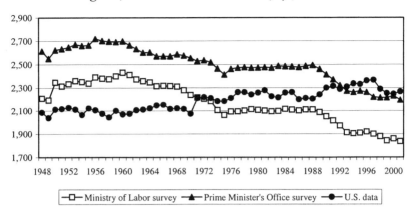

By contrast, the Workforce Survey conducted by the Prime Minister's Office polls households, not businesses, and therefore might gather more accurate data. But this survey is conducted only once a year (the third week of December), and workers may exaggerate the number of hours they worked. Both measures are routinely cited as accurate. Figure 7.1 shows the annualized results of both measures from 1948 to 2001, and for comparison, the annualized hours of United States workers according to employee surveys.[14]

The figure suggests four observations. First, Japanese workers always report higher figures than employers do; either workers exaggerate or employers underreport or both. Second, working hours peaked in Japan in the early 1960s, declined slightly during the 1970s oil shock, and declined again in the 1990s. Third, Japanese workers historically work more than their counterparts in the United States. In 1960, they worked, on average, approximately 620 hours more. Finally, by 1993, the number of hours reported by U.S. employees was higher than the number reported by Japanese employees.

14. Current Employment Statistics Survey (1971–2001); Employment and Earnings Survey (1948–1970). Both available at http://laborsta.ilo.org. Recent studies suggest that in the United States, although reference periods have an impact on data, "independent measures of working time largely corroborate the self-reported measures relied on by the standard surveys." Jerry Jacobs, Measuring Time at Work: Are Self-Reports Accurate?, Monthly Labor Rev., Dec. 1998, at 42, 50. Other survey data support the idea that Japanese workers historically work long hours; a 1990 auto industry survey found that Japanese workers work 2,275 hours, but the French and the Germans work between 1,650 and 1,750 hours. See Gavan McCormack, The Emptiness of Japanese Affluence, 80 (1990).

LABOR LAW

Japanese working hours are shaped by three specific aspects of Japanese labor law. First, the judicially created doctrine of abusive dismissal protects employee job security and in turn drastically limits an employer's ability to dismiss a worker. Second, revisions to the Labor Standards Act and the Temporary Measures Law to Promote Reduction in Working Hours in 1987, 1992, 1993, and 1998 limit the number of hours that employees legally may work. Finally, the enactment of the Worker Dispatching Law in 1985 (effective 1986), and the amendment of that law and the Employment Security Law in 1999, legalized temporary agency employment and liberalized job placement services. The first factor increased working hours; the latter two helped reduce them.

Dismissal

Japanese statutes historically provided few limits on employee dismissal. The Civil Code (art. 627) states that if parties to a contract have not provided otherwise, either party may terminate the contract on two weeks' notice. The LSA (art. 19) prohibits the dismissal of workers who are recuperating from work-related injuries and women on maternity leave, but virtually no one else. The LSA also extends the notice period in the employment context from two weeks to thirty days (art. 10), except when a worker is dismissed, according to section 20, with cause.

It is not the LSA but the judiciary, relying in part on this exception and in part on a constitutionally guaranteed right to work (art. 27), that places substantial limits on dismissal. After examining individual dismissal and group dismissal, I discuss the court's role in the larger labor process, and then turn to exceptions to the rules that results from that role.

Individual dismissal. Beginning in 1950, district courts interpreted section 20 of the LSA to require just cause for dismissal.[15] As Foote explains, "The position is that, regardless of the language of Section 20, there is an implied requirement that discharges be supported by just cause; discharges without just cause are deemed invalid."[16]

---

15. *Iwata v. Tokyo Seimei Hoken Sōgō Gaisha,* Tokyo District Court, 1–2 Rōminshū 230 (May 8, 1950).

16. Foote, *supra* note 6, at 643.

In the early 1950s, courts expanded the just cause analysis to adopt an "abuse of rights" approach, holding that dismissals that abuse employee rights were illegal. By employing this approach—one with statutory justification in a general Civil Code provision (art. 1) to the effect that "no abuse of rights shall be permitted"—courts fashioned a much more subjective approach to determining the legality of dismissals.[17]

The subjective abuse-of-rights analysis has led to a much more stringent approach to employee dismissals. The Supreme Court's decision in the 1977 *Kōchi Broadcasting* case is instructive and typical.[18] In that case, a radio station dismissed an announcer after he overslept twice in a two-week period. In some jobs, such a lapse might not be significant, but in this case, the particular announcer's slumber prevented him from reading the 6 A.M. news. The announcer then tried to cover up his error. In finding that the dismissal was an abuse of the employer's right to dismiss, the court noted that although the oversights damaged the "social credit of the company," plaintiff apologized in both cases, and "the dead air time was not so long." As for the cover-up, the Court held that he was "not to be strongly blamed," because it came "as a result of his awkward position because of his repeated mistakes in a short period."

This abuse-of-rights analysis pervades employee dismissal jurisprudence. Courts have found dismissals to be abusive in cases in which an employee makes several serious bookkeeping errors and engages in personal phone conversations during working hours,[19] and when a salesman enters a coffee shop in the middle of the day.[20] As the Supreme Court explained, "If, under the specific circumstances of the case, the dismissal is unduly unreasonable so that it is not appropriate based on the common sense of society, the dismissal will be void."[21] Because the "common sense of society" is determined by giving great weight to facts

17. Among academics, there was much debate about management's right to dismiss employees. Some of the leading employment law treatises of the time favored free dismissal rights for management. See Mitsutoshi Azuma, Kaikō [Dismissal] (1956); Takashi Yonezu, Kaikōkenron [Dismissal Rights], in Sengo Rōdōhō Gakusetsushi [A History of Labor Law Scholarship], 657, ed. Tsuneki Momii (1996).

18. *Shioda v. Kōchi Broadcasting Co.*, Supreme Court, 258 Rōdō Hanrei 17 (Jan. 31, 1977).

19. *A v. Seikō Kagaku*, Tokyo District Court, 617 Hanrei Jihō 72 (Nov. 20, 1967).

20. *Taguchi v. Takahashi Building K.K.*, Osaka District Court, 617 Hanrei Jihō 92 (Oct. 9, 1970).

21. *Shioda v. Kōchi Broadcasting Co.*, *supra* note 18.

favorable to employees, the result is an extremely restrictive dismissal regime.

In 2003, many of these common law principles were codified. The LSA was revised to state that dismissal must be based on "reasonable grounds" and must be acceptable "in light of social norms,"[22] placing decisions squarely in the hands of the judiciary (and showing quite clearly how messy the interaction of law and social norms can be). If the standard is not met, dismissal constitutes an abuse of right. Although case law has yet to emerge, it seems likely that the relevant "social norms" will be those that have been shaped and buttressed by fifty years of common law cases.

Group dismissal. Also without explicit statutory support, courts have established a four-pronged test for determining the legitimacy of economically motivated group dismissals. First, an employer must show a genuine need to reduce the size of the workforce. Some courts only require a high degree of business difficulty, but others have allowed firms to dismiss only if the failure to dismiss would "inevitably lead to bankruptcy."[23] Second, courts require employers to show that the necessary personnel reduction can be accomplished only by dismissal, and not by other means, such as transfers or layoffs. Third, the selection of workers to be dismissed must be fair and reasonable. Finally, the procedures for dismissal must be proper.[24]

The *Sanyō Electric Company* case is a minor one, but it shows how hard it is to fire workers.[25] In *Sanyō*, as a result of economic hardship brought on by the rising yen, trade friction, and competition from cheap imports, the defendant company dismissed twelve hundred staff members. The Osaka district court noted that the business environment was bad and that some sort of measures may have been necessary. But it stated that nonetheless "the company as a whole would have had enough reserve capital to endure the situation" and that the company should have "made every effort" to clarify which persons truly needed to be eliminated, and even

22. Rōdō Kijunhō no Ichibu o Kaisei Suru Hōritsu [Law to Revise the LSA], Law no. 104 of 2003.

23. Kazuo Sugeno, Japanese Labor Law, 408 (1992).

24. See, e.g., Kazuo Sugeno, Rōdōhō, 450–53 (5th ed. 1999). For cases applying the standard, see *Ikeda v. Sanyō Denki K.K.*, Osaka District Court, 558 Rōdō Hanrei 45 (Feb. 20, 1990); *Hirata v. Hitachi Medico,* Tokyo High Court, 354 Rōdō Hanrei 35 (Dec. 16, 1980).

25. *Ikeda v. Sanyō Denki K.K.*, Osaka District Court, 558 Rōdō Hanrei 45 (Feb. 20, 1990).

then, they should have been given the option of voluntary resignation. Because the defendant did not make "sufficient effort to examine ways to avoid dismissal," the dismissals were deemed invalid.[26]

The courts' role. Scholars have proposed various theories to explain the role of the judiciary in the dismissal context. Foote argues that the courts, in response to cases brought by workers, *created* norms[27]; despite the image of judicial inactivity in Japan, employment rules are created not by statute or administrative guidance but by courts, and they express an overall theme of maintenance of stability in relationships. Other scholars subsequently have argued that "judges' doctrinal adjustments do not stand in isolation from the activities that shape and reshape employment relations, such as employee-labor relations, advocacy lawyering, and foreign legal influences."[28] Signs that the Tokyo District Court attempted to relax the four-pronged test in 1999 and 2000, a move not followed by other regional courts but occurring precisely when restructuring of employment relations became critical to economic turnaround,[29] further suggests a lack of judicial isolation.

The historical evidence strongly suggests that courts were not enforcing longstanding *preexisting* social norms, because lifetime employment was simply not present in prewar Japan.[30] Beyond that observation, the more precise relation between judicial policy and exogenous factors is difficult to entangle. Gilson and Roe's theory that the courts "enforced the post-War practice as it developed . . . buttress[ing] the post-War lifetime

---

26. The doctrine is applied quite broadly. It extends to fixed-term contract employees because courts have long held that the renewal of fixed-term contracts on a regular basis may create a "regular employment" relation. See, e.g., *Toshiba Electric Co. v. Maeda*, Supreme Court, 28-5 Minshū 927 (Jul. 22, 1974); *Ikeda v. Sanyō Denki K.K.*, Osaka District Court, 558 Rōdō Hanrei 45 (Feb. 20, 1990). In 1991, the Osaka High Court went a step further, reversing the District Court to hold that the dismissal doctrine applied to a one-year contract that had never been renewed, despite the company's financial distress and the fact that the employee in question was not very competent. *Tonomizu v. Ryūshin Taxi K.K.*, Osaka High Court, 581 Rōdō Hanrei 36 (Jan. 16, 1991).

27. Foote, *supra* note 6.

28. Kettler and Tackney, *supra* note 6, at 3–5.

29. Satoshi Nishitani, Seiri Kaikō Hanrei no Hōseisakuteki Kinō [The Legislative Function of Group Dismissal Cases], 1221 Jurisuto 29, 31–32 (2002).

30. See, e.g., Sheldon Garon, The State and Labor in Modern Japan (1987); Andrew Gordon, The Evolution of Labor Relations in Japan: Heavy Industry, 1853–1955 (1985).

employment norm by raising the costs to any firm that wanted to change the deal"[31] does not take a firm stance on the issue, and it has been adopted by labor historians.[32] Whatever the precise cause, it is clear that judicially created rules concerning employment forced compliance and spread such employment practices throughout the country.

Exceptions: acceptable dismissals. Courts are said to have enforced a labor-management bargain: in exchange for job security, workers gave up power to controvert management with respect to many other relevant and important issues.[33] In accordance with the bargain, courts allow dismissals when workers oppose management on labor-related issues.

Take overtime work. In *Hitachi* (1991),[34] the Court affirmed the validity of a dismissal of an employee who declined a request to work overtime. A plant union had entered into an Article 36 agreement with management to allow overtime. The employee had previously been insubordinate, and in this particular instance the overtime requested was not the result of a booming economy but was necessary to correct errors that arose from the employee's prior negligence. The Court, finding that the overtime provision was a result of the management-labor bargain, held that the company thus was authorized to request overtime work.[35] The Court simply upheld the preexisting labor-management bargain: job security for control.

31. Gilson and Roe, *supra* note 7, at 526.

32. See, e.g., Andrew Gordon, The Wages of Affluence: Labor and Management in Postwar Japan, 184 (1997) (noting that courts gave "legal force to what was concurrently taking root as an implicit customary bargain"); Moriguchi, *supra* note 5, at 65 (courts "legitimized" and "consolidated" the practice).

33. The bargain may be rational, because workers are risk-averse and prefer job insurance, or, as Kazuo Koike, Masahiko Aoki, and Yoshiro Miwa have all separately argued to some degree, they may receive additional rents as the controlling group of the firm. Kazuo Koike, Understanding Industrial Relations in Modern Japan (1988); Yoshiro Miwa, Firms and Industrial Organization in Japan, 205 (1996); Masahiko Aoki, Information, Incentives, and Bargaining in the Japanese Economy (1988).

34. *Tanaka v. Hitachi Seisakusho,* Supreme Court, 594 Rōdō Hanrei 7 (Nov. 28, 1991).

35. Employees may be dismissed if they oppose a transfer. *Sasaki v. Kōwa*, Nagoya District Court, 31-2 Rōminshū 372 (Mar. 26, 1980); *Ishiguro v. Nippon Stainless Steel Co.*, Niigata District Court, 485 Rōdō Hanrei 43 (Oct. 1986). The refusal to accept certain modifications to working conditions may also lead to dismissal. *Yoshikawa v. Shuhoku Bus Co.*, Supreme Court, 22 Minshū 3459 (Dec. 25, 1968); *Nagai v. Aerotransport* (The Scandanavian Airlines Services Case), Tokyo District Court, 1526 Hanrei Jihō 35 (April 13, 1995).

Statutory Reductions in Working Hours

By the 1960s, the consequences of extreme working hours were evident. Japanese workers were beginning to notice that despite having one of the most productive economies in the world, they enjoyed relatively few gains in the form of reduced time at work. Although the "death from over-work" (*karōshi*) syndrome was not to become a major social issue until the early 1980s, health-related problems ostensibly caused by overwork had begun to appear.[36]

In the early 1970s, the Ministry of Labor attempted to reduce working hours with informal regulation. In 1976, the Central Labor Standards Council formally recommended a reduction in working hours but argued that because of the diversity of working practices and industries, continued informal regulation was preferable to direct legal regulation. The Ministry of Labor continued to hold the position that reductions in hours were best achieved by negotiations between management and labor and that the ministry's role was simply to facilitate such negotiations. But by 1980, the ministry had reversed course, leading to four important developments.

First, in 1982, the ministry proposed a revision of the LSA that would reduce the work week from forty-eight hours in an eight-day week to forty-five hours in a nine-day week. As the debate became a serious public policy issue, labor insisted on a five-day, forty-hour week. Business interests encouraged the ministry to stay out of the debate, but the ministry faced additional pressures for reform. Besides pressing labor interests and a growing domestic public sentiment in favor of reform, the international community had begun to point to excessive Japanese working hours as a possible cause of Japan's growing trade surplus. By linking domestic and international agendas, the labor-influenced ministry was able to submit a working-hours reduction bill to the Diet in 1987. The bill, a revision of the LSA, was a compromise between labor interests, which continued to insist on a forty-hour week, and managerial interests, which continued to oppose any reduction at all. The LSA was amended to establish the forty-hour rule in principle, but according to the Supplementary Provisions of the LSA, this rule was a "goal" to be phased in incrementally. The

36. See, e.g., Note, Kaiulani Eileen Sumi Kidani, Japanese Corporate Warriors in Pursuit of a Legal Remedy: The Story of Karoshi, or "Death from Overwork" in Japan, 21 U. Haw. L. Rev. 169 (1999).

Supplementary Provisions called for the reduction of hours by Cabinet Order "in stages, considering workers' welfare, working hour trends, and other circumstances" (arts. 131–32). As a result, the baseline standard was forty-six hours for the first three years after the amendments took effect in April 1988.[37]

Second, beginning in 1991, the Ministry of Labor proposed that regional Labor Standards Offices, in consultation with local Labor Standards Councils, be given the authority further to reduce working hours to an "appropriate" level. The bill, named the Temporary Measures Law Concerning the Promotion of Reduction in Working Hours,[38] was approved on a fast track, on June 19, 1992, and included explicit language stating that the Ministry of Labor "shall strive to consider the view of the workers" (art. 8(5)).

Third, in 1993, under further pressure from domestic and international interests, the Diet passed a further set of amendments to the LSA and the Temporary Measures Law. Over the opposition of managerial interest groups, the 1993 legislation successfully established for the first time a forty-hour, five-day week, subject to certain exceptions and incremental implementation plans. Thus, by 1993, the forty-hour week, subject to overtime at 125 percent of standard pay and various other exceptions, had become the legally mandated norm.

Finally, in September 1998, in a large-scale overhaul of the LSA, the Diet amended the act to provide that the Minister of Health, Labor, and Welfare may limit overtime hours. The minister did so, providing a maximum of 360 such hours per year.[39]

Temporary Employees

Before passage of the Employment Security Act of 1947, "labor bosses" who farmed out employees to client companies for low pay often created

---

37. See Daniel H. Foote, Law as an Agent of Change? Governmental Efforts to Reduce Working Hours in Japan, in Japan: Economic Success and Legal System, 251, 269–70, ed. Harold Baum (1997).

38. Rōdō Jikan no Tanshuku no Sokushin ni Kansuru Rinji Sōchihō, Law no. 90 of 1992.

39. Rōdōshō Kokuji [Notification of Ministry of Labor] no. 54 (Dec. 28, 1998). Additional measures changed working hours for women. Before 1998, the LSA (art. 64-2) limited women's overtime work to 6 hours a week and 150 hours a year and prohibited work on weekends and holidays. In 1998, amendments (art. 133) made the system applicable on the worker's request in certain situations. That system expired in March 2002 and was re-

hazardous working conditions for workers, many of whom had little choice but to accept if they wanted work.[40] The Employment Security Act sought to regulate the practice by prohibiting "worker dispatching," the causing of a worker employed by one person to engage in work for another under the direction of the latter (art. 44). The act also banned most private job placement services. Although *public* placement services existed, and private services continued to function with special permission of the Minister of Labor, permission was allowed for only twenty-nine specific occupations, effectively creating a public monopoly over job placement (art. 5). The enactment of the Worker Dispatching Law[41] in 1985 (effective 1986) and the amendment of that law and the Employment Security Law[42] in 1999 substantially liberalized both laws.

Worker dispatch. The dispatching of workers was clearly illegal under the Employment Security Law. But in practice, it flourished underground, and companies attempted to avoid legal issues by contracting with supplying firms for work and allowing the supplying firm to maintain a supervisory role.[43] These practices created issues of employment security and ambiguity as to legal responsibility. In an attempt to protect dispatched workers, the Diet legally recognized them in the Worker Dispatching Law of 1985.

Although the law legalized worker dispatch, it maintained two substantial limits on such work. First, pursuant to a related Cabinet Order, it specifically applied to only sixteen specific forms of work, such as secretarial services, filing, cleaning, machinery operation, and computer programming (arts. 4, 59). A 1999 amendment, enacted to comply with International Labor Organization Convention 181's negative listing requirement, eliminated the sixteen categories. The law now lists only the

---

placed by more gender-neutral amendments to the Child and Family Care Leave Law. Pursuant that law, among other things, male and female workers with family responsibilities are exempt from overtime. See Ryuichi Yamakawa, Labor Law Reform in Japan: A Response to Recent Socio-economic Changes, 49 Am. J. Comp. L. 627, 638–40 (2001).

40. Kazuo Sugeno, Koyō Shakai no Hō [Employment Society and Law] 206 (1996).

41. Rōdōsha Hakenhō, Law no. 88 of 1985.

42. Shokugyō Anteihō, Law no. 141 of 1947.

43. Kazuo Sugeno, Japanese Labor Law, 164 (1991); Shigeru Wakita, Rōdōhō no Kisei Kanwa to Kōsei Koyō Hoshō [Liberalization of Working Hours and Guaranteeing Fair Work], 81–138 (1995).

jobs for which dispatched workers may *not* be employed, such as construction, port labor, and medical jobs, but each category is rather broadly crafted.

Second, the law divides dispatch services into "general" and "specified." General dispatch services are for short-term workers who register with an agency. Although specified services are only required to give notice to the Ministry of Labor, general services must be formally licensed (arts. 5–7).

Job placement. The Employment Security Act prohibited the private taking of applications for employment and acting as a go-between to mediate between employer and employee (art. 5). Because job-placement services fell under that definition just as worker dispatch services did, they were prohibited under the law. The only exception to the rule was a small cadre of placement businesses with specific permission from the Minister of Labor to operate in twenty-nine permissible categories of workers such as artists, nurses, chefs, pastry cooks, bartenders, interpreters, models, and the most recently added category (1990), sightseeing-bus conductors (art. 4). But in the 1980s and early 1990s, the Japanese labor market began to change. In response to changing demographics, intensified global competition, and a much more fluid workforce, policy makers began to consider potential options.

Amendments to the 1999 Employment Security Act liberalized private job-placement services in three principal ways. First, it eliminated the general prohibition on such services. Although placement services must still register with the Ministry of Labor, registration requirements have been eased significantly, and registration terms have been extended from one year to three (art. 32).

Second, like the worker dispatch provisions, the amended law contains only a negative listing of categories of workers for which private job-placement agencies cannot serve, including security guards, technicians, and a variety of jobs for recent high school graduates. Like the worker dispatch provisions, the negative listings are quite broad.

Third, the 1999 legislation deregulated placement fees. Prior to passage of the amendments, private services could only charge the amounts listed in an official schedule, up to a maximum of 10.1 percent of six months' wages (art. 24). The amended law maintains maximum fees but allows fees to differ from those listed in the schedule.

EFFECTS

Recall the data about postwar working hours presented above. Those data roughly correlate with the institutional factors I have discussed: hours rose and remained high following court decisions limiting dismissal and fell through the 1980s and 1990s with the introduction of statutory working hour limits and liberalization of the market for temporary employees. In this section I show how those three sets of legal institutions—dismissal rules, reductions in working hours, and rules regarding temporary employees—combine with economic and social factors to effect change in working hours in Japan.

Dismissal

Nondismissal rules. Scholars of the Japanese employment system have long noted the tendency of Japanese firms to substitute variable for fixed employment costs by hiring fewer workers and moderating their hours.[44] What they have not yet done is make the subsequent link to the role of legal institutions in creating the need or the incentives for the buffer.

As shown above, the judicially created nondismissal policy, whether a result of judicial activism or merely a reflection and subsequent distribution of a developing bargained norm, substantially limits the ability of employers legally to dismiss employees. As a result of the inability to dismiss, employers have historically been unable to vary the number of employees with the workload. Employers thus face two options. If they hire too many workers, those workers might be busy in good times, but they will be idle in bad times, and employers will be forced to internalize their costs. If they hire too few workers, this smaller cadre will force lower internalized costs in bad times but will have to work many more hours in good times. Employers in Japan historically have chosen the latter option, and as a result, workers are forced to work extremely long hours during period of need. If they refuse, in accordance with the nondismissal bargain, they can be fired.

Recent overtime data tend to support the claim. In 1989, when the Japanese economy was booming, annual overtime for companies with more than 500 workers was 246 hours. After the bubble burst, average

---

44. See, e.g., Clair Brown et al., Work and Pay in the United States and Japan, 194 (1997).

overtime in 1993 was 153 hours.[45] As Yasuo Suwa explains: "Overtime work functions as a sort of invisible work force which will minimise the number of surplus employees during business downturns. . . . Total work hours in Japan, in fact, tend to be quite responsive to business fluctuations: they become longer during business booms and shorter in recession."[46]

For this system to work, employers must exercise intense scrutiny at the hiring stage to find hard workers and weed out lazy ones. This is exactly what Japanese employers do. Of course, the evidence of future hard work available to employers at hiring time may not be as reliable as, for instance, billable hours in a law firm at the time of the partnership decision. Although many companies do not rely heavily on university grades in hiring (university students, once admitted, are not expected to work hard), they do rely heavily on the reputation of the university an applicant attended. Employers thus use the entrance examination as a sort of proxy for hard work; they are unlikely to take a chance on a smart student from a lesser school. Employers also rely quite heavily on grades from high schools for applicants for whom a university education is not required.[47]

Employees also self-select for hard work. Just as hard-working young lawyers flock to large law firms that demand high billable hours, so, too, do young Japanese workers join firms that suit their workstyle. There is evidence to suggest that if these young workers decide that the pace is not for them, they leave the firm; for males in their twenties, turnover rates at Japanese firms are 20 to 25 percent.[48]

Lazy workers not cut out for large firms have three basic options. First, they can quit and work for small firms, which are not subject to the nondismissal bargain. Large firms ordinarily cannot meet the "genuine need" standard necessary to lay off workers; small firms can more easily do so. Second, they can continue in their sloth until their employer transfers them to a small subsidiary or otherwise related firm, which can fire

45. See Yoshio Higuchi, Trends in Japanese Labor Markets, in Japanese Labour and Management in Transition, 27, 34, ed. Mari Sako and Hiroki Sato (1997).

46. Yasuo Suwa, Flexibility and Security in Employment: The Japanese Case, 6 Int'l J. Comp. Labour L. & Indust. Rel. 229, 251–52 (1990).

47. James E. Rosenbaum and Takehiko Kariya, From High School to Work: Market and Institutional Mechanisms in Japan, 94 Am. J. Soc. 1334 (1989).

48. Kazuo Koike, Human Resource Development and Labor-Management Relations, in The Political Economy of Japan, 1:289, 296, ed. Kozo Yamamura and Yasukichi Yasuba (1987).

them.[49] Third, in a few cases, they remain as *"madogiwazoku,"* or "window-gazers," who show up for work every day and are not terminated, in large part because of the difficulty of dismissal.

Anti-poaching rules. Recall again the data about working hours in the post-war era. Hours were high during the postwar growth period and fell during the energy crisis and again following the bursting of the economic bubble. What prevents employees from leaving during good times such as the postwar growth period to go to firms with shorter hours? What keeps them at firms during bad times? One possible answer is the court-buttressed nondismissal bargain, according to which employees normally cannot be fired (unless they don't submit to overtime). The uniform application of the bargain among large forms ensures that employees would be no better off at other firms.

But as Gilson and Roe note, a historically closed external labor market also plays an important role in shaping Japanese labor practices.[50] Gilson and Roe see the closed external labor market, or "no-poaching rule," which mitigates labor mobility, as a product of several factors: managerial fear of worker demoralization due to the hiring of outsiders, managerial fear of retaliation from other firms that would lead to labor strife, and perhaps even policies of the Japanese government.[51] As for the latter, Gilson and Roe cite no direct evidence of government involvement, but, theorizing from government desire for workplace stability, informal enforcement in other areas, and what they call the illegality of head-hunting activities, suggest a relation and call for further investigation.

Something like this has got to be there, of course; companies are unlikely to agree by the tens of thousands to choke the labor market. In fact, three government institutions create the closed market that Gilson and Roe posit: job placement, head-hunting rules, and retirement packages.

<hr>

49. As James Lincoln and Christina Ahmadjian note, "Establishments with more than 100 employees [transfer] male employees out at 2–3 times the rate of smaller organizations." James Lincoln and Christine Ahmadjian, Shukkō (Employee Transfers) and Tacit Knowledge Exchange in Japanese Supply Networks: The Electronics Case, in Knowledge Emergence: Social, Technical, and Evolutionary Dimensions of Knowledge Creation, 10, ed. Ikujiro Nonaka and Toshihiro Nishiguchi (2000). The bursting of the bubble economy led to the creation of many affiliate firms and subsequent transfer of employees. Many of these workers were eventually dismissed as the economy declined. Wakita, *supra* note 43, at 159.

50. Gilson and Roe, *supra* note 7.

51. Ibid. at 526–28.

It is important to distinguish between job placement services and head-hunting activities. As the leading Japanese practice-oriented treatise explains, "headhunting *per se* is not illegal."[52] Head-hunting has long been seen as outside the scope of the Employment Security Act, and leading commentators argue that in part because head-hunters do not take applications from those seeking employment, they are engaged in consulting and not the sort of job-placement services contemplated by the act.[53] Although some head-hunting agencies registered with the Ministry of Labor just as job-placement services did, others did not.[54]

By contrast, job-placement services, as discussed above, historically have been regulated tightly by the Ministry of Labor via the occupational category and licensing requirements of the Employment Security Act. Private licenses are difficult to obtain, and the widely available public placement services have never engaged in poaching, serving instead as search services for unemployed blue-collar workers.[55] The lack of job-placement services limits the free flow of labor and buttresses the no-poaching rule.

Still, head-hunting rules, as Gilson and Roe indicate, warrant further investigation. Headhunting *might* be illegal depending on how it is carried out. Courts have strictly construed employees' duties of loyalty to restrict poaching. In the *Rakuson* case, for instance, an employee secretly poached most of the company's employees to join the employee's new venture. The Tokyo District Court, which focused not on the employee's status but on his actions, held that such actions, if "beyond reasonable

52. Rōdōhō Jitsumu Handobukku [Labor Law Practice Handbook], 45, ed. Mitsuo Miyamoto et al. (2nd ed. 2000).

53. Sugeno, *supra* note 40, at 64–65.

54. In a 1994 Supreme Court case concerning fee amounts charged by a head-hunting agency, the court held that an agency, because it "mediates" relations between employers and employees, was bound by the fee provisions of the act. *Tokyo Executive Search v. Sakamoto*, Supreme Court, 849 Hanrei Times 269 (April 22, 1994); see Micho Tsuchida, Rōdō Shijō no Ryūdōka o Meguru Hōritsu Mondai [Legal Problems of the Fluidization of Labor Markets], 1040 Jurisuto 53, 61–62 (1994). The court's decision, regarded by many commentators as "too broad," placed head-hunting fees in legal limbo until the act's 1999 liberalization. Sugeno, *supra* note 40, at 66. Head-hunting and "scouting" firms clearly must now register with the Ministry of Labor.

55. See e.g., Tetsu Sano, Korekara no Kōkyō Shokugyō Shōkai [The Future of Public Placement Services], 1173 Jurisuto 66 (2000); Takashi Araki, Changing Japanese Labor Law in Light of Deregulation Drives: A Comparative Analysis, 36 Japan Labour Bulletin 1 (1997).

limits" (like *Rakuson*'s secret poaching) incur tort liability.[56] In other cases, courts have similarly found poaching by *former* employees to give rise to tort liability (but not contract liability) when it exceeds "reasonable limits" or is done in bad faith,[57] and that managers who quit and take employees with them may violate fiduciary duties to the firm.[58] Such limits could help create or support a closed external market.

Japanese firms often pay lump-sum retirement bonuses and severance fees on an employee's termination. Employers routinely insert a standard provision in employee contracts and firm work rules to the effect that this payment will be reduced if the employee retires to take a job with a company in the same line of business. The clauses are extreme but legal. The Supreme Court, finding that such payments are a combination of reward and deferred wages, approved a Solomonic halving of a bonus in one case: the employee got the reward for meritorious service but not the deferred wages.[59]

Statutory Working Hours

As the maximum number of hours allowed under the LSA decreased beginning in 1987, average hours worked in Japan began to fall. In fact, working hours fell at a greater rate there than in any other industrialized nation.[60] Of course, the law may have been as much a reflection of trends as a cause. But statutory revisions are a significant part of the story in explaining how norms governing working hours are incorporated and distributed through society.

56. *Media Trading Company K.K. v. Rakuson K.K.*, Tokyo District Court, 1399 Hanrei Jihō 69 (Feb. 25, 1991).

57. See Michio Tsuchida, Rōdō Shijō no Ryūdōka o meguru Hōritsu Mondai [Legal Problems of the Fluidization of Labor Markets], 1040 Jurisuto 53, 60 (1994); Yoshiyuki Tamura, Rōdōsha no Tenshoku, Hikinuki to Kigyō no Rieki [Worker Job Change, Head-Hunting, and Corporate Profits], 1103 Jurisuto 106, 109 (1996).

58. See J. Mark Ramseyer and Minoru Nakatazo, Japanese Law: An Economic Approach 114 (1999) (citing *Takuda v. Nihon Setsubi K.K.*, Tokyo District Court, 835 Kin'yū Shōji Hanrei 23 [Oct. 26, 1989]).

59. *Sanko-sha Case*, Supreme Court, 958 Rōdō Keizai Hanrei Sohuho 25 (Aug. 9, 1977).

60. John M. Evans et al., Trends in Working Hours in OECD Countries, Labour Market and Social Policy Occasional Paper No. 45, OECD, Feb. 21, 2001, at 23. On institutional changes in the United States that lead to reductions in working hours, see Dora L. Costa, Hours of Work and the Fair Labor Standards Act: A Study of Retail and Wholesale Trade, 1938–1950, 53 Ind. & Labor Relations Rev. 648 (2000).

Temporary Employment Arrangements

The historical limitations placed on fixed-term contract employees, dispatched workers, and job-placement services have two principal effects on working hours. First, the historical inability of employers to use such nonstandard employees as a labor buffer means that permanent, regular employees are forced to perform that function. Second, in addition to the real effects on working hours of regular employees, the reliance on regular employees may lead to higher average working hour statistics, because the pool of surveyed workers is less likely to include part-timers than it is in other industrialized countries.

In each case, it is likely that the liberalization of such arrangements that began in the mid-1980s contributes to the visible trend of reduced working hours. As more nonstandard employees are hired, working hours are shifted to them from regular workers.

Nonstandard workers *are* being hired. In 1990, 10 percent of people aged fifteen to thirty-four were "freeters," a combining of "free" and the German *arbeiter* [laborer] that describes part-time workers. According to the 2003 White Paper on the National Lifestyle, a decade later that 10 percent had grown to 21.2 percent, with 4.17 million young people "freeting" from job to job.[61] As those employees come to constitute a greater portion of the workforce, average hours across the entire workforce should decrease.

Social Factors

The legal institutions that I have described in this chapter do not explain the totality of working hours. Worker opinion in Japan, as elsewhere, is heterogeneous.[62] Legal institutions form only one part of the mix of many factors that affect working life in Japan. Social factors form another.

Recent empirical evidence offers support for the importance of social factors. Relying on German and U.S. survey data, Linda Bell and Richard Freeman found a possible explanation for differences in hours worked:

61. Kokumin Seikatsu Hakusho [White Paper on the National Lifestyle], ed. Naikakufū (2003), available at http://www5.cao.go.jp/seikatsu/shitepaper/h15/honbun. The government defines the denominator of young people to exclude students and "housewives."

62. See, e.g., Keiichi Kuwahara, Nihonjin no Rōdō Jikan [Japanese Working Hours], 145 (1979).

stated simply, some people just like to work.[63] Might Japanese workers work long hours because of preference or because norms prevent complaining? Stated more broadly in the context of this chapter's claims, perhaps the legal institutions discussed herein have no direct causal force but instead are redundant reflections of societal preferences or of bargains between management and labor,[64] some of the effects of which might be seen even in the absence of law.

This argument is important. Although sociocultural factors might be difficult to quantify and "prove" precisely, the lack of evidence does not disprove the fact that such forces might nevertheless be at work. I offer one argument and two pieces of evidence in response.

The argument is that social factors, in particular, underlying norms (in this case, the acceptability of long hours) that lead to judicial and legislative change, are unlikely to be unanimous. The expression of norms in the form of legislation or judicial opinions has the effect of standardizing existing practices among groups that might otherwise not follow the norm. Although some groups might still disobey the law just as they would disobey norms, legal and financial penalties offer disincentives in addition to existing social sanctions against such behavior.

In the case of working hours, labor law, through sanctions against dismissal, creates a universal need for workers in large firms to work long hours. Of course, law does not supply the motivation for hard work; some work hard because they like to, some because others do, some because they do not want to be transferred to less prestigious positions or ulti-

---

63. Linda A. Bell and Richard B. Freeman, The Incentive for Working Hard: Explaining Hours Worked Differences in the U.S. and Germany, NBER Working Paper 8051 (Dec. 2000); see also Linda Bell and Richard Freeman, Why Do Americans and Germans Work Different Hours?, in Institutional Frameworks and Labor Market Performance: Comparative Views on the U.S. and German Economies, 101, ed. Friedrich Buttler et al. (1995).

64. Despite their activism in the 1950s and 1960s, labor unions in Japan have been relatively quiet for the past four decades. Some commentators view this silence as a sign of weakness; labor's voice is fragmented, while the voice of business is unified. See T. J. Pempel and Keiichi Tsunekawa, Corporatism without Labor? The Japanese Anomaly, in Trends toward Corporatist Intermediation, 231, ed. Philippe C. Schmitter and Gerhard Lehmbruch (1979). Others view the silence as a sign of power; labor's alignment with the ruling Liberal Democratic Party mitigates the need for exercise of voice. See Sheldon Garon, The State and Labor in Modern Japan, 243 (1987). Union organization rates have fallen from 35 percent in the 1960s to below 24 percent in recent years. See Kazuo Sugeno and Yasuo Suwa, Labour Law Issues in a Changing Labour Market, in Japanese Labour and Management in Transition, 53, 62, ed. Mari Sako and Hiroki Sato (1997).

mately fired, and, for that matter, some because they prefer work to their families. The selection and self-selection processes of hiring at Japanese firms help ensure that workers are properly sorted to fill the legally induced need.

As for evidence, first, survey data at least tentatively suggest that the dismissal rules' effects on working hours are not a universal expression of Japanese preferences. When asked by the *Yomiuri Shinbun,* one of Japan's national newspapers, "Why do you think working hours in Japan have not become shorter?," 17 percent of respondents said that "Japanese people love to work," and 23 percent said that "employees feel guilty if they leave work earlier than others." But the largest group, 57 percent, responded that a "large workload" was the cause.[65] In a survey by the Prime Minister's Office, workers who used only one of their five allotted vacation days in a year were asked why they had not taken vacation time. The most common reason given was not something directly based on culture but the simple realization that "later I'd just be busier" (25.7 percent), and the second most common reason was that the worker had "planned to save the time for illness or urgent matters" (17.8 percent). A similar survey by the Tokyo Chamber of Commerce found that 36 percent of respondents, the largest group, gave the former answer,[66] and another by the Ministry of Labor found that 38.2 percent gave such an answer (and 22.9 percent saying that the workplace was simply not conducive to vacation).[67]

The second piece is that the experience of Japanese workers in subsidiaries of Japanese companies in the United States often differs dramatically from that of Japanese workers in firms in Japan. Workers in U.S. subsidiaries do not have lifetime employment commitments and fre-

---

65. Yomiuri Shinbun Poll, May 30, 1993, available at the Roper Center for Public Opinion Research, University of Connecticut.

66. See Takeshi Fujimoto, Nihon no Rōdōsha [Japanese Workers], 71 (1990).

67. Kōji Ishii, Rōdō Jikan to Nihon Keizai [Working Hours and the Japanese Economy] (1982). Might Japanese workers simply be more loyal? Relying on other survey evidence, the most detailed study of Japanese and American comparative labor practices finds that "the pattern of differences in organizational commitment and job satisfaction between Japanese and U.S. employees runs strongly counter to the behavioral evidence of a highly committed Japanese labor force. The organizational commitment of the Japanese is either equal to or slightly lower, and their job satisfaction is far lower, than that of our American sample." James R. Lincoln and Arne L. Kalleberg, Culture, Commitment, and Control: A Study of Work Organization and Work in the United States and Japan, 182 (1990). This evidence suggests that company loyalty does not explain the entire picture.

quently are laid off.[68] Many Japanese workers dread a return to Japan after an overseas posting, because working hours outside of Japan, where subsidiaries tend to be more adequately staffed, are not as grueling.[69] The only particular scrutiny adopted by U.S. subsidiaries when hiring appears to consist of covert attempts to screen potential union members, not detailed background investigations.[70]

One likely explanation for the differences between U.S. and Japanese practices might be culture. Japanese subsidiaries in the United States might adopt U.S. cultural practices, even if their management is Japanese. I find this explanation to be unlikely in many cases, especially given the frequent turnover of Japanese management, many of whom have neither the time nor the inclination to "Americanize." Instead, the differences in practice suggest that the institutional argument has considerable predictive power. A more likely reason for the difference is that Japanese-run institutions in the United States function under the influence of U.S. institutions. Japanese labor laws only apply in Japan, and Japanese subsidiaries in the U.S. accordingly look more like U.S. firms.

CONCLUSION

Why does Daddy have to work so late? Japanese workers work extremely long hours in part because socially supported institutions prevent worker dismissal in bad times and because other options for buffering supply and demand in the workforce are limited. But there are two silver linings. First, dismissal rules provide workers with job security in many situations. Second, recent changes in laws governing working hours and temporary employees suggest that one of the benefits of a booming economy—reduced working hours— might be attainable by legal reform. In each case, social norms play a powerful role, but only through careful analysis of legal institutions can the underlying relation, and potential ways of improving Japanese working life with better institutional design, be understood.

68. Duane Kujawa, Japanese Multinationals in the United States (1986).

69. See, e.g., Yoshi Noguchi, Dropping out of Tokyo's Rat Race, N.Y. Times, Mar. 1, 1992, at C11.

70. See Gregory M. Saltzman, Job Applicant Screening by a Japanese Transplant: A Union-Avoidance Tactic, 49 Ind. & Labor Relations Rev. 88 (1995).

CHAPTER EIGHT

DEBT-SUICIDE

On a cold night in February 2003, Kazuyoshi Saitō stood on the platform of the Utsunomiya line waiting for the next express train. He knew the schedule precisely, and he also knew that the train did not stop at that station. His intent, on this night as on the two previous occasions that he had come to the station, was to gauge precisely when he should jump in front of the speeding train in order to maximize his chances of death and minimize his chances of merely being injured. Doing so, he reasoned, would be the best way to relieve himself of the $300,000 in debt that he had incurred in the past decade—a debt that his annual income of $30,000 was unlikely to wipe out any time soon.

Having confirmed his timing calculations, he stopped by a local convenience store, bought a newspaper and a bottle of whiskey, and returned to his cluttered apartment, the rent for which he had not paid in four months. In the newspaper, he read for the first time stories about a new legal process called "civil rehabilitation." He had heard of it before but had not followed the news closely enough to know much about it; his problems were bigger than that. But as he read, he learned of debtors who had chosen the new process as an alternative to bankruptcy. He had never considered himself a candidate for bankruptcy; that would only make his life more miserable, and it was miserable enough as it was. But "civil rehabilitation" sounded more appealing, and he didn't think that his neighbors and friends, or at least those who still remained, would shun him as they might had he filed for bankruptcy.

The following day, instead of jumping in front of the train according to his original plan, he contacted a lawyer. He soon filed for civil rehabilitation, sought psychological counseling at the urging of his attorney, and gave up thoughts of suicide.

Sadly, many debtors in Japan jump. In 2003, 34,427 Japanese committed suicide—about 94 per day, a figure that, as we will see below, is high by international standards.[1] Of these, 10,387 left suicide notes. Police who investigate the suicides divide the notes by category based on the primary reason for suicide mentioned in the notes. The largest group, 3,890 victims, claimed that health problems were the cause. The second largest group, 3,654 victims, or about 10 per day for a country with a population half that of the United States, explicitly blamed economic factors as the primary motivation. If the percentage of those who cite economic factors for their suicide is the same among the victims who do not leave notes, the number of such victims would reach 33 per day—33 people killing themselves every day because of the economy—and the number of unsuccessful attempts is estimated to be ten times the number of completions.[2]

Stories about these debt-suicide victims have appeared with increased frequency. Japanese morning "wide" news-variety television shows (*waido*) feature family members of debt-suicide victims telling sad tales with follow-ups from reporters telling the next potential victims, "You don't have to die!" In a 2002 report, the *New York Times*, noting that "as many as two million Japanese are effectively bankrupt," finds that statistics are skewed because "every year thousands of people in distress commit suicide, police statistics show, rather than face their debt collectors, friends, and families in shame."[3] The Minister of the Economy blames "the system for the high number of debt-caused suicides in Japan, calling it unimaginable in the West, where businesses are allowed to fail yet people make a fresh start on life."[4]

This chapter examines this complex relation of suicide, debt, and insolvency law in Japan.[5] Of course, for most people, suicide and reliance on

---

1. The figures are from Keisatsuchō Seikatsu Anzenkyoku Chiikuka, Heisei 15nenchu ni okeru Jisatsu no Gaiyō Shiryō [Statistical Outline of 2003 Suicides] (2004), available at http://www.npa.go.jp/toukei/chiiki2/jisatsu.pdf.

2. Yoshitomo Takahashi, Chūkōnen Jisatsu [Middle-Aged Suicide], 7 (2003).

3. Ken Belson, Struggling in Debt, Sacrificing Pride, N.Y. Times, Dec. 28, 2002, at B1, B3.

4. Yuri Kageyama, In Tough Times, Suicides over Debts Surge in Japan's Shame Culture, Associated Press, Mar. 6, 2003, available on LEXIS.

5. A related and growing body of work that attempts to gain insight into the obviously complex relation among indebtedness, law, health, and happiness includes Teresa A. Sulli-

insolvency law are not "everyday" events. But for most people, debt is, and for many people in Japan, huge amounts of debt are as everyday as rice and miso soup. I focus on the connection to insolvency law to show how legal institutions influence everyday debt. I include suicide in the inquiry not only because it makes an interesting story but because it shows an extreme version of the ways institutions matter.

Pretend for a moment that all people in financial distress are rational; a heroic assumption, perhaps, but a good place to start. Such persons must choose between suicide and life. If life isn't worth living, suicide is the choice. In deciding whether life is worth living, a debtor considers many factors, including the monetary and social costs of bankruptcy, the possibility of life insurance payout to his or her family, and so on. For many people, bankruptcy tips the scales, making future life so unappealing that suicide is their choice.

Based on this underlying relation, my data suggest a causal relation between insolvency law and suicide in Japan. The relation is indirect; law is seldom if ever a dominant factor in an individual's decision to commit suicide. But the data, many of which relate to the creation of an efficient and relatively socially acceptable insolvency regime in 2001, show that law plays a role both in controlling debt and in mitigating the social stigma of indebtedness, each of which alters the suicide calculus. Identifying the exact causal process is difficult. Some rational persons might perform the calculation from the previous paragraph. The evidence that I have gathered tentatively suggests that even if they do not, because both debt and stigma may lead to stress, depression, and social alienation for some people, and each of *those* is in turn a major cause of suicide, legal change affects suicide rates.

The relation is by no means simple; human responses to debt, debt-related law, and depression are varied and ambiguous, the framework for debt and suicide decisions has a sociocultural context, and separating issues of social stigma from issues of economic efficiency when examining the effect of legal reform is difficult if not impossible. I merely propose that for some people, some of the time, in some circumstances, law is a rel-

---

van, Elizabeth Warren, and Jay Lawrence Westbrook, The Fragile Middle Class: Americans in Debt (2000); Melissa B. Jacoby, Teresa A. Sullivan, and Elizabeth Warren, Rethinking the Debates over Health Care Financing: Evidence from the Bankruptcy Courts, 76 N.Y.U. L. Rev. 375 (2001); Melissa B. Jacoby, Does Indebtedness Influence Health? A Preliminary Inquiry, 30 J. Law, Medicine & Ethics 560 (2002).

evant part of the mix. That modest conclusion aside, I confess at the outset that there is no grand theory of life and death in the conclusion; no law-times-alpha-equals-joy equation awaits in an appendix.

I first discuss suicide in the Japanese context, both generally and in the more specific context of debt. Then I analyze Japanese legal remedies for consumer debt and attempt to determine the relation between the two by exploring the quantitative and interview evidence. Finally, I discuss the implications of the relation.

SUICIDE

Even casual observers of Japan usually know something, or will claim to know something, about Japanese suicide. Kamikaze pilots are well known, such movies as *Shogun* and *The Last Samurai* popularize the image of suicidal soldiers and servants, and popular media (recall Belushi's *Saturday Night Live* samurai) sometimes portray Japan as a country that regards taking one's own life as a decision on a par with choosing an appropriate breakfast cereal. This section takes a closer look by examining suicide data, suicide theory, and links to the economy.

Data

Suicide data are available from two primary sources: the police and the Ministry of Health, Labor, and Welfare. Police statistics show higher figures. Police gather data about deaths specifically for the purpose of classifying them as homicides, suicides, illness-related deaths, or accidents; Ministry of Health data come from death certificates filed by physicians and medical examiners. The latter process, as one psychologist explains, is problematic: "A large number of death certificates are filed by attending physicians, who, when they know the family, do everything they can to avoid writing 'suicide.' If a person commits suicide by leaping from a tall building, the death certificate might list the cause of death as a head injury, and the number of cases in which suicide by overdose is listed as 'accidental poisoning' is large."[6] Police data are likewise imperfect; it is difficult to know when an automobile accident is actually a suicide. But they appear to be more reliable than Ministry data.

6. Yoshitomo Takahashi, Jisatsu no Risuku Manejimento [Suicide Risk Management], 5 (2002).

Figure 8.1. Suicides and Suicide Rates, 1978–2003

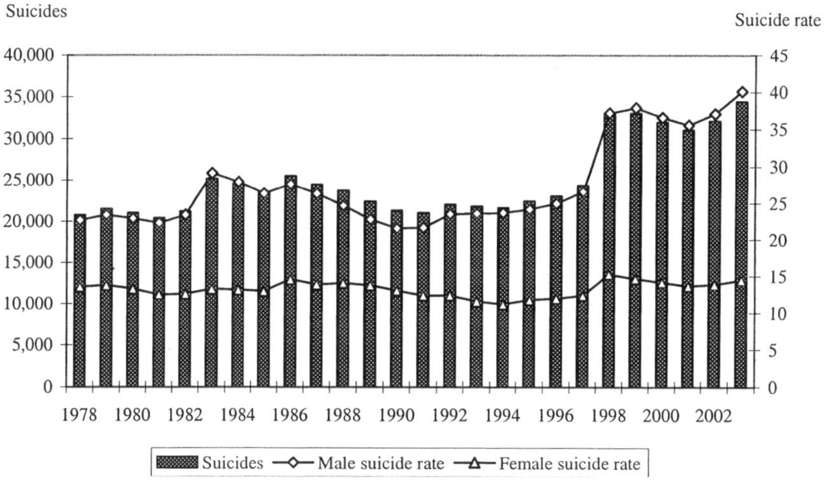

Figure 8.1 presents police data for the period 1978–2003 on suicide in Japan. As the figure shows, suicides rose slightly in the early 1980s, fell slightly during the late 1980s and early 1990s, and rose again at the end of the 1990s and the beginning of the twenty-first century. Male suicide rates, now more than forty per hundred thousand, are far higher than female suicide rates for any period.

To place these figures in context, consider suicide rates for the United States. In 2001, 30,022 persons committed suicide, a number roughly equal to the Japanese figures but based on a national population base roughly twice Japan's. The suicide rate per 100,000 in 2001 was 10.8; males were 17.6, females 4.1. The highest rate was among white males, at 19.5, still far lower than rates for Japanese males. In contrast to Japanese trends, U.S. rates decreased during the 1990s from 12.4 steadily to 10.7.[7]

Placed in a broader context, Japan's male suicide figures are among the highest in the industrialized world, despite the fact that Japanese life expectancy is also among the highest. Extreme caution is warranted in examining comparative suicide data because different systems may have different notions of what constitutes suicide. That stated, according to 2004 World Health Organization (WHO) data, the Canadian rate for males is 18.4, the German 20.4, the French 26.1. Of the ninety-nine countries sur-

7. Elizabeth Arias et al., Deaths: Final Data for 2001, National Vital Statistics Reports, vol. 52, no. 3, at 8, 52 (Sept. 18, 2003), available at http://www.cdc.gov/nchs/data/nvsr/nvsr52/nvsr52_03.pdf.

Table 8.1. Rank of Suicide among the Top Five Causes of Male Death

Age group	Rank of suicide (% of all deaths)
10–14	3 (8.4)
15–19	2 (19)
20–24	2 (33.5)
25–29	1 (37.3)
30–34	1 (33.8)
35–39	1 (29.1)
40–44	2 (21.2)
45–49	2 (16.4)
50–54	2 (12.9)
55–59	3 (9.7)
60–64	4 (4.9)

Source: Ministry of Health, Labor, and Welfare, Jinkō Dōtai Nenpō, 1999, available at http://www1.mhlw.go.jp/toukei-i/toukeihp/11nenpo_8/deth8.html.

veyed by the WHO, only ten have higher rates than Japan's—but those countries are all transition economies with different macroeconomic characteristics, and research suggests that those characteristics matter.[8] The data show no regional patterns with respect to Japan; the Chinese rate is 13.0, the Korean 20.3.[9] In short, there appears to be quantitative evidence to support the myth: Japanese figures are quite high.

Japanese suicide rates also demonstrate age-specific patterns. Table 8.1 shows the ranking of suicide among the leading causes of death for males in different age groups as recorded by the Ministry of Health, Labor, and Welfare. Japan also maintains data about suicides by age group. Police data show that juvenile suicide (that by persons aged nineteen and under), often as a result of school-related factors such as bullying (22.6 percent) and rarely as a result of economic factors (2.6 percent), though problematic, accounts for only 2 percent of total suicides. Suicides of persons under age forty have declined or remained constant over the past quarter-century; twentysomethings account for 10 percent of total suicides, thirtysomethings for 12 percent. But suicides by those between the ages

8. Elizabeth Brainerd, Economic Reform and Mortality in the Former Soviet Union: A Study of the Suicide Epidemic in the 1990s, 45 European Econ. Rev. 995–1006 (2001). India has a similar economic suicide problem. See It Is a Crisis Rooted in Economic Reforms: Interview with Utsa Patnaik, Frontline, June 19–July 2, 2004, at 62.

9. All data are from the World Health Organization at www.who.int/mental_health/prevention/suicide/en/figures_web0604_table.pdf

of forty and forty-nine have increased from 3,641 in 1968 to 5,419 (16 percent of total suicides) in 2003, suicides by those between the ages of fifty and fifty-nine have increased from 2,753 to 8,614 (25 percent), and suicides of persons more than sixty years of age increased from 6,024 to 11,529 (33 percent).[10]

Explanations

If Japanese suicide rates are peculiarly high, might those rates be high for peculiarly Japanese reasons? Given the cultural mystique of Japanese suicide, an examination, if cursory, of the literature seems appropriate. Consider Jack Seward's popular work *Hara-Kiri: Japanese Ritual Suicide* (1968). Seward traces the Japanese method of self-destruction, if not the practice itself, to A.D. 285, with the advent of Buddhism. Buddhism's "fatalistic acceptance of death" combined with Shinto's "simple primitive animism" to form a moral code institutionalized as *bushidō*, or the Way of the Warrior. Bushidō raised *hari-kiri*, or more formally *seppuku*, to an honorable death sentence.

Maybe so. But new evidence uncovered by Thomas Conlan strongly suggests that suicide was a part of samurai lore not because of honor but because they feared more gruesome deaths at the hands of captors.[11] And Japanese suicide clearly should not be viewed as a purely masochistic or macho exercise; the abundance of lesbian double suicides of the 1930s, for instance, was a revolt against traditional Japanese gender roles.[12]

Maurice Pinguet offers a more complete account of Japanese suicide. Like Seward, Pinguet contrasts the Japanese historical warrior ethic and a "tradition of sacrifice" with that of Christianity, which forbade suicide.[13] Unlike Seward, Pinguet suggests that bushidō did not die; rather, it continued with such tragic personae as the author Yukio Mishima, who dramatically took his life in 1970. Sociologist Mamoru Iga reaches similar conclusions, finding differing "value orientations" for Japanese and Americans. Iga argues that Japanese value orientations such as monism,

10. Keisatsuchō Seikatsu Anzenkyoku Chiikuka, *supra* note 1; see also Takahashi, *supra* note 6, at 4–8.

11. Thomas Donald Conlan, State of War: The Violent Order of Fourteenth-Century Japan, 37 (2003).

12. Jennifer Robertson, Dying to Tell: Sexuality and Suicide in Imperial Japan, 25:1 Signs 1 (1999).

13. Maurice Pinguet, Voluntary Death in Japan, 100 (1993).

groupism, accommodationism, and authoritarian familism produce un-realistically high aspirations. When people in Japan cannot reach their goals, they feel that "there is no way out." Add to this despair social con-straints on "outwardly-directed aggression" and romanticization, and suicide may become a popular solution.[14]

Pinguet's and Iga's propositions are difficult both to test and to apply. Their focus on the suicides of Japanese writers (Mishima, Kawabata, Arishima, Akutagawa, Dazai) as "highly representative of Japanese cul-ture"[15] is a bit of a stretch, unless one considers national culture to revolve around the famous, the eccentric, and the long-dead (the youngest was born in 1925; most were born in the nineteenth century). More important, their hypotheses also may explain too much. Blanket theories aid little in discovering why a few people in Japan commit suicide while the vast ma-jority of people do not; these are stereotypes, not causes.

Many scholars writing in Japanese offer a less romantic view that fo-cuses more on differing causes. Psychologist Yoshitomo Takahashi, for instance, the most prolific Japanese authority on the subject, disputes three hallmarks of stereotypical Japanese suicide. First, Takahashi notes the common perception by non-Japanese that Japanese suicide victims are systematically taking the knife to their bowels in ritual *seppuku*, then notes that he has never seen such a thing in twenty years of practice.[16] Sec-ond, despite romanticized stories of *shinjū*, joint suicide pacts (murder-suicide included), Takahashi finds that the actual rates of shinjū as a per-centage of suicides is the same in the United States as in Japan. Finally, he strongly disputes the notion that many Japanese use suicide as a method of taking responsibility for a group. Media accounts to the contrary, he finds that such suicides are almost always about failure and shame, not responsibility, and that depression is often a contributing factor.[17]

Other Japanese scholars working in various disciplines also avoid the stereotypes, and accordingly they reach varied conclusions. Attorney Hi-roshi Kawamoto has forcefully argued that whatever the background so-cial causes, stressful working conditions in Japan lead to a high number of

14. Mamoru Iga, The Sword in the Chrysanthemum, 114–86 (1986).

15. Ibid. at 70.

16. The data support his experience; only about 2 percent of suicides are done with sharp objects. Ministry of Health, Labor, and Welfare, Jinkō Dōtai Chōsa [Vital Statistics], avail-able at http://wwwdbtk.mhlw.go.jp/toukei/data/010/2001/toukeihyou/0003844/t0065997/mc360_001.html.

17. Takahashi, *supra* note 2, at 86–87.

suicides.[18] Other experts cite psychological factors, economics, age, sex, age, marital status, available suicide methods, and suicide-related costs.[19] Following those studies, I now turn to one factor raised by Japanese experts in explaining patterns and trends in the data: in many cases, it's the economy.

The Economy

In the summer of 2003, three Osaka residents (a sixty-one-year-old cleaning company worker, his sixty-nine-year-old wife, and her eighty-one-year-old brother) leapt in front of an oncoming train on Japan Railways' Kansai Line to their deaths. The suicide note sent by the wife to a friend explained why. According to the four-page letter, the husband had borrowed $200 from various sources; the amount to be repaid now totaled $1,500. Debt collectors called the house every night, and when the couple said that they could not pay, the less savory ones threatened to "get it from their neighbors." She concluded, "We have decided to apologize with our lives."[20]

Such stories abound, especially following a media concentration on the issue as a "trend" beginning in 2003. The accounts also leave little doubt that many people commit suicide for reasons that include financial distress. Studies by Japanese psychologists of suicide motivation likewise show that although interpersonal relations are often the primary motive, economic hardship also plays a significant role at a rate of about 10 to 15 percent, roughly equivalent to the numbers cited in the introduction and detailed below.[21]

Is the relation widespread enough to be seen in the macroeconomy? Consider first the data about motives of suicide victims (Japan is one of the few countries to maintain such data). As I detail below, since 1978, the National Police Agency has classified suicide as related to family prob-

18. Hiroshi Kawamoto, Karō Jisatsu [Death by Overwork] (1998). The Supreme Court has ruled that death by overwork gives rise to an actionable tort claim. *Kōno v. Dentsu K.K.*, Supreme Court, 1707 Hanji 87 (Mar. 24, 2000).

19. See Karin Amamiya, Jisatsu no Kosuto [The Costs of Suicide] (2002); Ayanori Okazaki, Jisatsu no Kuni [Suicide Nation] (1958).

20. Munen no Tegami [A Regretful Letter], Mainichi Shinbun, June 15, 2003, at 13.

21. Hiroko Suzuki, Kyūmei Kyūkyū Senta- ni Okeru Jisatsu Kitosha no Jittai [An Empirical Analysis of Suicide Attempts at an Emergency Lifesaving Center], in Jisatsu Kito [Suicide Pact], 146, 149–52, ed. Teruhiko Higuchi (2002).

Figure 8.2. Economic Suicides, 1978–2003

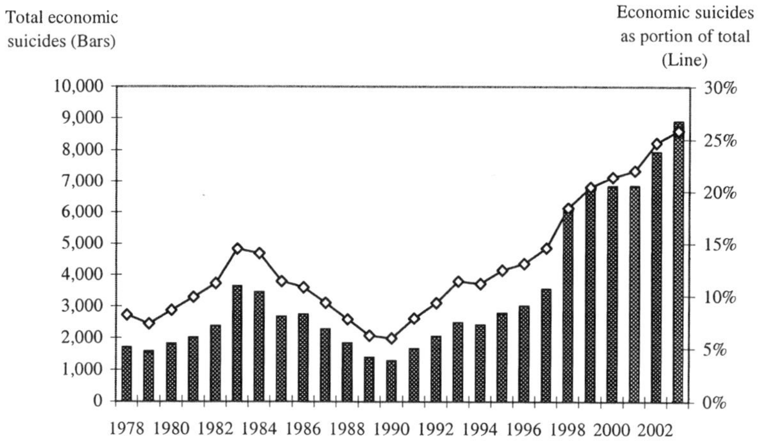

Total economic
suicides (Bars)

Economic suicides
as portion of total
(Line)

lems, health, economic hardship, job stress, male-female relationships, school, alcoholism and mental illness, or "other."[22] For reasons that I also discuss below, these data are imperfect, but they provide a useful baseline for analysis. Figure 8.2 shows the total number of economically based suicides as well as the number of such suicides as a percentage of total suicides from 1978 to 2002.

As the figure shows, economically based suicide has risen dramatically in recent years, both in raw numbers and as a percentage of total suicides. It is age-specific; despite recent bleak job forecasts, young people seldom do it. Among note-leavers in 2003, 39 percent of male economic suicides are committed by men in their fifties, 24 percent by men in their forties, and 20 percent by men in their sixties.[23] But the data cluster differently according to type of employment; the same data show that one-third are self-employed, another one-third are unemployed, and another one-third are company employees.

Compare these data with the data for macroeconomic performance in figure 8.3.

Figure 8.3 shows the total number of suicides, the number of economic suicides, and two macroeconomic measures: bankruptcy and GDP growth. Suicide increased when GDP growth dropped dramatically in

22. See David Lester and Yukio Saito, The Reasons for Suicide in Japan, 38 Omega 65, 66 (1998–1999).

23. Keisatsuchō Seikatu Anzenkyoku Chiikuka, *supra* note 1.

Figure 8.3. Suicide and the Macroeconomy, 1990–2003

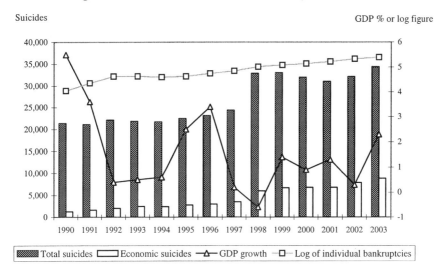

1998, a period that marked the end of the "golden" recession, in which ordinary people were rarely affected, and the beginning of a "real" recession, in which they often were so. Bankruptcies and suicides both rose, so the data do not show a clear substitution effect. But other connections are difficult to determine with any precision; there are no obvious linear relations. Although we know that some people kill themselves because financial matters, that relation is not particularly clear in the macrodata, and more detailed inquiry is required to unravel any potential relation among debt, law, and suicide.

DEBT AND INSOLVENCY

When the Japanese economy was booming in the 1980s, individual debt was not a widespread problem. In 1980, consumer debt, at approximately ¥1.5 trillion, made up only 11.73 percent of household expenses. By 1990, however, as the economic bubble burst, consumer debt rose to ¥6.3 trillion, accounting for 27.37 percent of household expenses. Debt levels increased throughout the 1990s but subsided to 1990 levels by 2000.[24] These amounts—and the numbers of bankruptcies that accompany them—are

24. Ken'ichi Nakamura, Shōhisha Shin'yō Shijō no Kyōsō to Kōritsusei [Efficiency and Competition in the Consumer Debt Market], 5 (Dec. 2002), available at http://www.esri .cao.go.jp/jp/archive/e_dis/e_dis030/e_dis022a.pdf.

lower than in the United States, but many observers believe that they suggest a Japanese debt epidemic nonetheless.

Regardless of macro comparisons, it is difficult to determine when debt levels are excessive for legal and economic purposes, much less for the emotional purposes that might drive debt-ridden persons to suicide. Kenji Utsunomiya, a prominent bankruptcy attorney, estimates that 1.5 million to 2 million people are effectively bankrupt but have not yet filed.[25] If that is so, then many others must be in debt trouble but not "effectively bankrupt."

Data collected by the National Consumer Affairs Center offer additional clues. The center, a special-status corporation organized by the government that counsels about half a million people each year about such issues as tainted beef, fraudulent sales tactics, and cancellation of foreign travel after 9/11, keeps data concerning incidents of such counseling at its local offices. As figure 8.4 shows, the incidence of debt-related counseling increased steadily from 1989 to 2001.[26] During the same period, the total number of counseling incidents rose from 165,697 in 1989 to 624,762 in 2001.[27] But the number of debt-related counseling incidents also steadily rose as a percentage of all counseling incidents, from less than 1 percent in 1989, to between 2 and 3 percent in 1997, to more than 5 percent in 2001. Because the center advertised debt counseling services to the same extent as other services, it is unlikely that the growth came merely from increased awareness.

The typical debtor seeking counseling, according to the center, is 37.2

25. Kenji Utsunomiya, Shōhisha Kin'yū [Consumer Finance], 3 (2002). The same may be true in the United States; Michelle White estimates that at least 15 percent of American households could benefit from filing, about ten times Utsunomiya's figure; see Michelle J. White, Why Don't More Households File for Bankruptcy?, 14 J. L. Econ. & Org. 205 (1998).

26. Kokumin Seikatsu Senta-, "Tajū Saimusha Mondai" Chōsa Kekka Ni Tsuite [Regarding the "Multiple-Debt Problem" Survey], June 21, 1999, available at http://www .kokusen.go.jp/cgi-bin/byteserver.pl/pdf/n-19990621_1.pdf; updated with data from Kokumin Seikatsu Senta-, Shōhi Seikatsu Sōdan ni Miru 2001 no 10dai Kōmoku [10 Topics in 2001 Consumer Counseling], Dec. 5, 2001, available at http://www.kokusen.go.jp/pdf/ n-20011205_3.pdf; and Kokumin Seikatsu Senta-, Shōhi Seikatsu Sōdan ni Miru 2002 no 10dai Kōmoku [10 Topics in 2002 Consumer Counseling], Dec. 6, 2002, available at http:// www.kokusen.go.jp/cgi-bin/byteserver.pl/pdf/n-20021206_2.pdf.

27. Kokumin Seikatsu Senta-, Shōhi Seikatsu Nenpō 2002 [Consumer Affairs Yearbook 2002], available at http://www.kokusen.go.jp/pdf/n-20021007_3.pdf.

Figure 8.4. Debt-Related Counseling Incidents, 1989–2001

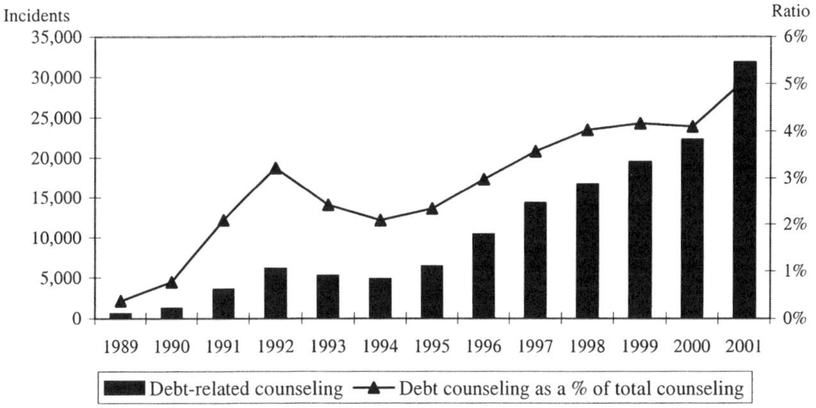

years old, male (56 percent are), and employed in a salaried profession.[28] A more detailed portrait is created by my interviews (presented below) and in a profile of five "rich debtors," all "salarymen" in their twenties and thirties, in a popular weekly magazine. Four had a debt balance of approximately ¥30 million ($30,000) each. Of these four, one had a take-home monthly salary of ¥1.5 million ($15,000), but the others had take-home salaries of ¥290,000, ¥220,000, and ¥170,000, respectively, none of which left much room for debt repayment after expenses. Their experiences were varied; one borrowed to buy brand-name goods, a second just couldn't make ends meet, a third debtor had a gambling problem, and a fourth invested the funds in his business. The fifth was a combination of virtue and vice; half of his debt came from paying for his parents' medical expenses; the other half was incurred when he was "cheated" by a female high school student whom he met on a mobile-phone dating network ("I thought I was answering a survey to win a brand-name necklace, but before I knew what was happening, I bought it"; he used the network so often that his fees reached ¥370,000, or $3,700, in three months).[29]

High interest rates and erratically enforced usury laws mean that many such debtors face interest rates of up to 40 percent from formal lenders. The average consumer lending company charges 33.1 percent for short-

28. Kokumin Seikatsu Senta-, "Tajū Saimusha Mondai" Chōsa Kekka Ni Tsuite, *supra* note 26.

29. Kōshaku Kanemochi Hakusho, Spa!, June 10, 2003, at 50.

term loans. Historically, loan agreements between private individuals have had virtually no limits on interest rates.[30]

Most debtors have multiple loans from multiple sources, which can range from legitimate to very questionable. The Japan Consumer Credit Industry Corporation maintains data about the more legitimate sources; it found consumer credit in 2001 to have reached a record ¥74 trillion, or about $740 billion. Of this amount, about ¥35 trillion is made up of sales on credit, including ¥23 trillion in credit card sales and ¥12 trillion in sales contract credit. The remaining ¥39 trillion consists of consumer finance, of which ¥14 trillion is made up of loans secured by bank or postal accounts, ¥10 trillion is made up of cash advances on credit cards and similar transactions, and ¥4 trillion is made up of bank loans. The ¥11 trillion yen remainder consists of loans from consumer finance companies.[31] Information in the market is highly segmented; in most cases, lenders from different market segments performing credit checks learn only about specific defaults and not credit details, because information-sharing is scarce.[32]

As table 8.2 shows, consumer finance companies are ubiquitous and have a large client base with mostly unsecured loans. Industry reports show that the total number of branches has tripled in five years with the addition of ATMs.[33]

Although most activities of the big five consumer finance companies are legitimate, the industry as a whole, which has about thirty thousand registered lenders, has a questionable reputation. Some observers consider some sectors of the consumer finance industry to differ little from organized crime; their designation as *sarakin* (salaryman financing) "conjure[s] up images of loan sharks, gamblers in need of quick cash and burly men with punch perms demanding payments—or else."[34] Stories—and

30. Kokumin Seikatsu Senta-, "Taju Saimusha Mondai" Chōsa Kekka Ni Tsuite, *supra* note 26, at 9; see also Financial Services Agency, Karisugini Ihōna Kin'yū Gyōsha ni Gochūi [Exercise Caution Around Illegal Finance Companies], available at www.fsa.go.jp/notice/noticej/karisugia.html (detailing maximum legal interest rates of 109.5 percent).

31. Nihon Kurejitto Sangyō Kyōkai, Nihon no Shōhisha Shin'yō Tōkei [Consumer Credit Statistics of Japan], 30 (2003).

32. See Ronald J. Mann, Credit Cards and Debit Cards in the United States and Japan, 55 Vand. L. Rev. 1055, 1081 and n. 97 (2002).

33. TAPALS Hakusho 2002, 3 (2003), available at http://www.tapals.com/archive/pdf/hakusho-2.pdf.

34. Philip Brasor, Credit Companies Target the Debt-Ridden Poor, Japan Times, May 19, 2002, at 1.

Table 8.2. Top Five Consumer Finance Companies

	Fujitsu	*Acom*	*Promise*	*Aiful*	*Sanyo Shinpan*
Number of branches	1,710	1,741	1,507	1,529	958
Number of employees	3,433	4,321	3,844	3,477	1,085
Annual advertising expenses	¥16 billion	¥20 billion	¥21 billion	¥17 billion	¥3 billion
Loan balance	¥1.65 trillion	¥1.5 trillion	¥1.23 trillion	¥1.16 trillion	¥285 billion
Unsecured loan balance	¥1.65 trillion	¥1.42 trillion	¥1.22 trillion	¥921 billion	¥285 billion

Source: Kenji Utsunomiya, Shōhisha Kin'yū [Consumer Finance], 5, 53 (2002).

subsequent extortion convictions based on those stories—of employees of such legitimate firms, often backed up by organized crime syndicates, instructing borrowers to sell a kidney or an eyeball to repay debts do little to help their image.

Below legal sarakin, and sometimes working in concert with them, is a fascinatingly greasy, well-functioning underground loan market. The terms of loans from these lenders vary, but representative terms include ten-day interest rates of 300 percent and annual rates of 10,000 percent.[35] In addition to true loan sharks, market players include bankruptcy fixers (*seiriya*), introducers (*shōkaiya*, brokers who receive a fee of 25 to 50 percent for introducing debtors to new loan sources), cooperating lawyers (*teikei bengoshi*, lawyers who work with fixers and brokers), repo men (*toritateya*), and goods brokers (*kaitoriya*, brokers who give debtors quick cash by purchasing goods—usually electronics and tickets—with debtors' credit cards, paying them 30 to 40 percent of the goods' value and selling the goods at specialty resale shops). This activity spawns other subindustries; brokers gather information from sarakin on repeat debtors and sell it to other sarakin for further exploitation.

To get a sense of the scope of illegal sarakin operations, consider three relevant types of data. First, the National Consumer Affairs Center began keeping records of sarakin-related counseling incidents in 1999, when it recorded 19,399 consultations. By 2003 the number had grown to 114,992 consultations, roughly a fifth of the center's activity.

Police keep the other two relevant data sets First, police record the number of "underground finance incidents" (*yami kin'yū jiken*), defined

35. See Yami Kin'yū Bokumetsu Kirifudani [Killing the Underground Loan Market], Yomiuri Shinbun, July 18, 2003, at 3.

as incidents involving illegal interest rates and unlicensed lenders. In 2002 they recorded 222 such incidents involving twelve thousand victims and a gross damage amount of approximately $158 million, which works out to about $13,000 per victim.[36] Second, in the early 1980s, police maintained specific data about "sarakin suicides," which could include both legal and illegal sarakin. In 1984, police recorded 1,164 suicides that they deemed to be related to sarakin debt repayment, or about one-third of total economic suicides (as reflected in figure 8.2 above). According to their data, 90 percent of such suicide victims were male, 56 percent were company employees, and 67.8 percent were married. A small percentage, 8.6 percent, committed suicide simultaneously with another person. Most sarakin suicides (89.9 percent) were committed by debtors, but a few were committed by spouses (5.1 percent) or children (2.2 percent) of debtors. Police somehow also determined that 12.1 percent of victims were harassed by creditors, 48.2 percent were not, and that this factor was unknown in 39.7 percent of cases. Sarakin debt collection methods used on eventual victims included personal contact (13.6 percent), phone calls (29.7 percent), and mailings (9.2 percent) and usually were used at the debtor's home (45 percent). Although this level of detail is interesting, it is speculative, the large number of unknowns is troublesome, and police no longer categorize so strictly.[37]

What legal options are available for debtors with multiple debts from multiple sources? Japanese corporations historically have had a plethora of legal options for dealing with excessive debt, including bankruptcy, litigation, and four kinds of reorganization. For individuals, however, only one feasible legal choice existed before April 2001: bankruptcy.[38]

Individual bankruptcy in Japan roughly parallels Chapter 7 filings in

36. Ibid.

37. See Kenji Kiyonaga, Iwayuru Sarari-man Kin'yū Saikensha no Jisatsu no Bunseki [An Analysis of Sarakin Suicides], 27:2 Kagaku Keisatsu Kenkyūjo Hōkoku 70 (Dec. 1986). Another type of data comes from the National Consumer Affairs Center, which recorded 97,120 counseling incidents related to sarakin in 2002, a figure that represents 11.7 percent of all counseling incidents and an increase over the previous year's record of 7.3 percent. See Kokumin Seikatsu Senta-, Shōhi Seikatsu Nenpō 2003 [Consumer Affairs Yearbook 2003], available at http://www.kokusen.go.jp/pdf/n-20031003_3.pdf.

38. Individuals could choose composition instead of bankruptcy, but historically they have not. See Theodore Eisenberg and Shoichi Tagashira, Should We Abolish Chapter 11? The Evidence from Japan, 23 J. Legal Stud. 111, 116 and n. 18. One reason why may be that composition does not stay the enforcement by debtors of secured claims. Ibid. at 119–20. The use of other options, including informal compromise and formal conciliation, has in-

the United States. At the commencement of the bankruptcy, a trustee (almost always a lawyer) takes control of the debtor's assets to liquidate them for creditors, in much the same way that a U.S. trustee does.[39] According to the Bankruptcy Act (arts. 157–69), the trustee arranges meetings of creditors much like a "section 341 meeting" in the United States. Creditors submit proof of claims that are subject to approval of the trustee and of the court (arts. 228–29). Ultimately, the judge issues a discharge (arts. 87–98).

Although the systems are facially similar, many differences arise—and most of them point to the fact that the Japanese system is more onerous. Consider the following four differences. First, unlike the U.S. system, in which bankruptcy proceedings commence upon filing, the process does not start in Japan until "two weeks to six months later, when the court finds that the debtor has met the indicia of bankruptcy."[40] Second, in the U.S. system, an automatic stay is issued at commencement. But in Japan, as Kent Anderson explains, "[D]ebtor's assets are only protected upon application for and granting of a 'preservation measure.' Preservation measures are generally directed at specific assets or proceedings rather than blanket protection. . . . Related to the lack of an automatic stay, all secured creditors have the right to proceed against assets outside of the insolvency proceedings. Further, those with rights of setoff and title ownership of property held by the debtor are similarly free to control the relevant assets without specific permission from the court."[41] Third, unlike the U.S. system, in which discharge is automatic (and often done by mail),[42] Japan's Bankruptcy Act (art. 366) requires a judicial order. Finally, unlike the nondiscriminatory U.S. system, the Japanese bankruptcy regime limits the activities of persons discharged from bankruptcy, prohibiting them from becoming, among other things, a lawyer, a guardian

---

creased in recent years. See Kent Anderson and Stacey Steele, Insolvency, in Japan Business Law Guide ¶¶19-601 to 19-644, ed. Veronica Taylor (2003).

39. Hasan hō [Bankruptcy Act], Law no. 71 of 1922, arts. 6, 142; see also Teresa A. Sullivan, Elizabeth Warren and Jay Lawrence Westbrook, As We Forgive Our Debtors: Bankruptcy and Consumer Credit in America, 26–33 (1989) (describing a typical U.S. Chapter 7 case).

40. Kent Anderson, The Cross-Border Insolvency Paradigm: A Defense of the Modified Universal Approach Considering the Japanese Experience, 21 U. Penn. J. Int'l Econ. L. 679, 704 (2000).

41. Ibid. at 705–6.

42. Sullivan et al., *supra* note 39, at 30.

of a minor, a custodian, a supervisor of a guardian, an executor of a will, a trustee, a notary, a patent agent, a certified public accountant, or a corporate director.[43]

Since the late 1990s, courts have eased the burdens of Japanese consumer bankruptcy law. For instance, pursuant to a Tokyo District Court rule implemented in April 1998 (and copied in Kawasaki and Yokohama courts), commencement is officially granted in simple cases when a lawyer files the case; the debtor need not show up in court. Courts have also experimented with collective discharge procedures that greatly expedite cases.

The biggest boost to consumer insolvency was not judicial: the Japanese legislature in November 2000 (effective April 2001) with great fanfare created a second option for individual debtors: civil rehabilitation.[44] Civil rehabilitation parallels Chapter 13 proceedings in the United States. The debtor may choose either "small-scale" or "salaried income" proceedings. The Ministry of Justice explains that the small-scale option is designed for farmers and the self-employed, and the salaried income option is for the "salaryman"; the primary difference is income regularity.[45] Pursuant to the act (art. 221), debtors in either category may file if they have less than ¥30 million (about $300,000) in unsecured debt. In principle, the debtor continues to control her assets (art. 38(1)), subject to an affirmative duty to act fairly and faithfully (art. 38(2)). The court may appoint a supervisor, and no formal judicial proceeding is required (art. 54).

Civil rehabilitation allows a debtor to negotiate a rehabilitation plan with creditors. In general, the plan must provide for repayment in three years to unsecured creditors of the larger of (a) a percentage of the debt,

---

43. See Anderson, *supra* note 40, at 706 and n. 109.

44. Civil rehabilitation technically became an option for individuals with the passage of Minji Saisei Hō [Civil Rehabilitation Act], Law no. 226 of 1999, effective April 2000, because that law makes eligible all persons, both natural and artificial. Few individuals used the provisions. See Kent Anderson, Small Business Reorganizations: An Examination of Japan's Civil Rehabilitation Act Considering U.S. Policy Implications and Foreign Creditors' Practical Interests, 75 Am. Bankr. L.J. 355, 366 and n. 60 (2001). It was not until the individual framework was set up by an amendment to that law, Minji Saisei Hō Nado wo Ichibu wo Kaisei suru Hōritsu, Law no. 225 of 2000, that individual civil rehabilitation became truly feasible, because the amendment provided for home mortgage exemptions and summary proceedings.

45. See Ministry of Justice, Dai 150kai ni oite Seiritsu shita "Minji Saisei Hō nado no ichibu wo Kaisei suru Hōritsu" ni Tsuite [Regarding the Civil Rehabilitation Law Passed in the 150th Diet Session], http://www.moj.go.jp/HOUAN/houan08.html.

usually one-fifth, or (b) an amount equal to two years' disposable income (for salaried income proceedings) (arts. 221–45). In most cases, home mortgages are excluded from the total amount of allowable debt, are extended for up to ten years, and are not subject to creditor vote (arts. 196–206). Creditors approve the plan with a majority vote (summary approval procedures are often available with creditors' consent). The court confirms the rehabilitation plan, it is executed, and the remaining debt is discharged (arts. 221–45).

Japanese Supreme Court survey data for thirty court districts at the end of one year of operation of the statute illuminate individual civil rehabilitation patterns. Contrary to initial estimates that farmers would be the most likely users of the law, more than 70 percent of filings were "salaried income" proceedings.[46] Nearly one-half of filers had income of ¥2 million to ¥4 million ($20,000 to $40,000). Fewer than 1 percent of filers had income exceeding ¥10 million yen, fewer than 3.5 percent had income of less than ¥1 million yen, and average income was ¥3.6 million yen, putting most filers squarely in the middle class. Average debt was ¥8.46 million yen, and more than half of filers had debts of ¥3 million to ¥9 million; the average number of creditors was eleven, and more than two-thirds of filers had between five and fifteen. Average time from filing to execution was 152 days, with a minimum in 583 surveyed cases of 68 days and a maximum of 289 days.[47]

In general, bankruptcy in Japan, like Chapter 7 in the United States, gives a (mostly) fresh start to people willing to make substantial sacrifices by eliminating some debts, and civil rehabilitation, like Chapter 13, offers an opportunity for people to pay their debts. But "fresh starts" aside, the actual workings of the bankruptcy and civil rehabilitation systems do not differ dramatically; length and costs of proceedings are roughly the same. Nor do future lenders differentiate between former bankruptcy filers and former civil rehabilitation filers; deadbeats are deadbeats. Instead, the primary difference lies in the *perceived* difference. Again Kent Anderson, discussing the corporate context, is instructive:

[W]ith the [Civil Rehabilitation Act's] passage there was a renewed interest in and commitment to proactively reforming, merging, and liquidating troubled

---

46. Takeshi Hatano and Hideaki Iwanami, Kojin Saisei Jiken no Gaikyō [Outline of Individual Rehabilitations], 741 NBL 17, 20 (2002).

47. Ibid. at 20–27.

businesses. This enthusiasm was captured by the courts, which have promised
to expedite cases, debtors, who have initiated more reorganizations than ever
before, creditors, who have promised to be more active and cooperative, academics, who have sung the praises of the act and its intended purpose, the bureaucrats who have promoted use of the [act], and even the media, which [have]
publicized it in, among other ways, a prime-time television special on its use. In
short, the enactment of the [act] was a symbolic gesture to a more expedient,
user-friendly, and affirmative reorganization scheme.[48]

As the bankruptcy system is liberalized via reforms scheduled to be
enforced in 2004, substantive differences between the two systems may
decrease further.

In the United States, Chapter 13 is considered "less stigmatizing" than
Chapter 7,[49] and, as orchestrated perceptions have taken root, the same
appears to be true in Japan. As one company employee told a Japan Economic Newswire reporter, "I thought of (filing papers with the court) for
personal bankruptcy, but I could not do that because my family was concerned about keeping up appearances. I opted for the 'individual version'
of the civil rehabilitation process, questioning myself about the morality
of paying back the money I borrowed."[50] I address the issues of stigma
and ease of filing in more detail below.

Bankruptcy and civil rehabilitation filings both have increased in recent
years. The number of individual bankruptcy filings rose from 160,741 in
2001 to 214,996 in 2002 and 251,799 in 2003. In the same period, the number of individual civil rehabilitations rose from 6,210 to 13,498 to 23,612,
a much larger increase in terms of percentage but perhaps not so remark-
able given the smaller numbers.[51]

Above, I charted macroeconomic indicators and individual bankruptcy
and found an equivocal relation. Now that the outlines of consumer insolvency options have been sketched, we can examine another potential rela-

48. Anderson, *supra* note 44, at 363.

49. Sullivan et al. *supra* note 39, at 34.

50. New Law Makes Declaring Personal Bankruptcy Easier, Japan Economic
Newswire, July 7, 2002, available on LEXIS.

51. Takeshi Hatano and Noriaki Kitazawa, Kinnen no Tōsan Jiken Mōshitate no Gaikyō
[Outline of Recent Bankruptcy Petitions], 760 NBL 32, 33–34 (2003); Chieko Tsutsumi and
Hiroyuki ōbayashi, Heisei 15nen ni okeru Tōsan Jiken Mōshitate no Gaikyō ni Tsuite [Re-
garding 2003 Bankruptcy Filings], 784 NBL 34, 35 (2004).

Figure 8.5. Monthly Suicides Relative to Bankruptcy and Rehabilitation Petitions, April 2001–March 2002

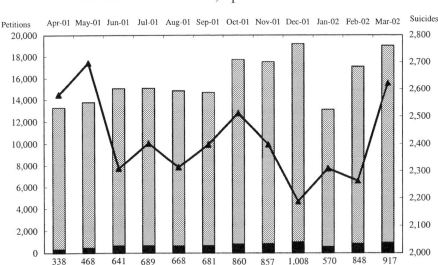

tion: that between civil rehabilitation petitions and suicide. Figure 8.5 shows the monthly data for the first year of the civil rehabilitation scheme's existence and compares them with bankruptcy and suicide data.[52]

As the figure shows, rehabilitation petitions are roughly correlated with individual bankruptcy petitions, suggesting a bifurcated market and not a substitution effect. Although this finding might be merely an early year effect, because norms of filing have not yet settled, it is potentially important. One possible interpretation is that potential petitioners are not choosing between civil rehabilitation and bankruptcy but between civil rehabilitation and some other option, perhaps not filing at all, or perhaps suicide. But once again, forming firm conclusions, especially about the relation between suicide and petitions, is difficult.

52. Looking at the first year's data requires caution because special circumstances that may have led to the law's enactment are difficult to quantify. Monthly data require additional caution; filings may increase at the end of the year for tax-related reasons, and studies conducted in Japan have shown an increase in suicides in the spring (and for that matter, on average, on Fridays and between 6 P.M. and midnight). Ayanori Okazaki, Jisatsu no Kuni [Suicide Nation], 51–58 (1958).

UNRAVELING THE RELATION

We now can unpack the relation between insolvency law and suicide. I first attempt to do so at the macro level by examining the results of regression analysis. I then turn to the micro level, looking primarily at data gathered from interviews. The two approaches produce complementary results.

Quantitative Data

I construct a multiple regression model to estimate the effects of bankruptcy and related laws on suicide rates. I make no grand claims based solely on these regressions. But if the regressions suggest some correlation that does not conflict with other available evidence, I am inclined to regard them as useful and perhaps important. They also raise some interesting lines of inquiry in this sensitive area for field research (which can help determine whether any observed correlations might be spurious), and for that reason I present them first.

Variables. I hand-collected data about each of Japan's forty-seven prefectures. For reasons that I discuss below, the primary dependent variable is the annual suicide rate,[53] which I subdivided into male and female suicides. As discussed above male and female suicide rates differ dramatically. For economic suicides, the discrepancy is quite stark. In 2002, of the suicide victims who left notes, 42 percent of the men blamed economic problems; only 12 percent of the women did. Of the note-leaving victims who blamed the economy, only 8 percent were female.[54]

The independent variables, which largely follow other established studies of suicide, attempt to control for various other potentially relevant social and economic phenomena and are as follows:

As for law, I include measures of the number of bankruptcies and civil rehabilitation petitions filed in district court. The correlations are difficult to predict. Both might be positively correlated with suicide, because each

53. The data are from Ministry of Health, Labor and Welfare, Jinkō Dōtai Chōsa [Vital Statistics], at http://wwwdbtk.mhlw.go.jp/toukei/data/010/2001/toukeihyou/0003840/ t0065823/mc190_001.html and http://wwwdbtk.mhlw.go.jp/toukei/data/010/2002/ toukeihyou/0004214/t0082288/jc040_007.html.

54. Keisatsuchō Seikatsu Anzenkyoku Chiikuka, *supra* note 1.

might be measuring the number of persons in financial distress. But both might also be negatively correlated, because some accounts suggest that suicide in fact substitutes for formal legal actions. Or the two measures might differ, because less stigma may be attached to rehabilitation than to bankruptcy, which could mean a negative correlation for rehabilitation and an uncertain result for bankruptcy.

With regard to balance sheets, I control for income and debt. Income is a well-studied variable in suicide studies. Controlling for debt levels is an admittedly imperfect attempt to control for the number of persons in a prefecture who are under financial strain.

Finally, I control for divorce, unemployment, and mental health care.[55] The divorce rate has often been used in quantitative suicide studies. A significantly positive correlation is often observed, perhaps because divorce is a "primary source of individual trauma that might precipitate suicidal behavior."[56] Still, the direction of correlation is not necessarily a foregone conclusion in Japan, where social and economic forces are said to trap women in bad marriages with some frequency. Studies that have shown unemployment to be negatively correlated to mortality find nonetheless that unemployment is positively correlated to suicide,[57] and I expect to find a similar correlation.

Mental health care is widely available in Japan, but it generally takes place in mental institutions, which are largely devoted to elderly patients (many with Alzheimer's), people with obvious brain disorders, and people who have already attempted suicide. Although the number of outpatients has increased over the past four decades (and the number of admitted patients has decreased), outpatient care is still not widely practiced or sought out by potential suicide victims or their loved ones. Most suicide counseling in the professional psychology sector, if it occurs at all,

55. Of course, I do not assume that I have included all relevant social factors. A recent study, for instance, shows reduced suicide rates in Kobe following the 1995 earthquake discussed in chapter 3; see Toshiki Shiori et al., The Kobe Earthquake and Reduced Suicide Rate in Japanese Males, 56(2) Archives of Gen. Psychiatry 282 (Mar. 1999). One possible explanation offered by the authors is that in postearthquake Kobe, there were fewer high buildings from which to jump.

56. See e.g., Bijou Yang, The Economy and Suicide: A Time-Series Study of the U.S.A., 51:1 Am J. Econ. & Soc. 87–99, 89 (1992).

57. Christopher J. Ruhm, Are Recessions Good for Your Health?, 115:2 Q. J. Econ. 617–50, 633 (2000).

occurs on an outpatient basis, so I use the number of mental health outpatients as an independent variable.[58]

Still, readers are cautioned not to compare this number directly to U.S. numbers. Mental health care in Japan is relatively new, and it comes with significant stigmas attached. Treatment for depression is rare, antidepressant drugs are not widely accessible,[59] and the process by which "Japanese psychiatrists in private practice see patients for five to 10 minutes for just medication management after the patients wait for one to two hours" is said to typify the "mechanical non-human communication between Japanese mental health professionals and their patients."[60] The situation appears to be changing gradually; popular books about depression abound, and television commercials ("My doctor said, 'It's depression. You must have been in a lot of pain'") inform viewers that depression is a treatable malady. But mental health nonetheless continues to have a different place in Japan.

Results. The results of the regressions, presented in table 8.3, may be interpreted as follows.[61] For total suicide rates, the only significant relations were a negative correlation to divorce and a positive correlation to unemployment. The latter was predicted, but I was unsure about the former, and the relation merits further study in the sex-specific panels. Liabilities were negative and marginally significant.

Female suicide rates exhibited one significant relation: a negative relation to divorce. Consider three interpretations. First, the correlation might indicate many unhappy marriages in which spouses feel trapped (and thus divorce, rather than causing stress, relieves it), perhaps because

58. See Gohei Yagi and Akira Tanabe, Nihon Seishinshō Chiryō Shi [History of Japanese Mental Health Care], 288–310 (2002).

59. Peter Landers, Drug Companies Push Japan to Change View of Depression, Wall St. J., Oct. 9, 2002, at A1. As of 2003, Zoloft and Prozac were still unavailable in Japan except through an exception to the drug laws that allows importation of prescription drugs from outside of Japan for personal use. Luvox, a Prozac-class drug, became available in 1993, see ibid.

60. Kari Huus, Japan's Chilling Internet Suicide Pacts, available at http://www.msnbc.com/news/922190.asp.

61. Regressions are ordinary least squares. I also experimented with, but do not report, time-series analysis and lagged variables as well as two-stage least squares, with results that differed little from those given above.

Table 8.3. Correlates of Suicide in Japan, 2001–2003

Explanatory variables	Total suicide rates		Female suicide rates		Male suicide rates	
	Standardized coefficient	t-stat	Standardized coefficient	t-stat	Standardized coefficient	t-stat
Bankruptcy	.199	1.024	.187	.856	.187	1.003
Civil rehabilitation	−.139	−.914	.018	.103	−.323	−2.742***
Divorce	−.569	−2.863***	−.640	−2.862***	−.490	−2.567**
Debt	−.122	−.776	−.095	−.537	−.124	−.816
Income	.007	.049	.084	.539	−.027	−.204
Mental health outpatients	.318	1.862*	.094	.490	.387	2.363**
Unemployment	.534	2.941***	.369	1.805*	.560	3.211***
Intercept		3.219***		2.834***		3.080***
Adjusted R^2	.325		.145		.378	
Observations	47		47		47	

Sources: *Bankruptcy:* Shihō Tōkei Geppō, available at http://www.courts.go.jp. *Civil rehabilitation:* Takeshi Hatano and Hideaki Iwanami, Kokin Saisei Jiken no Gaikyō, 741 NBL 17, 18–19 (2002); Takeshi Hatano and Noriaki Kitazawa, Kinnen no Tōsan Jiken Mōshitate no Gaikyō [Outline of Recent Bankruptcy Petitions], 760 NBL 32, 33–34 (2003); and Chieko Tsutsumi and Hiroyuki Ōbayashi, Heisei 15nen ni okeru Tōsan Jiken Mōshitate no Gaikyō ni Tsuite [Regarding 2003 Bankruptcy Filings], 784 NBL 34, 35 (2004). *Divorce:* Jinkō Dōtai Tōkei, ed. Kōseisho (2002). *Debt:* Sōmushō Tōkeikyoku, Shakai Seikatsu Kihon Chōsa Hōkoku (2002). *Income:* Sōmucho Tōkeikyoku, Kakei Chōsa Nenpō (2001). *Mental health outpatients:* Kōsei Rōdōshō Daijin Kanbō Sōkei Jōhōbu, Iryū Shisetsu Chōsa/Byōin Hōkoku (2002). *Unemployment:* Ministry of Health, Labor, and Welfare, available at http://wwwdbtk.mhlw.go.jp/toukei/data and at Kōsei Rōdōshō, Rōdō Keizai Hakusho at reference page 29 (2002).

Note: *Bankruptcy* is the total number of individual bankruptcies filed in district court per 1,000 persons. *Civil rehabilitation* is the total number of individual civil rehabilitation petitions filed in district court per 1,000 persons. *Divorce* is the divorce rate. *Income* is average disposable income per worker's household. *Liabilities* is average liabilities per household. *Mental health outpatients* is the total number of outpatients in mental hospitals per 1,000 persons. *Unemployment* is the employment rate.
*, **, and *** indicate significance at the 90 percent, 95 percent, and 99 percent levels, respectively.

contested divorce is hard to obtain in Japan.[62] Second, and more broadly, the correlation might suggest that prefectures in which the stigma against divorce is strong have less stigma against suicide; prefectural variation might result from differing demographics, norms, or histories.

62. Japanese divorce law provides for easy consensual divorce, but gaining consent of a reluctant spouse may be difficult and costly. Courts historically prohibit divorce when the

A third possible explanation follows from Durkheim's classic study of suicide. Durkheim theorized that suicide rates go up when people are too detached from social networks (egoistic suicide) and when people are too close to them (altruistic suicide).[63] Either might apply here. On one hand, divorce might allow spouses—especially women, whose time is more likely to be spent on family tasks than on broader social networks—to rejoin other meaningful social groups. On the other, divorce might loosen the social bonds that might encourage "altruistic" spousal suicide, in which spouses commit suicide together, or in which one spouse commits suicide to spare the survivor from incurring his debts, a life-insurance-based phenomenon in Japan that I discuss in the next section.

Male suicide rates were significantly correlated to four variables. First, civil rehabilitation was negatively correlated, at least tentatively suggesting that it provides an option other than suicide for persons in financial distress. Second, divorce was negatively correlated, perhaps for the reasons discussed above. Third, the number of mental health outpatients was positively correlated. Finally, I found a highly significant positive relation to unemployment.

Note that in no specification was a significant correlation to bankruptcy observed. Although that finding is ambiguous, it does suggest at some level that the substitution relation between bankruptcy and suicide may be exaggerated and that suicide may be more dependent on other social and economic factors.

Two alternative measures. I used the annual suicide rate given above rather than the economic suicide rate for a simple reason: I do not trust police data categorization in a system in which police, who usually have no formal psychological training, are *required* to choose one motive, even if several motives exist (and on top of that, they might simply be lying, confused, or mistaken).

As other scholars have noted, there are no studies of the reliability of the categorization,[64] so I conducted my own investigation. I reviewed sui-

---

person at fault brings the action. See Taimie L. Bryant, Marital Dissolution in Japan: Legal Obstacles and Their Impact, 17 Law in Japan 73 (1984).

63. Emile Durkheim, Suicide: A Study in Sociology (1897), trans. John A. Spaulding and George Simpson (1951).

64. David Lester and Yukio Saito, Predicting the Time-Series Suicide Rate in Japan by Motive: A Brief Note, 45 Omega 149, 150 (2002).

cide notes in two locations: one urban, one rural. In the urban location, I was allowed to review sixty-two suicide notes. The notes that I read were gloomy, as I expected, and, most relevant for judging the reliability of the data, tended to contain multiple explanations. I categorized the notes by motive, as police do. But when I checked my categorization against that of the police administrator in charge of categorizing the letters, I found that we differed in more than one-third of the cases. I detected no particular police bias in favor of one explanation or another. The administrator made principled (but to me, unconvincing) arguments for his categorization, and of course our disagreement does not mean that I am correct. But perhaps because neither of us truly had expertise in interpretation, we were unable reach a satisfactory resolution.

I then examined twenty-one letters at a rural location in Kyushu. At this location, in addition to finding categorization to differ from that explained to me in the urban location, I detected what I believe to be a systemic bias: in cases of ambiguity, police tended to choose explanations that did not shame the decedent or the family. Recall the classifications: family problems, health, economic hardship, job stress, relationships, school, alcoholism and mental illness, and "other." Police seemed to eschew explanations of alcoholism and mental illness and family problems in favor of economic- and health-based explanations. This is troubling; the primary reason cited by other experts for using police data instead of cause-of-death data gathered from medical examiners by the Ministry of Health is that the former avoid such problems and the latter do not.[65] When I asked the officer about this classification, he said he thought that my claim had some merit but that such biases would only occur in cases with notes when the classification was ambiguous, and in cases without notes, police take the age, sex, and occupation of the victim into account when determining the reason for suicide—hardly encouraging comments for serious data analysis.

Moreover, suicide-note data may be biased in several systematic ways independent of classification errors. Older victims tend to leave notes more often than younger victims, and men tend to leave notes more often than women.[66] One Japanese study has found that unsuccessful suicide attempters leave notes more often than successful victims.[67] Although this

65. Takahashi, *supra* note 6, at 5.

66. Keisatsuchō Seikatsu Anzenkyoku Chiikuka, *supra* note 1.

67. Kenshirō Ōhara, Isho [Suicide Notes], in 1 Jisatusgaku 175, 184–86, ed. Kenshirō Ōhara (1974).

finding could be based on the "cry for help" nature of unsuccessful attempts, another interpretation might be that suicide notes are simply biased by the relative difficulty of completing the act in a gunless society.[68] Some notes are also addressed specifically to the police, and it is not inconceivable that some victims would modify their notes for that audience or strive to create explanations that would make sense to that audience. Noteless cases, in which police tend to rely on statements of family, friends, and coworkers, are even more suspect.

Accordingly, I chose not to rely on the economic-suicide data, but I ran the regressions separately using those data nonetheless. The results were remarkably similar; the small differences from the gross annual suicide rate regressions (stronger correlations for civil rehabilitation and unemployment for males) do not merit reproduction of the results here.

Of course, the gross annual suicide rate that I use also might be problematic. It is possible that police inaccurately categorize accidents and suicides; if a body is found at the base of a tall building and there are no witnesses, it might be difficult for police to determine whether the victim fell or jumped. Police officers to whom I spoke at least seemed confident in their ability to classify such incidents, perhaps because hanging is a common method of suicide and accidental asphyxiation by hanging is unlikely.[69] I also have little reason to suspect a systematic bias in favor of accidents instead of suicides in rural locations, because suicide rates in Japan are *higher* in rural than in urban areas.[70]

68. Nearly three-fourths of male victims die of asphyxiation by hanging. The other methods most frequently used by men are, in descending order of frequency, jumping from tall buildings, carbon monoxide poisoning, overdose, self-injury with a sharp object, jumping in front of a train, and drowning. Nearly two-thirds of women also choose hanging, up from a little over half five years ago, followed by jumping off tall buildings, overdose, carbon monoxide poisoning, jumping in front of a train, and self-injury with a sharp object. Ministry of Health, Labor, and Welfare, Jinkō Dōtai Chōsa [Vital Statistics], available at http://wwwdbtk.mhlw.go.jp/toukei/data/010/2001/toukeihyou/0003844/t0065997/mc360_001.html.

69. It is unlikely but not impossible. The DSM-IV estimates deaths of two persons per million population per year from all kinds of hypoxyphilia (sexual arousal by oxygen deprivation), of which autoerotic asphyxiation by hanging is a subset. Diagnostic and Statistical Manual of the American Psychiatric Association §302.83, at 529 (4th ed. 1994). The estimate for Japan for all hypoxyphilia would thus be 125 persons per year, less than one-half of one percent of the annual suicide total.

70. See Takahashi, *supra* note 2, at 39; Tsutomu Yamamoto, Contemporary Social Problems in Japan: A Study of the Suicide and Depopulation Problems, 1 Int'l J. Japan. Soc. 19

Table 8.4. Unexplained Deaths and Suicides, 1991–2001

Year	Unexplained deaths	Suicides
1991	75,224	21,302
1992	78,803	22,372
1993	81,580	22,171
1994	83,749	22,472
1995	90,747	23,198
1996	91,452	24,051
1997	94,232	26,006
1998	107,173	33,925
1999	114,267	33,664
2000	116,164	32,674
2001	119,396	31,768

Source: Koichi Hiraiwa and Sumiko Abe, Jisatsu Yosoku to Sono Hantei Kijun [Forecasting Suicide and the Decisionmaking Standard], in Jisatsu Kito [Suicide Pact], 207, 208, ed. Teruhiko Higuchi (2002).

Still, when I asked police what kind of person they considered likely to commit suicide, some cited cases of people experiencing stress, depression, shame, or debt, but many responses were straight out of Durkheim, including "people who don't have ties to society" and "people who think that this is the only way out for their families." These opinions might affect police officers' decisions about whether the death was a suicide.[71]

Accordingly, I examined a second alternative data set that does not rely on suicide coding. Police have a separate data category for deaths that cannot be explained. As table 8.4 shows, these unexplained deaths are roughly correlated to suicide rates. Accordingly, in addition to running the regressions with the annual suicide rate, sex-based categories, and economically based suicides as the dependent variables, I also ran regressions using the unexplained death rate as the dependent variable. Once again, I found no significant differences.

Summary. To be sure, the data are far from perfect. But taken together, these results suggest three tentative conclusions. First, many nonlaw fac-

_____

(1992). In another regression I controlled for urban as opposed to rural differences using several different measures. The correlation was negative but insignificant and did not result in significant differences in the other variables.

71. The same appears to be true of U.K. coroners; see Steve Taylor, Suicide and the Study of Durkheim, 65–94 (1982).

tors such as unemployment appear to matter. Second, in no category was a statistically significant relation observed between suicide and bankruptcy. Suicide thus does not appear to substitute directly for bankruptcy—if anything, more bankruptcies means more suicides, suggesting that both are measures of financial distress (and perhaps also casting doubt on the rationality of the victims). Finally, the regressions suggest that the Civil Rehabilitation Law may nevertheless be helpful in controlling suicide, at least for men, who are most likely to use it. The law's impact appears to be small, perhaps because the system is so new, but it is statistically significant nonetheless.

Field Research

The regression results are intriguing evidence of a correlation between male suicide rates and insolvency law. To gain further evidence for or against such a relation, and to explore the reasons why such a relation might exist, I interviewed people with information about suicide victims.

Unable to interview the group of people with whom interviews might have been most probative, victims, I spoke instead with a total of ninety persons, as categorized in table 8.5, in rough order of distance from the victim (and coincidentally or otherwise, also in rough order of willingness to talk). As the table shows, the closest I got to suicide victims was speaking with victims of failed suicides. Of course, I preserve anonymity for family members and debtors.

Most categories are self-explanatory, but four deserve elaboration. No lawyer is specifically licensed to do bankruptcy work; "bankruptcy lawyer" refers to a practitioner who professes to have a specialty. A "lawyer substitute" is a judicial scrivener, licensed by the state to perform simple legal tasks, including simple bankruptcies. "Debt counselors" normally work for nonprofit organizations that refer debtors to attorneys, some of whom take cases on a pro bono basis. "Suicide counselors" are mostly volunteers; suicide counseling is relatively new: the first hotline opened in Tokyo in 1971, and about seventy-five hundred counselors now work for forty-seven round-the-clock centers throughout the country.[72]

In addition to conducting the interviews, I also attended bankruptcy

---

72. Yukio Saitō, Sōdan no Genba kara—Yobō e no Mondai Teiki [From the Counseling Front: Problems of Prevention, in Sarari-man no Jisatsu [Salaryman Suicide], 37, ed. Yoshitomo Takahashi and Hiroshi Kawahito (1999).

Table 8.5. Interviewees

Interview group		Number
Police who investigate suicides		8
Counselors	Bankruptcy lawyers and lawyer substitutes	8
	Debt counselors	12
	Social workers	9
	Mental health professionals (psychologists)	9
	Suicide counselors	4
Families of suicide victims		15
Debtors	Debtors who told me they considered suicide	18
	Debtors who did not tell me they considered suicide	4
	Debtor-victims of failed suicide attempts	3
Total		90

and civil rehabilitation hearings and observed debt-counseling sessions and suicide-counseling hotlines. I also was permitted to observe a group therapy session (a rarity in Japan) for families of victims of suicide, several of whom contacted me then or later to discuss my project. None of this activity was exactly a barrel of laughs, but it did yield interesting insights.

To this evidence I also add news accounts and the relevant empirical work of other scholars, primarily Japanese psychologists. I primarily rely on these works, rather than discussions of suicide by non-Japanese scholars or of non-Japanese subjects, both because Japanese experts are closer to the problem and because the perception of the problem in Japan is important for understanding stigma.

I first consider the evidence regarding suicide as an option for debtors. I then examine evidence regarding the potential efficacy of legal change. Finally, I examine evidence that pertains to potential explanations.

Suicide as a way out of debt. Interviewees uniformly stated that suicide, like bankruptcy, often is perceived by people with serious debt problems as an acceptable and serious option. According to a psychologist, Takahiro Horibe, who has worked with many debt-ridden patients:

Some people become very desperate after taking on large debts. When they sit down to compute the amount of time that it will take to repay their debts, they often realize that they will never be able to do so. Moreover, many excessive debtors have more problems than debt alone; they typically find themselves in these situations when they lose their job and must borrow to make mortgage payments or rent payments. It's not the debt per se that's the problem, it's the enormous stress that the debt creates. Once a person arrives at that hopeless state, they can either suck it up and go into bankruptcy, or they can say "Why bother? It won't make any difference. I'm a failure." For these people, suicide is the easiest answer.

For Horibe, then, the process seems quite natural; debt leads to stress, stress leads to suicide. A case study in a textbook for psychologists who deal with suicide issues puts a more human face on Horibe's general analysis, and for that reason merits quotation at length:

50-year-old male.

Has chronic diabetes, and has injected himself with insulin for several years. He runs a small printing firm, but business has been poor, leaving him with multiple debts. He became difficult to deal with and irritable, marital problems occurred, and he divorced two years ago. His wife left the house. Six months ago, his business went under, and he took on the debts as an individual. To pay them, he borrowed money from friends and sarakin. His health worsened, and he began to eat and bathe irregularly.

Debt collecting efforts became intense, he thought "I want to get out of this," and he overdosed on insulin. A few hours later, he was discovered unconscious and admitted to the hospital. He regained consciousness and was detained in the hospital to control his diabetes. He was referred to a psychologist for depression. His depression was severe, but he responded relatively well to medication, and he returned to a level of normalcy. But his debt situation never changed, and he began to become self-destructive.

As for his debt problem, because it was a cause of his depression, he was referred to a social worker to fix his problems of environment. The social worker recommended personal bankruptcy and a plan to protect his wages, and the patient agreed. He returned to his normal insulin routine, and was released from the hospital.[73]

In both Horibe's analysis and the case study, then, debt played an important role in the onset of psychological conditions that lead to suicide and suicide attempts. Note also that in the case study, filing for bankruptcy was considered an element of treatment.

73. Kentoku Chō, Sōnenki no Jisatsu [Suicide in the Prime of Life], in Jisatsu Kito [Suicide Pact], 34, 44–45, ed. Teruhiko Higuchi (2002).

The psychologists that I interviewed agreed about the basic reasons why suicide is seen as a way out of debt; they said that the road from debt to suicide meanders through stress, depression, and occasionally irrationality. Some debtor-victims voiced agreement. Consider the following email, which I received from Inoue, a forty-seven-year-old office worker who found himself deep in debt but eventually chose bankruptcy:

There was no way that I could have paid my debts unless I won the lottery. So I used to play the lottery quite a bit, and I borrowed even more to do it. . . . My debt got so high that I realized I only had two choices: go bankrupt or "end it." So I looked into bankruptcy and a friend of mine told me that it took him 4 years and his lawyer was a shady guy and he wound up poor as dirt and I thought "why would I want such a thing? I need an answer *now,* not four years from now." . . .

So I started reading [suicide manuals] and so on to try and figure out some painless way of ending things; hanging seems so violent so I started importing drugs from Thailand to mix into a death potion. . . . I became really lonely and depressed about the whole thing even though I had read that people who decide to commit suicide usually get happy at the end because they've reached a decision, so I thought that maybe I wasn't really ready yet because all I felt was pain, just extreme emotional pain. . . . [After seeing a telephone number on a television program,] I then called a suicide hotline, and they referred me to a debt specialist who convinced me that maybe bankruptcy wouldn't be so bad and that I could start over and that a lawyer could get me out of my high-interest loans because the interest charged was too high under the law. . . . Looking back on it now, I think that the whole suicide thing was kind of stupid, but that's how I thought back then; it was all really, really gloomy.

But while psychologists spoke in terms of depression and stress, other interviewees spoke of a different path. Consider the following words from a debt counselor:

To be honest, I get really frustrated with some of the [debtors] with whom I work. I do this job because I want to help people work through their problems. But by the time that some people finally get around to coming in to seek practical answers, they already have a very fatalistic attitude toward the whole process. They hate themselves for taking on so much debt, their families, if they have told them the problem, have told them that they're failures and so on, and they believe it. They believe that they're worthless people simply because they borrowed a lot of money. . . . In some cases, they are subject to harassment from their creditors. . . . Part of my job is trying to convince these people that legal solutions like bankruptcy are better solutions than suicide, and that suicide destroys anything positive that remains in their lives.

Like the psychologists, the debt counselor also saw an indirect relation between debt and suicide. But for the debt counselor, debt leads to a lack of self-worth, and a lack of self-worth leads to suicide. These concepts are not necessarily related, and the ways in which different people discuss them might be reflected in the different ways people treat or respond to debt.

Not all interviewees focused on the internal emotional relation of debt to death. Consider the words of a police officer who has studied and investigated many suicides:

Officer: You read the same suicide note over and over again. Guy loses job. Guy can't pay the bills. Guy borrows from loan sharks at some crazy interest rate that he can't possibly repay. He thinks about bankruptcy but decides that would be too much of an inconvenience [*meiwaku*] for his family and friends, so he hangs himself.

Q: What do you think about such things?

Officer: Hmmm. . . I sympathize with these guys. I wish for their families' sakes that they'd swallow a little pride and just go to a lawyer or something to take care of it, but it's not like I don't understand what they're going through, and not everybody can pay a lawyer. Most people just figure, hey, my time is up. . . . Sometimes I respect them for doing it; I wouldn't have the guts.

The officer adds two important items to the mix of emotional factors. First, he notes that some victims consider the impact of their decision on family and friends. This concept of "burdening" people (meiwaku) in one's social circle was raised by many interviewees; many people seem to believe that killing oneself creates less of a burden, or perhaps less of a lasting burden, than living with a debtor. Of course, this motivation need not be exclusive (people can be depressed and think of family members simultaneously), rational, or even wholly altruistic, but it was widely expressed. As one failed suicide attempter told me: "I wasn't thinking clearly at all, of course. But I still thought of my family and how embarrassed they would be to find out how much I owed, and how I got myself into this situation in the first place. . . . They knew nothing about it. But the lenders were threatening to tell them—to tell my neighbors too. My mother was too proud for all of that; it would be such a burden [to put her through it]. I thought that if I committed suicide, those problems would go away and they would never find out about it."

Second, the officer says that he respects the victims and that their actions take courage. Although not a dominant theme of my interviewees, several people (all of whom, coincidentally or not, were over the age of fifty or were talking about such persons) expressed the idea that suicide was some combination of "traditional," "honorable," "selfless," and "courageous." If so, then suicide as a debt-reduction option might be more easily understood, and if such beliefs are widespread, the process by which individuals go from debt to death might be as much about social norms as internal emotional processes. Either motivation, of course, suggests that law needs to address responses to debt, and not debt alone.

Law's response. These data thus suggest that many debtors consider both bankruptcy and suicide. But they do not *necessarily* suggest that the two are substitutes. People who think that bankruptcy is "easy" might choose it without ever seriously considering suicide, and some people might commit suicide no matter what. Other people might not ever consider bankruptcy or even trace their psychological problems to their financial ones. In all cases, initial perceptions and predispositions may guide the set of choices.

This ambiguity prompted a second line of inquiry regarding whether making bankruptcy rules more debtor-friendly, either by civil rehabilitation (as has been done) or some other means, might lead to a decrease in the suicide rate. Some of the above responses already hint at such claims. Moreover, debt counselors uniformly stated that such changes would make major differences (I was told, without hyperbole, that "change in bankruptcy law is the one policy change that could actually have an effect on human lives"). This opinion is reflected in policies such as that of the "Network to Eliminate Debt Suicides," which explicitly advocates bankruptcy and civil rehabilitation as alternatives to suicide. Other interview responses varied from yes to maybe to no; I consider each in turn.

Among those who said yes, some thought that a different kind of bankruptcy system would make a substantive difference. The wife of one suicide victim told me: "I am angry at my husband for having killed himself, but I'm also angry at him for being too proud to be bankrupt. So you have to go to court and get a lawyer or whatever . . . who cares about such things? . . . [The problem is the] politicians who run this country for corporations and not people . . . they don't think about how difficult it is to be an ordinary person who owes lots of money . . . instead of helping people with debts they try to help [consumer finance companies] be more successful and kill us all. . . . If there had been some easy alternative to bankruptcy, some way that he could have gotten a break just for a little while, he'd still be alive."

Other debtors and victims' family members made similar statements. An adult daughter of a suicide victim told me that "better law would have kept my father from losing his life" and pleaded with me both to press for bankruptcy reform and to publicize the system in Japan. The president of a small printing company told me that he agonized over whether to chose bankruptcy or death but that making bankruptcy "more simple" would have made the choice much easier.

Still, many interviewees offered vague answers as to precisely how the bankruptcy regime should be, or should have been, improved. They wanted bankruptcy to be "easier" but were not sure exactly what that meant. Some were not even sure what was so difficult about the existing system, though they knew it to be expensive and time-consuming. As I suggest in the next subsection, I suspect that some of the ambiguity might stem from the fact that some of the perceived difficulty of the bankruptcy regime is related to social and not to legal or monetary factors.

Not all interviewees were so vague; some, in fact, pointed explicitly to civil rehabilitation as a solution. According to one bankruptcy lawyer:

The civil rehabilitation system has probably saved thousands of lives. And I have evidence. Before civil rehabilitation, clients would come in, I would tell them about bankruptcy options, and often they wouldn't come back. Some of them went to other lawyers, some of them just borrowed more and more, and some of them just ran away in the middle of the night [yonige]. But I know for sure what happened to at least two of them; they killed themselves. That must sound stupid to an American, but that's what Japanese people do; they just give up. . . . But after civil rehabilitation [was promulgated], the clients stay with me. They hear the solution, they hire me, and we take care of it. . . . Now I can convince them that it's not worth dying over.

And according to Hasegawa, a twenty-eight-year-old worker with credit card debt equal to a year's salary: "I was really depressed because of all the debt and because of the prospect of having to declare bankruptcy.

How could I face my family and friends? I thought about killing myself; at least that way cremation would be the only real expense. But I got some advice [from a debt counseling center] and decided to do civil rehabilitation. It's not such a big deal."

Responses that explicitly pointed to civil rehabilitation as a source of change were by no means the norm; only eleven interviewees—but all of the lawyers (who might have an interest in promoting the system)—raised the issue without prompting. Because the rehabilitation option has been available for such short period of time, the dearth of volunteered responses is not surprising, but it is noteworthy that all those who raised the issue made similarly positive statements.

The above interviewees are concrete examples of the way legal change can affect life-or-death decisions for some people. But opinions differed, and many interviewees—the maybes—stated that debtors' problems went beyond mere debt. According to a psychologist:

Psychologist: Bankruptcy law cannot fix mental health. People who commit suicide need treatment, not lawyers. . . . People who want to commit suicide will commit suicide, and people who want to erase their debts will erase their debts. They are two different categories.

Q: Are you saying that the only solution for patients considering suicide is medical treatment?

Psychologist: No, no, some people will kill themselves because they're lonely; a friend could be all the treatment they need. Others will kill themselves when they hear that they have cancer or some other horrible disease just so they don't have to go through it. And yes, some people might be persuaded to spare themselves if something could be done about their financial problems, so maybe some kind of law that easily did so could actually have an effect, but the law would matter not because it solved the debt, but because it changed their outlook. But if a person has resigned himself to suicide, I wouldn't think that law would have a huge effect. The law would have to have an effect before that stage.

This mental health professional, then, like others whom I interviewed, reflects the indirect causal philosophy that seems to underlie the treatment plan for the fifty-year-old in the case study quoted above. Bankruptcy, though not a solution per se, may have an indirect effect on psychological factors such as depression and stress, and by that mechanism might reduce suicides. It also may simply imply, as the case study suggests, that some people need both mental health care *and* bankruptcy reform, and that providing either alone is only a partial solution.

Some interviewees were even more cautious about the relation. According to a suicide counselor: "Changing the law might help some people find a way out. But many people that I talk with have more problems than just debt. They feel completely isolated from society, have real problems talking about their fears, and don't have close friends. The debt is only part of the problem, so solving that would only be a partial solution." For these persons, then, legal change might be insufficient. In a similar vein, a debt counselor added:

You could fix the rules on bankruptcy all you want and some people would still kill themselves over debt. Some would do it because they just get really desperate. Some are ashamed and don't want to bother anybody [*meiwaku wo kaketakunai*]. And lots of them have debts to sarakin that bankruptcy law can't fix. You can't go to a loan shark and say "the law says this, the law says that, you have to follow it." . . . Lawyers could play a much stronger role in dealing with the loan sharks, but people who go to sarakin are unlikely to go to lawyers; they aren't looking for legal solutions. . . . So some people are committing suicide to avoid having their throats cut, not to avoid bankruptcy. Maybe some are avoiding bankruptcy, though; it's not something we can say for sure for the entire group of people.

This debt counselor makes one insightful point and one questionable one. The insight comes in the third sentence, as he discusses the shame of bankruptcy. For some people, the problem might not be the insolvency mechanism itself but *any* mechanism that brings shame by publicly announcing the debt. For those people, it is unlikely that any amount of tinkering with insolvency institutions that does not involve extensive privacy protections would be insufficient. In small and close-knit communities, there might be no sufficient protection.

But the counselor's statement about sarakin is open to question. Although it is true that insolvency law might not pose a threat to most sarakin who function outside of private law, other interviewees strongly stated that people who seek insolvency-related legal help, whether from attorneys, debt counselors, or the courts, also received aid from those actors, police, and other enforcers in handling sarakin. The insolvency data used in the regressions presented above might thus be correlated not only because insolvency correlates with suicide but also because seeking help for insolvency reduces sarakins' influence, which in turn reduces suicide.

Other interviewees offered other nonbankruptcy-related explanations for suicide that suggest causal variation. They stated that the "real" problem in debt-related suicide is not an inefficient bankruptcy system but depression, loneliness, gambling, liquor, the sex industry, creditor harassment, or the illegal loan market. Many family members said that the relatives who killed themselves did not want to burden the family with their problems and chose the private solution of suicide instead, a characterization that implies that some people would avoid public insolvency at any cost. Some debtors said that when they were considering suicide, they realized that bankruptcy was complex but had no idea what it actually entailed. One debtor told me that he did not even realize that the root of his problem was money, and a man who attempted suicide told me that bankruptcy never crossed his mind as a possibility; both are cases in which even the most procedurally efficient or debtor-friendly insolvency law reform would appear to have little effect.

Quantitative data support such nondebt co-explanations. A study of ninety-three suicides at a Tokyo hospital from 1991 to 1993 showed that among young people (under age thirty-nine), 45 percent were schizophrenic and 33 percent were clinically depressed. Among people aged forty to fifty-nine, 45 percent were depressed, 16 percent were schizophrenic, and another 10 percent were suspected depression cases.[74] Another study, based on surveys of 420 family members of suicide victims in Fukushima Prefecture in 1997, found that the broader problems were loneliness and stress from a variety of sources that included economic hardship but also included many other factors.[75] The indirect approach— economic and social institutions that lead to psychological problems that lead to suicide—is common among Japanese mental health professionals for a wide range of issues that include unemployment and other workplace-based problems.[76]

74. Kantoku Hara, Chūnen no Jisatsu no Byōri [Pathology of Middle-Aged Suicide], 505–8 (2000).

75. Koichi Hiraiwa and Sumiko Abe, Jisatsu Yosoku to Sono Hantei Kijun [Forecasting Suicide and the Decisionmaking Standard], in Higuchi, *supra* note 73, at 207, 210–16.

76. See, e.g., Nobuo Kuroki, Jisatsu no Rōsai Hoshō no Genjō [The Current State of Suicide and Workers' Compensation], in Higuchi, *supra* note 73, at 170; Mayumi Sugawara, Jisatsu Kitosha wo Torimaku Kankyō—Shokuba ni Okeru Mentaru Herusu [Environmen-

This evidence suggests two possible relations. On one hand, if nondebt reasons explain many debt-induced suicides, mere tinkering with insolvency law without broader institutional overhaul might not generate large positive effects. On the other, the interview data largely tend to support, or at least do not contradict, the quantitative evidence, which suggests that insolvency reform could affect potential suicide victims positively by reducing one factor in debt-related suicides, namely, debt, which could in turn reduce the nondebt factors. This analysis dovetails nicely with evidence from the United States, in which Melissa Jacoby insightfully notes potential adverse health-related consequences from the law's approach to debt enforceability, debt collection, and debt encouragement.[77]

In short, the interviews and regressions appear to be consistent with a claim that bankruptcy and suicide are not necessarily substitutes. Though the two may be substitutes for some people, they appear to be two separate decisions for others; some people might choose between filing and not filing for bankruptcy, and again between life and suicide. But easing the rules for eliminating debt by a mechanism such as civil rehabilitation might have a significant effect on the suicide decision for some people.

Explanations. The quantitative and interview data suggest a relation between certain kinds of law and some suicides. But without an understanding of what is so bad about insolvency that it has a connection to life and death, formulating solutions is difficult. My research and interviews suggest two primary explanations for why law might be related to suicide: inefficiency of the bankruptcy system and stigma regarding bankruptcy. For many people in Japan whom I interviewed, the explanations are inseparable; about half mentioned both concepts, and systemic inefficiency might simply be a reflection of the social stigma. Still, I separate the two here for analytical purposes. I complete the analysis with an examination of the efficiency and stigma of suicide.

About half of the interviewees stated that bankruptcy is problematic because it is inefficient. Some offered only general assessments ("it is difficult"), which might pose more of a psychological barrier than known inefficiencies. But many explicitly named various systemic problems: bankruptcy was said to involve high attorneys' fees, to favor creditors,

---

tal Issues for Suicide Victims: Mental Health in the Workplace], in Higuchi ed., *supra* note 73, at 217.

77. Jacoby, *supra* note 5, at 564–67.

and to be time-consuming, difficult to understand, and unhelpful to debtors.

Reliable numbers are available for the first factor, attorneys' fees. A typical bankruptcy in Tokyo is said to cost approximately $4,000 if done by a lawyer and $2,000 if done by a judicial scrivener. Subject to income and other restrictions, the Japan Legal Aid Association offers assistance for a reduced price; a completed bankruptcy runs $2,050 if by an attorney and $1,040 if by a judicial scrivener.[78]

The other systemic factors are more difficult to quantify in all but broad relative terms, and civil rehabilitation may in fact differ little. But the perception is common, and anecdotal evidence abounds. Kensuke Suzuki published an account of his bankruptcy that echoes sentiments raised by my interviewees and illustrates these systemic inefficiencies.[79] According to Suzuki's book, the Kobe earthquake turned his $17 million cigarette import business to rubble, leaving him with personal debts of about $20,000 to banks and $8,500 to a credit card company, in addition to company debts. He liquidated his company but specifically rejected personal bankruptcy because he thought it too time-consuming and expensive. Instead, he "constantly" considered suicide as a solution, especially while behind the wheel of his car; he could see no other way out. But he found a newspaper article about a new kind of "summary" bankruptcy. The year was 2001, before the introduction of civil rehabilitation, and the system was little more than the relaxation of bankruptcy rules by the Tokyo District Court discussed above, but, because the process could be completed in three months, this "was a kind of bankruptcy I had never heard of."[80] Even this simplified process was not easy; it could only be done in the Tokyo court and not the Tokyo branch court near his home, and he soon learned that he could not apply pro se. He consulted several lawyers, each of whom refused his case because of his inability to pay their fees. He then consulted a nonlawyer who billed himself as a "professor of law" for representation. The professor demanded an up-front fee to be wired to his bank account, announced that the case would be handled by a student, and admonished Suzuki not to discuss the fee arrangements publicly because they violated fee rules. Thinking this a bit shady, Suzuki refused.

78. See, e.g., Yutaka Shōzui, Kojin no "Hasan" ha, Kazoku no "Hasan" de aru! [Personal Bankruptcy Equals Family Bankruptcy], in Yami Kin'yū [Underground Finance], 42, 60, ed. Manabu Inoue (2002).

79. Kensuke Suzuki, Hasan Kara no Saiki [Return from Banrkuptcy] (2002).

80. Ibid. at 161 and passim.

Eventually, with the help of a local nonprofit organization, Suzuki found a lawyer who agreed to take his case pro bono. He applied for summary bankruptcy in 2002 and claims to have emerged a new man, now running a $400,000-a-year international shipping business. His story is clearly one of success, but each step of this process required substantial initiative to battle systemic inefficiencies, and many troubled debtors who consider suicide simply do not have Suzuki's resolve.

Although the system is still new and unknown to many, civil rehabilitation is said to be more efficient than bankruptcy. One debt counselor explained:

Many people who come in for counseling have no idea what bankruptcy is like, or hear only the horror stories and worst-case scenarios. So when the come in, they automatically are opposed to bankruptcy. "Just give me anything but bankruptcy," they'll say. "Bankruptcy will be worse than the loan sharks, I'll have even less financial freedom [*kubi ga motto mawaranakunaru*, literally, my neck will turn even less], and I'll be dead before it ends." I spent a lot of time [in my job] telling such persons that bankruptcy really isn't so bad, when in fact I know that it really is time-consuming, costly, and sometimes unfair. . . . Civil rehabilitation makes my job much easier. When people come in to see me now, they don't have such a negative view of the process. They know that civil rehabilitation is supposed to be easier, quicker, and they won't lose everything. So from the beginning, they seem to have a much healthier attitude.

Returning to Hasegawa, the twenty-eight-year-old debtor who chose civil rehabilitation instead of suicide, claiming that civil rehabilitation is "not such a big deal":

Q: Why is it not such a big deal?

Hasegawa: It's so much easier. You just fill out a few forms and you're basically done. I knew it wouldn't take a long time and that I eventually would be free of debt.

Q: And that differs from bankruptcy?

Hasegawa: Bankruptcy is completely different; it's all about who gets what and how much blood they can suck out of you. And it takes forever, like pulling a bandage off your arm one millimeter at a time. That was the process that I dreaded; I needed to get out *now*.

Q: So much that you considered suicide?

Hasegawa: Yes. I thought that bankruptcy and suicide were my only options. I didn't really want to commit suicide, and maybe I really wouldn't have had the guts to go through with it. Maybe I would have just run away or something instead. But I just really didn't want to go through bankruptcy.

A bankruptcy lawyer offered a similar perspective: "Some people would do anything to avoid bankruptcy; it's like going to the dentist, you put it off and put it off until you're in so much pain that going to the dentist is much worse than if you had just gone in there early. . . . Bankruptcy is painful like that; people don't want to lose their homes and they don't want to go to court and they don't want to live as a bankrupt person for several years while the court decides their fate. . . . For people who are nervous or depressed or just kind of crazy, these bankruptcy costs are so high that suicide becomes more and more realistic. . . . Civil rehabilitation is much cheaper [and] easier [than bankruptcy], and that makes the choice [between life and death] easier as well. "

As these three opinions suggest, bankruptcy for some people is such a costly option that suicide becomes realistic. These persons might not be thinking clearly; at this stage many are suffering from severe stress and depression. But several interviewees expressed the idea that it is the economic cost of bankruptcy that makes it so undesirable. If so, a less costly mechanism such as civil rehabilitation seems much more appealing.

Other interviewees cited the social stigma that accompanies bankruptcy. We already know that debt-related stigma is significant in Japan. Lenders, as we have seen, threaten debtors with revelation to neighbors of their debts, and a favorite sarakin tactic is to roll by the debtor's house in a soundtrack, publicizing his finances over a megaphone ("Tanaka doesn't pay his debts!").

Measuring stigma is extraordinarily difficult. Still, my interviews suggest that many people avoid bankruptcy, whether by civil rehabilitation or by suicide, not because of cost-related issues but because of the stigma of being adjudicated bankrupt. More directly, about three-fourths of interviewees mentioned stigma and related social factors attaching to bankruptcy. Several stated that civil rehabilitation has less stigma, suggesting, at a minimum, that the large amount of publicity surrounding the enactment of the system made many conscious of its existence.

Consider first the words of Osaka lawyer Tatsuya Kimura, a specialist in solving debt problems. In an interview published in a book about underground debt, Kimura responded to questions about the demerits of filing for personal bankruptcy: "Regular employees of the government or of a large corporation must be careful; if the news comes out that an employee has filed for bankruptcy, he is in danger of being fired or relegated to lower assignments. But because there are other methods besides personal bankruptcy, there is no need to worry. Still, if you think about it, even with these limits to the bankruptcy system, after the debts are paid, at least a debtor can live a normal human life. Delaying bankruptcy for one year delays normal life for five."[81] Kimura's description of the social sanctions of bankruptcy is stark: file, and lose your job. The firing, as we saw in chapter 7, might not be legal if bankruptcy is the stated reason for the termination, but employers can offer other reasons or simply reassign. Interviewees who told me of such events explained that employers considered debtors to be bad decision makers and potential troublemakers. Although some debtors agreed that bankruptcy should be undertaken despite its great cost, many postponed or avoided it for precisely the stigma-related consequences that Kimura encourages them to overlook. Consider Suzuki, a fifty-two-year-old former debtor who now is something of a missionary for civil rehabilitation:

Suzuki: The reason that I chose civil rehabilitation over bankruptcy is simple: I didn't want to be branded as someone who was bankrupt. I can't imagine anything more embarrassing than that; it's like admitting to the entire world that you're a complete and total failure. I might as well have AIDS or leprosy.

Q: But some people might think that you were solving your problems through bankruptcy, right? They might say, "Oh, it's a shame that he got into such problems. But isn't it wonderful that he is being so manly (*otokomae*) in solving them?"

Suzuki: Nobody would say that. Or at least nobody I know. Maybe that's what rich people do, or foreigners or something, but nobody I know. Bankruptcy means you're a loser for life. My wife would have divorced me for sure.

Q: But civil rehabilitation was OK?

Suzuki: Oh, civil rehabilitation is completely different. I wouldn't say that it's honorable, but people don't despise you for it. . . . Even the word is better; bank-

---

81. Noriyuki Imanishi, Minna Tatakaisugirunya! [Stop Resisting!], in Yami Kin'yū, *supra* note 78, at 108, 113.

ruptcy means that I am broken [it uses the character for "broken" or "losing"], but civil rehabilitation means that I am "reborn."

The adult son of a man who committed suicide before the Civil Rehabilitation Law's enactment expressed similar sentiments in the following sad terms: "My father was a very proud man. He thought that if he declared bankruptcy, everyone would think of him as a failure; our neighbors, his co-workers, even me. . . . He claimed in his note that he was [killing himself] so that my family wouldn't be shamed. . . . Now [my seventeen-year-old brother] will have to try and find a wife whose parents don't mind that his father committed suicide . . . but maybe [the future wife's father] will share my father's old way of thinking and think that his death was honorable. . . . I guess that with either [suicide or bankruptcy], he would be a failure to some people, and in his mind, bankruptcy was worse."

And as a debt counselor lamented: "Japanese society has the line between shameful and not shameful completely reversed. How can it be so shameful to go to court and try to [make] things better? But yet that is what's shameful, and suicide is not as shameful. . . . Either way, people will know that you did something to get yourself into debt, and now the creditors are not getting paid. Making the choice to kill oneself instead of filing a few papers is such a tragic waste of human life."

Finally, consider this sad excerpt from the suicide note of the president of a small company: "My financial debts are simply more than I can bear. To those whom I hurt by borrowing more and more even when I knew it was impossible to pay it back, I'm sorry (mōshiwakenai). I wish I could pay it back but I cannot, and I do not want to shame my family . . . a man does not live in shame. Bankruptcy is a cowardly act . . . I will do no such thing. . . . I will end my life with dignity, and I will remember all those who were kind to me. I will never forget my family and I thank you for all you have done for me over the years. . . . [Son,] take care of your mother."

These statements leave little doubt that some people believe bankruptcy to entail significant social sanctions both to themselves and their families, so significant that the sacrificial act of suicide is more attractive. Even interviewees who, like the debt counselor and the family member, decried the stigma recognized it nonetheless, suggesting that social stigma erodes a meaningful postbankruptcy "fresh start."[82]

82. To speculate a bit, I suspect that the stigma reflects the general relative lack of second chances in Japan. Long-term employment arrangements and sticky labor markets make sec-

Reduction of insolvency's social stigma might be one of the primary benefits of civil rehabilitation. True, some interviewees were unfamiliar with the new regime, and, although the regressions show a correlation to suicide, widespread change has not yet occurred and may not occur soon. But among those who knew of the system, civil rehabilitation was seen as much less stigmatizing than bankruptcy, and accordingly it might be less taxing. The formal sanctions that attach to bankruptcy in the form of disenfranchisement do not exist in the newer system, and many interviewees stated that social sanctions also are lower, despite the fact that stigma reduction was never a stated goal of the reform. Lower social sanctions may thus help explain why some of even the most troubled debtors—those who would commit suicide because of their situation—might choose it in order to avoid taking their own lives in situation in which bankruptcy might not have had the same effect.

Bankruptcy, then, is viewed by many people as inefficient and stigma-causing. But what of the comparative efficiency and stigma of suicide?

If a debtor's goal is to eliminate his debts, suicide would seem to do a pretty good job. But institutions can make suicide even more effective in debt elimination. Until now, we have looked at debtors as if they existed in isolation, but interviews with family members show the importance of viewing the victim in context. Consider the choice set of a debtor with a family. If he lives, his family struggles with his debt as he undergoes bankruptcy. But if he dies—in Durkheim's classic altruistic suicide mode—his family is likely to get an insurance payout. If his death looks accidental, payout is assured. Even if the death is clearly a suicide, in stark contrast to the United States, payout in Japan is likely.

The Japanese Commercial Code (art. 680) provides that insurers need not pay in suicide cases. But Japanese life insurance contracts normally have no exclusion of benefits for suicide provided that the victim has held the policy for a minimum period of time, usually one, two, or three years.[83] Japanese insurers usually invoked the Commercial Code only if it became apparent that the victim planned to commit suicide at the time he bought the policy; the benevolence, according to the Japanese Life In-

---

ond chances unavailable for most. In this immobile system, scars are lasting, and opportunities for redemption are often few. Japanese law codifies this idea by disenfranchising filers for life (even if it has no real consequences for most); as discussed above, bankruptcy law prohibits discharged debtors from assuming certain jobs and responsibilities.

83. See Amamiya, *supra* note 19, at 64–69. Most life insurers raised the exclusion period from one year to two in 1999 in response to rising suicide rates.

surance Association, results from the feeling that "we should focus on the life of the spouse after the primary insurer commits suicide."[84] In one case, a sixty-one-year-old company president took out ten policies with one-year exclusions for a total of $20 million. He killed himself (or fell from a construction site, at least) about a year later. Insurers refused to pay. The victim's wife brought suit, and the Supreme Court, in a landmark 2004 ruling, held that the contract trumps the statute and the insurers whose policies were issued more than one year before the death must pay.[85] Presumably insurers prefer to litigate the outlying claims rather than be the first market player to delete the suicide exemption altogether.

Thus, although bankruptcy might be an inefficient legal option for limiting debts, another option, life insurance, is available. If the goal is debt reduction, it can be quite effective. Large insurance policies often provide families with financial security even if victims' debts are satisfied using the proceeds, a factor that helps explain why nearly 6 percent of all life insurance payouts in Japan are suicide-related.[86]

Now turn to the social stigma of suicide. Suicide is often romanticized in Japan. The abundance of suicide manuals available in bookstores indicates a certain level of social acceptance, Buddhism may provide a justification because of reincarnation, and survey data indicate that many Japanese people consider suicide an acceptable solution to difficult problems.[87] If bankruptcy entails social stigma and suicide does not, perhaps it is little surprise that some people choose suicide.

Still, there are signs that the romanticization of suicide in Japan is diminishing. When the elderly president of a chicken farm came under fire in 2004 for covering up a bird flu outbreak, he and his wife committed suicide. The Japanese public found little to applaud in the action. Many expressed sympathy, but others said that their actions were "no longer acceptable" and that their actions were designed to evade responsibility.[88] If the social stigma of suicide increases, we might expect to see more insolvencies declared.

84. Brian Bremner, Sorry, We're Not Paying, Business Week, June 3, 2002, available at http://www.businessweek.com/magazine/content/02_22/b3785143.htm.

85. Party names not given, Supreme Court, No. 2001(O)734, 58:3 Minshū (Mar. 25, 2004).

86. Amamiya, *supra* note 19, at 64–69.

87. See Iga, *supra* note 14, at 149–58.

88. See, e.g., person-on-the-street interviews at http://www.japantoday.com/e/tools/print.asp?content=popvox&id=466.

IMPLICATIONS

Evaluating the Civil Rehabilitation Law

The variety and ambiguity of interviewees' responses implies that formulating responses (legal or otherwise) to debt-suicide is no simple task. In some cases, the Civil Rehabilitation Law provides debtors with an option other than bankruptcy or suicide. Accordingly, regardless of the overall efficiency or fairness of the law, the quantitative and interview evidence presented in this chapter suggests that this particular reform of insolvency law has saved lives. Bankruptcy costs more in terms of both institutional strain and social sanctions than suicide; civil rehabilitation costs less.

Still, the varied and ambiguous responses given by my interviewees regarding their wants in an insolvency law system and the way in which such a system might affect their behavior suggests that civil rehabilitation might be effective because it coexists with bankruptcy to provide varied options for varied people. If so, then the key to institutional design is not reaching a single solution but providing multiple solutions for persons who have different needs.

The multiplicity of responses also suggests a potential pitfall of insolvency law reform: we might *want* insolvency to be difficult and stigmatizing, for at least three reasons. First, easier insolvency would lead to increased filings, and increased filings hurt creditors and increase costs for other borrowers. Second, as an insolvency law regime is relaxed, individuals might take on more debt, increasing the overall number of persons in financial distress. Finally, creditors might make loans more difficult to obtain. Recent empirical evidence suggests that lenders will respond to lax insolvency laws by reducing amounts that they lend, a process that imposes costs on borrowers at the time of loan origination.[89] Some consumers might be willing to pay these costs to obtain the insurance of bankruptcy availability, but those costs might also increase emotional distress. Similarly, creditors might charge higher interest rates, which could again trouble borrowers. Any combination of these processes could conceivably lead to an increase rather than a decrease in suicides.

89. Karen M. Pence, Foreclosing on Opportunity: State Laws and Mortgage Credit, May 13, 2003, available at http://papers.ssrn.com/sol3/papers.cfm?abstract_id=410768.

Some commentators feared these problems in Japan.[90] The little evidence we have (marginally increased filings after both Tokyo bankruptcy court rule relaxation and legislative reform) suggests that more filers will emerge, but so far, corollary symptoms such as increased debt and higher interest rates have not occurred. Although bankruptcy rates have increased in recent years in Japan, they still are comparatively quite low, suggesting that modest changes would be unlikely to have large effects on rational lenders. Still, it is important for policymakers to recognize the potential perverse danger of insolvency law liberalization, and, by small steps, to create a menu of options for a variety of debtors.

Perhaps more significantly, nothing in this chapter is intended to suggest that a primary purpose of insolvency law is suicide prevention. Though the deaths are undoubtedly tragic, bankruptcy's linkages to suicide are much less clear than its linkages to debt reduction. There can be no doubt that bankruptcy can reduce debt, and the focus of bankruptcy law in Japan and elsewhere should not be on preventing suicides. What this chapter has attempted to show is the extent to which law can affect behavior—the worst consequences of bad law. Designing a bankruptcy law to reduce suicide would be foolhardy, but improving bankruptcy law is laudable even if it does not necessarily control suicide rates.

Japanese Responses to Legal Change

As discussed above, cost and social stigma are two primary explanations for why people turn to suicide instead of insolvency. Consider first the cost explanation. If people are choosing life instead of death because the legislature has altered the cost calculus, that cause-and-effect pattern provides still further evidence for the premise that Japanese actors respond to legal change. Writing with Curtis Milhaupt, I have argued that Japanese corporate actors respond to such changes.[91] Our claim was directed primarily against nay-saying observers of the Japanese economy who claim that institutional reform will be insufficient to pull Japan out of its economic rut. But in legal scholarship about Japan, individuals, not corporations, historically have been the subject of arguments regarding non-

90. Debt-Saddled Japanese Get a Break, Nikkei Weekly, April 9, 2001, at 1.
91. Mark D. West and Curtis J. Milhaupt, Economic Organizations and Corporate Governance in Japan: The Impact of Formal and Informal Rules (2004).

responsiveness to legal change. Individuals are often said to base their relations on and conduct their affairs according to social factors, not legal ones.[92] The evidence presented in this chapter (which complements evidence from our studies of love hotels and working hours) suggests that relatively small legal changes—tinkering with the insolvency regime—in some cases will have profound effects, indeed, life-and-death effects, on individuals.

Now consider the social explanation. If people are choosing life instead of bankruptcy because civil rehabilitation has altered the social calculus of insolvency, that cause-and-effect pattern implies that small legal changes can have enormous consequences for a few people and probably also have consequences of a lesser magnitude for many others. Altering the formal institutional regime appears either to have diminished the social sanctions that accompany insolvency or to have created a new, no-stigma form of insolvency. Either description of the change implies a strong role for law in the shaping of social norms, a particularly important finding in Japan.

Of course, improvement of the insolvency regime alone is unlikely to be sufficient. Japan's problems with consumer finance, both legal and illegal, run so deep that more broad-scale institutional changes are likely to be necessary. One rather obvious place to start would be Japan's vast underground debt regime. Some minor relevant revisions were enacted in 2004, including giving administrators the ability to refuse applications for registration as legal lenders from persons with ties to organized crime, a voiding of contracts with an annual interest rate of more than 109.5 percent, and increased penalties for usury and unregistered operations. That's great, but what Japan really needs is facilitation of finance by legitimate institutions to drive the mob out of business.

CONCLUSION

Recall the story with which this chapter began, that of Kazuyoshi Saitō explicitly choosing courts instead of death. The speed and drama with which Saitō reached his decision might be unique, and I suspect that his retelling of that story to me might be slightly exaggerated. The absolute reliance on the Civil Rehabilitation Law is probably also rare, because the

92. See, e.g., Takeyoshi Kawashima, Nihhonjin no Hō Ishiki [Japanese Legal Consciousness] (1967).

law is still quite new. But Saitō's incentive structure might not be unique at all. True, some people are destined for suicide; others may be destined for bankruptcy. But the evidence presented in this chapter has shown that sometimes insolvency law can be a matter of life or death. The relation is complex, and many people need mental health care, drugs to treat depression, and the love of friends and family much more than they need bankruptcy reform. But even in Japan, where the stigma of suicide is low and the stigma of insolvency is high, for some people, some of the time, and for reasons that are often varied and ambiguous, law appears to make a difference in the ultimate decision.

CHAPTER NINE

CONCLUSIONS AND IMPLICATIONS

Against the backdrop of everyday Japan, this book has analyzed law in order to understand society and society to understand law. Four basic underlying themes emerged.

First, law is plentiful in everyday Japan. I have avoided some obvious places to look for law: birth, marriage, death. Of course, law functions in those arenas; statutes determine available baby names (you can't name your child "Cancer," for instance), the status of couples, and burial sites, and an analysis of how it does would be interesting but perhaps unsurprising in the modern state. But we have found law in some rather unexpected places: sex, sumo, and suicide. Even outside of the traditional litigation context, and even setting aside the big corporate players and business transactions that we might expect to generate contracts and lawsuits, law flourishes in everyday Japan.

Second, norms also are plentiful in everyday Japan. Those norms interact with law in many different ways. We saw in the lost-and-found context and in the case of working hours how law may both complement and supplant social norms. We saw that close-knit groups such as sumo wrestlers rely heavily on norms to structure their activity but that ordering in a situation such as that of Kobe condominiums might be better left to law. The karaoke noise complaint case showed the futility of separating law and norms in decisions of whether to bring legal action. We saw how clever institutional design and promotion of something as basic as the Civil Rehabilitation Law can both rely on underlying norms and perhaps create new ones.

These norms are heterogeneous, even in Japan, and do not always function with absolute precision. Sumo wrestlers get angry and leave the association. The ubiquitous love hotels, seen by some as a scourge, have gained greater acceptance. Neighbors engage in bass-thumping midnight karaoke wars. Sometimes things don't work. Nor is there an easy way to characterize the relation between rules and norms—and that is precisely the point. Humanly devised constraints on behavior are necessarily varied, and academics and policymakers would do well to resist easy answers.

Third, and perhaps most important, these institutions are not only plentiful; they actually matter. Law structures the behavior of people in Japan even in the more mundane aspects of their lives. Sometimes, as in the cases of lost-and-found, karaoke, or insolvency, law plays a very direct role that can easily be observed. In other cases, such as employee dismissal rules that create long working hours or property rules that encourage consensus in condominiums, the causes and effects are more indirect.

This finding might be unsurprising; it would be much more surprising if we were to find that most of the people, most of the time, do *not* respond rationally to the incentives before them. But to many people who study Japan and, in particular, its law, Japan has been exempt from such principles. Rather than rely on abstract legal principles that don't fit the historically engrained tradition, the story goes, relationships prevail over legal rules, social custom over common law, and harmonious consensus over lawsuits. True, as we have seen, there are situations in which relationships trump rules, custom trumps law, and consensus trumps rancor. But in the midst, institutions matter.

Finally, all of this is messy stuff. Even in the limited context of the case studies presented here, I have not addressed the ways in which different institutional regimes interact: zoning rules create synergies between karaoke and love hotels, rules that affect working hours also can affect debt-suicide, and love hotel cleaning staff often deal with lost objects (usually jewelry, and owners have a low claim rate) in ways that require analysis of both love-hotel and lost-and-found rules. The addition of variables that create relations outside of the case studies would, of course, expose even more intricacy.

This degree of complexity might strike law-and-economics types as frustrating and law-and-society types as fascinating, but it should leave all with a few doubts. Using tools from both schools, we have seen that sometimes law works, sometimes it doesn't, and sometimes it does something different from what many people had in mind. Sometimes, as in the complicated questions of why people do not bring legal actions in karaoke cases, people who appear to be doing the same things for the same reasons are doing nothing of the sort. And sometimes, as we saw when trying to determine why people choose suicide instead of insolvency, people don't know what they're doing or why they're doing it. What an odd world this would be if those who examine such things took it upon themselves to tell them.

* * *

These findings have at least three significant implications.

First and most simply, the ubiquity of law in everyday Japan implies a need for a shift of focus in several areas. If we really want to know how law works in Japanese society, we should study things other than lawsuits and lawyers. Scholars of Japan who study things other than law have long recognized the value of examining the small things, and it is time for legal studies to catch up.

The implication applies beyond Japan, to the broader field of comparative law. Too often, comparative law scholarship and study are focused on the big things: big cases, institutional structures, and social upheavals. I recognize the difficulty of changing the focus: studies of U.S. law in comparative perspective, for instance, would be remiss if they did not analyze litigation rates and the cornerstones of American constitutional jurisprudence (as do most classes in Anglo-American jurisprudence at Japanese universities). But given the richness of available information from everyday Japan, one would think that the same lens might offer benefits if trained elsewhere as well.

Second, and more broadly, there is no place now (was there ever?) for a dichotomized view of Japanese law that sees all behavior as either economically motivated or socially encouraged. There is no zero-sum game. Sometimes law-and-economics offers better answers, and sometimes law-and-society does. Some may accuse me of an academic or (worse?) a lawyerly dodge in an attempt to satisfy both camps. But in fact, I am not proposing a shift to an all-pleasing middle-of-the-road approach as much as I am gently bashing both, encouraging an acknowledgment of the weaknesses of the dichotomy and a discarding of the worst of each school. Answers lie in the interplay, not the extremes.

Finally, the findings of this book suggest cause for optimism. As we have seen, law can greatly impact everyday lives of ordinary people, even in Japan. It would be surprising if every legal change could create the kind of effective institutional regime that we see, for instance, in the lost-and-found context. As we have seen from such diverse topics as love hotel regulation, employee dismissal policy, and bankruptcy law, results do not always materialize exactly as predicted. But the fact that people in Japan respond to law—and in some cases, respond with vigor—suggests cause for optimism in Japan's struggle with potentially more consequential issues. Policymakers and advocates for social change should be both excited and cautious about the ability of the law to confront such problems as the aging crisis, gender inequity, and insidious issues of class and race, each of which, for many people, constitutes everyday Japan.

INDEX

divorce, and suicide, 237
divorce law, 239n62
Donner, Arvin, 45–46
Dufwenberg, Martin, 20
Duggan, Mark, 62
Durex Global Sex Survey into Sexual Attitudes and Behavior, 145n2
Durkheim, Emile, 240, 243

earthquake insurance policies, 129
East Japan Railway, 18
economic suicide. *See* debt-suicide
Edo Period, 27, 156
egoistic suicide, 240
elder share regime, 57, 68–78; associate elders, 72; association revenues and elder distributions, 1989–1995, 73–74; combination of rules and norms, 83–86; creation of new rules, 86–88; defection from rules to norms, 80–83; elder name, 70; "elder name succession/ inheritance notice," 71; "elder stock," 57; foreigner question, 86–88; four rules to help certain wrestlers obtain shares, 71; leaving, 78; loyalty norms, 83; master elder shares, 70; remedial norms, 85; restrictions on share transfer, 70–71; rules and norms, 78–88; strict application of existing rules, 78–80
elder shares, 69–73; benefits and valuation, 73–78; pricing, 75–77; rented from another elder, 71–72; shrinking pool owing to increased longevity of elders, 76n41; "single-generation" or "lifetime" share, 71; total number of, 71
elders (retired wrestlers): in the best position to maximize revenue, 68–69; eligibility rules, 70; income linked to association's financial performance, 73–75; relinquish their shares at age sixty-five, 72; salaries as of 2003, 73
elementary education system, 47
Ellickson, Robert C., 59n5
embezzlement: entrusted-property, 26; lost-property, 11, 30; lost-property, prosecution and enforcement, 28–33
emergency phone number, use for non-emergency inquiries, 37n58

Employment Security Act of 1947, 203, 204, 205, 209; amendments to, 197, 205
Engel, David, 110, 120
enshuku, 158
Entertainment Law of 1948, 147, 159, 163; 1972 amendments, 159, 161; 1985 revisions, 162; regulation of adult entertainment, 159; regulation of love hotels, 163, 164, 166–70
entrusted-property embezzlement, 26
Environment Agency, recommendations for noise control regulation for late-night businesses, 93–94
Environment Dispute Coordination Commission, 98n39
"equal exchange" *(tōka kōkan)* rebuilding, 140–41
external labor market, 193
extortion schemes, 160
extralegal love hotels, 171, 172–74

Factory Law, 194
false loss reports, 38n63
family court, 30
family-owned businesses, 191
fashion health establishments, 166
female suicide rates, negatively related to divorce, 238–40
field work, 5
finder's receipt *(shutokumono azukarisho)*, 38
finder's report *(shutokutodoke)*, 38
fines, for lost-property embezzlement, 32
Flynn, Errol, 2
Foote, Dan, 193, 197, 200
foreign population, as social capital factor, 120–21
Freeman, Richard, 211
"freeters," 211
Fujikura, Koichiro, 97–98
"full service" *(honban)*, 166n51
Futagoyama stable, 67, 79n46
Futahaguro, 85n62
FW/PBS, Inc. v. Dallas, 165

geisha, 157
general honesty, 44–45
gifts, contractual and tax consequences, 4n8
Gilson, Ron, 193, 200–201, 208, 209